The Italian General Election of 2008

Also by James L. Newell

CORRUPTION IN CONTEMPORARY POLITICS (*editor with Martin J. Bull*)

CRIMINAL FINANCES AND ORGANISING CRIME IN EUROPE
(*editor with Petrus C. Van Duyne and Klaus Von Lampe*)

ITALIAN POLITICS: Adjustment under Duress (*with Martin Bull*)

ITALIAN POLITICS: Quo Vadis? (*editor with Carlo Guarnieri*)

ORGANISED CRIME ECONOMY: Managing Crime Markets in Europe
(*editor with Petrus C. Van Duyne, Maarten van Dijk and Klaus Von Lampe*)

PARTIES AND DEMOCRACY IN ITALY

POLITICA IN ITALIA: I fatti dell'anno e le interpretazioni, 2005 edition
(*editor with Carlo Guarnieri*)

SCANDAL IN PAST AND CONTEMPORARY POLITICS (*editor with John A. Garrard*)

THE ITALIAN GENERAL ELECTION OF 2001: Berlusconi's Victory (*editor*)

THE ITALIAN GENERAL ELECTION OF 2006: Romano Prodi's Victory (*editor*)

THE ORGANISATION OF CRIME FOR PROFIT: Conduct, Law and
Measurement (*editor with Petrus C. Van Duyne, Almir Maljevic,
Maarten van Dijk and Klaus Von Lampe*)

THREATS AND PHANTOMS OF ORGANISED CRIME, CORRUPTION AND
TERRORISM: Critical and European Perspectives
(*editor with Petrus C. Van Duyne, Klaus Von Lampe and Matjaž Jagar*)

The Italian General Election of 2008

Berlusconi Strikes Back

Edited by

James L. Newell

First published 2009 by
PALGRAVE MACMILLAN

Palgrave Macmillan in the UK is an imprint of Macmillan Publishers Limited,
registered in England, company number 785998, of Houndmills, Basingstoke,
Hampshire RG21 6XS.

Palgrave Macmillan in the US is a division of St Martin's Press LLC,
175 Fifth Avenue, New York, NY 10010.

Palgrave Macmillan is the global academic imprint of the above companies
and has companies and representatives throughout the world.

Palgrave® and Macmillan® are registered trademarks in the United States,
the United Kingdom, Europe and other countries.

ISBN-13: 978–0–230–22407–0 hardback
ISBN-10: 0–230–22407–5 hardback

This book is printed on paper suitable for recycling and made from fully
managed and sustained forest sources. Logging, pulping and manufacturing
processes are expected to conform to the environmental regulations of the
country of origin.

A catalogue record for this book is available from the British Library.

Library of Congress Cataloging-in-Publication Data

The Italian general election of 2008 : Berlusconi strikes back /
edited by James L. Newell.
    p. cm.
Includes bibliographical references and index.
ISBN 978–0–230–22407–0
  1. Elections – Italy – History – 21st century. I. Newell, James.

JN5607.I683 2009
324.945′093—dc22   2008052857

10 9 8 7 6 5 4 3 2 1
18 17 16 15 14 13 12 11 10 09

Printed and bound in Great Britain by
CPI Antony Rowe, Chippenham and Eastbourne

Contents

Part IV   The Outcome

Figures

Tables

Acknowledgements

I would like to thank each of the authors for their contributions and for their swift responses to requests for suggestions and comments on edited versions of initial drafts. The help of the staff at Palgrave in seeing the book through the various stages of the production process is also gratefully acknowledged. Naturally, responsibility for any errors remaining in the text at the end of the process lies with me. Finally, a debt of gratitude is owed to Serena for her usual considerable forbearance. Once again, it is to her that I wish to dedicate this book.

JAMES L. NEWELL
29 September 2008

Abbreviations

AN	National Alliance (*Alleanza Nazionale*)
CDA	Christian Democrats for Regional Autonomy (*Democrazia Cristiana per le autonomie*)
CdL	House of Freedoms (*Casa delle libertà*)
CDU/CSU	Christian Democratic Union/Christian Social Union (Germany)
CEI	Italian Bishops' Conference (*Conferenza Episcopale Italiana*)
CIACE	Committee for European Community Affairs (*Comitato interministeriale per gli affari comunitari europei*)
CIRCaP	Centre for the Study of Political Change (*Centro Interdipartimentale di ricerca sul cambiamento politico*)
CO.R.EL 2008	Electoral Referendum Committee 2008 (Comitato Referendum Elettorale 2008)
DC	Christian Democratic Party (*Democrazia Cristiana*)
D–FT	The Right–the Tricoloured Flame (*La Destra–Fiamma Tricolore*)
DS	Left Democrats (*Democratici di Sinistra*)
EC	European Community
EMU	Economic and Monetary Union
EU	European Union
FDP	Free Democratic Party (Germany)
FI	Go Italy! (*Forza Italia*)
GDP	Gross Domestic Product
ICI	local property tax (*Inposta comunale sugli immobili*)
IdV	Italy of Values (*Italia dei Valori*)
IMF	International Monetary Fund
IRES	Company Income Tax (*Imposta sul Reddito delle Società*)
IRPEF	Personal Income Tax (*Imposta sul Reddito delle Persone Fisiche*)
INPS	National Social Security Institute (*Istituto Nazionale della Previdenza Sociale*)
IRAP	Regional Business Tax (*Imposta Regionale sulle Attività Produttive*)
MPA	Movement for Autonomy (*Movimento per l'Autonomia*)
MS–FT	Social Movement – Tricoloured Flame (*Movimento Sociale – Fiamma Tricolore*)
NATO	North Atlantic Treaty Organisation
OECD	Organisation for Economic Cooperation and Development
NL	Northern League (*Lega Nord*)

PCI	Italian Communist Party (*Partito Comunista Italiano*)
PD	Democratic Party (*Partito Democratico*)
PdCI	Party of Italian Communists (*Partito dei Comunisti Italiani*)
PCdL	Workers' Communist Party (*Partito Comunista dei Lavoratori*)
PdL	People of Freedom (*Popolo della Libertà*)
PDS	Democratic Party of the Left (*Partito Democratico della Sinistra*)
PGs	parliamentary groups
PM	Prime Minister
PPI	Italian People's Party (*Partito Popolare Italiano*)
PR	proportional representation
PSI	Italian Socialist Party (*Partito Socialista Italiano*)
PSOE	Spanish Socialist Workers' Party (*Partito Socialista Obrero Español*)
RAI	Italian Radio and Television (*Radiotelevisione Italiana*)
RC	Communist Refoundation (*Rifondazione Comunista*)
SA	Rainbow Left (*LA Sinistra L'Arcobaleno*)
SC	Critical Left (*Sinistra Critica*)
SD	Democratic Left (*Sinistra Democratica*)
SDI	Italian Democratic Socialists (*Socialisiti Democratici Italiani*)
SMCs	single member constituencies
SPD	Social Democratic Party (Germany)
SVP	South Tyrolese People's Party (*Südtirolervolkspartei*)
TFR	Severance Pay (*Trattamento di Fine Rapporto*)
UDC	Union of Christian Democrats and Centre Democrats (*Unione dei Democratici Cristiani e dei Democratici di Centro*) / Union of the Centre (*Unione di Centro*)
UDEUR	Democratic Union for Europe (*Unione Democratici per l'Europa*)
UN	United Nations
UNAMA	United Nations Assistance Mission in Afghanistan
UNIFIL	United Nations Interim Force in Lebanon
UNSC	United Nations Security Council
VAT	Value Added Tax

Contributors

Daniele Albertazzi is Senior Lecturer in European Media at the University of Birmingham. He has recently co-edited (with Duncan McDonnell) *Twenty-First Century Populism: The Spectre of Western European Democracy* (Basingstoke: Palgrave Macmillan, 2008) and is co-editing (with Clodagh Brook, Charlotte Ross and Nina Rothenberg) *Resisting the Tide – Cultures of Opposition in the Berlusconi Years* (London, Continuum, 2009).

Donatella Campus is Associate Professor of Politics in the Faculty of Political Science 'Roberto Ruffilli' at the University of Bologna. She is the author of *L'elettore pigro. Informazione politica e scelte di voto* (Il Mulino, 2000) and of *L'antipolitica al governo* (Il Mulino, 2007) as well as of numerous articles dealing with political communication and electoral politics.

Michele Capriati is Professor of Economic Policy at the University of Bari. His research interests lie in the areas of regional development and processes of innovation in the organisation of enterprises with particular reference to economically disadvantaged areas. Recent works include: 'The economic context 2001–2006', in J.L. Newell (ed.) *The Italian General Election of 2006: Romano Prodi's Victory*, (Manchester: Manchester University Press, 2008); 'Sviluppo regionale e libertà effettive: una verifica empirica', *Rivista economica del Mezzogiorno*, no. 1, 2007; 'Expenditure in R&D and local development: an analysis of Italian provinces' (paper presented to the 45th Congress of the European Regional Science Association, Vrije Universiteit, Amsterdam, 23–27 August 2005).

Cristopher Cepernich is Lecturer in the Sociology of Communication at the University of Torino. Since 1995 he has been carrying out research in the field of political communication, in the Department of Political Studies. He is author of: *Le pietre d'inciampo. Lo scandalo come meccanismo sociale* (Aracne Editrice, 2008); 'Landscapes of immorality. Scandals in the Italian press (1998–2006)', *Perspectives on European Politics and Society* vol. 9, no. 1, 2008; 'Il postmoderno emergente. Manifesti e campagna "on line" nelle Regionali piemontesi del 2005', in *Il leader postmoderno* (ed. by C. Marletti, FrancoAngeli, 2006).

Alessandro Chiaramonte is Associate Professor of Political Science in the University of Florence. He has published numerous articles on elections, and electoral and party systems. He is the author of *Tra maggioritario e proporzionale. L'universo dei sistemi elettorali misti* (Il Mulino, 2005). He is also the co-editor, togheter with G. Tarli Barbieri, of *Riforme istituzionali e rappresentanza politica nelle regioni italiane* (Il Mulino, 2007) and, with R. D'Alimonte, of *Proporzionale ma non solo. Le elezioni politiche 2006* (Il Mulino, 2007).

Mark Donovan is a Senior Lecturer in the School of European Studies, Cardiff University. He edited the reader *Italy* (Ashgate, 1998) and co-edited, with David Broughton, *Changing Party Systems in Western Europe* (Pinter, 1998). From 2000–2005 he co-edited *Modern Italy*, the journal of the Association for the Study of Modern Italy. Most recently he co-edited, with James Newell, a special issue of *Modern Italy* on The Centre in Italian Politics.

Ilaria Favretto is Professor of Contemporary European History in the Faculty of Arts and Social Sciences of Kingston University (London). She is author of *The Long Search for a Third Way: the British Labour Party and the Italian Left since 1945* (London: Palgrave-Macmillan, 2003); and *Alle radici della svolta autonomista: Labour Party e PSI, due vicende parallele (1956–1970)* (Rome: Carocci, 2004). She is also co-editor, together with John Callaghan, of *Transitions in Social Democracy and Ideological Problems of the Golden Age* (Manchester: Manchester University Press, 2007).

Giovanna Antonia Fois has a PhD in European and Comparative Politics from the University of Siena. She is attached to the University's Centre for the Study of Political Change and her research interests are mainly focused on the European integration process and government elites.

Alfio Mastropaolo teaches Political Science at the University of Turin. His publications include: *La mucca pazza della democrazia, Nuove destre, populismo, antipolitica* (Turin: Bollati-Boringhieri, 2005) and *Italian Politics. The Center-Left's Poisoned Victory* (edited with J.L. Briquet, New York: Berghahn, 2007).

Duncan McDonnell is a research fellow at the Department of Political Studies in the University of Turin and the Department of Italian in the University of Birmingham. He is the co-editor (with Daniele Albertazzi) of *Twenty-First Century Populism: The Spectre of Western European Democracy* (Palgrave MacMillan, 2008). He is currently conducting research on the changes in Italian local politics over the past two decades and on populist parties in government in Italy and Switzerland.

James L. Newell is Professor of Politics, University of Salford. Recent books include *Parties and Democracy in Italy* (2000), *The Italian General Election of 2001* (ed. 2002), *Italian Politics: Quo Vadis?* (ed., with Carlo Guarnieri, 2005), *Italian Politics: Adjustment Under Duress* (with M. Bull, 2005), *The Italian General Election of 2006* (ed. 2008). He is co-editor of *European Political Science*, co-convenor of the UK Political Studies Association's (PSA's) Italian Politics Specialist Group, and a member of the PSA Executive Committee.

Gianfranco Pasquino is Professor of Political Science at the University of Bologna and Adjunct Professor of Political Science at the Bologna Center of the Johns Hopkins University. He is author of many books among which *Il sistema politico italiano* (Bononia University Press, 2002), *Sistemi politici* *comparati* (Bononia University Press, 2007, 3rd edition) and *Le istituzioni di Arlecchino elettorali* (Scripta web 2008, 5th edition) and, with Riccardo Pelizzo, *Parlamenti democratici* (Il Mulino, 2006).

Franca Roncarolo is Associate Professor of Political Science at the University of Turin, where she co-ordinates the online Political Communication Observatory, which monitors election campaigns and news coverage of politics. Her research interests focus in particular on the comparative analysis of political leadership in western democracies and changes in the relationship among politicians, journalists and citizens. She has published a number of articles and books on these issues, the most recent of which is *Leader e media. Campagna permanente e trasformazioni della politica in Italia* (Milan: Guerini, 2008).

Federico Russo holds a PhD in Comparative and European Politics from the University of Siena and he is currently carrying out research at the Centre for the Study of Political Change (University of Siena). His interests are mainly focused on legislative studies and representative roles with particular reference to Western European countries.

Luca Verzichelli is Professor of Political Science in the University of Siena. His research interests are the comparative analysis of political elites and parliamentary politics. His recent books include *Italian Politics 2005* (co-edited with Grant Amyot, Berghahn, 2006) and *Political Institutions in Italy* (with Maurizio Cotta, Oxford University Press, 2007).

Introduction: a Guide to the Election and 'Instructions for Use'

James L. Newell

Introduction

Shortly after the Italian general election of 2006, a book about the results appeared, entitled *Dov'è la vittoria?* (Itanes, 2006). A pun on the Italian national anthem (which includes a line asking, precisely, 'Where is the victory?') the title reflected the widely held – but in many respects, misleading – view that the centre left had lost an initial advantage to scrape a narrow vote lead over a more effective adversary, with the result that its victory was a partial defeat, and the identity of the 'real' winner uncertain.[1] The 2008 election has given rise to no corresponding senses of uncertainty. It was won by the media tycoon, Silvio Berlusconi, whose centre right coalition took 17,394,890 votes (as compared to 14,088,968 for the centre left) and had comfortable majorities (of 58 and 33 seats) in the two branches of Parliament, the Chamber of Deputies and the Senate respectively. The number of parties represented in the legislature declined dramatically, with the result that whereas there had been 14 groups in the Chamber at the end of the preceding legislature, the number now went down to six: the large Popolo della Libertà (People of Freedom, PdL) and the smaller Lega Nord (Northern League, NL) on the centre-right, and governing, side; the large Partito Democratico (Democratic Party, PD) and the smaller Italia dei Valori (Italy of Values, IdV) on the centre-left, and opposition, side; the Unione di Centro (UDC) located in the centre of the left-right spectrum, and finally, the so-called Gruppo Misto (Mixed Group) hosting the small number of independent deputies, and those representing the linguistic minorities and Italians resident abroad. This implied the likely emergence of clear-cut governing and opposition roles with the possibility of straight-forwardly adversarial patterns of interaction between cohesive majority and minority coalitions – in contrast to the more nearly consensual patterns of law-making of the past.[2] For the same reason, it was reasonable to think that the government that took office stood a good chance of lasting for the entire legislature – in contrast to the previously unstable coalitions which, since 1948, had held office for an average of 358 days each. In short, the election outcome held out the prospect of a radical break with the past – most significantly with the previous legislature which had been brought to an end by the collapse, in January, of the nine-party centre left coalition whose imminent demise media commentators had constantly predicted almost from the day it had taken office just 18 months previously. Now, Italy was said at last to have joined the ranks of the 'advanced democracies' with their elevated two-party concentrations of votes and seats (see the chapter by Chiaramonte).

If the Italian general election of 2008 thus merits attention because of its seemingly profound potential implications for the country's internal politics, then it also merits the close attention of outside observers for a second reason. This is the country's significance for the international political system and therefore – in a globalised world – for matters that must touch even the outside observer directly. Many, if not most states can merely adapt to international economic and political pressures created and sustained, ultimately, by the handful of powerful Western states – of which Italy is one of the most significant. In 2004, its Gross Domestic Product (GDP) at over 1.67 trillion dollars ($1,672,302,000,000) was the sixth highest in the world and amounted to over 5 per cent of the combined GDP of the 'high income' countries as defined by the World Bank.[3] It is one of the four largest states, in terms of population and GDP, of the EU. It contributes to 27 peace-keeping missions in 19 different countries where the experience its soldiers have acquired in international policing has allowed them to play a diplomatic role possibly at least as effective as that of diplomats by profession (Walston, 2008: 153–154).

It is therefore the hope of this author that readers from a wide range of backgrounds will find material of significance in this book whose purpose, like those dedicated to the two previous Italian elections (Newell, 2002; 2008c) is to take an 'intellectual photograph' of the event in such a way as to explain how it came about and make clear its implications for the Italian political system as a whole. In order to assist in achieving this objective, the remainder of this chapter is devoted to providing the essential background information to enable the reader to engage without difficulty with the more specific analyses in each of the chapters that follow. Doing so requires carrying out a number of tasks, the first of which is to describe the institutional backdrop against which the election took place.

The institutional framework

The 1948 Constitution, which sets out the institutional geography of the Italian Republic, reflects the constitutions of most other liberal democracies in establishing a tripartite division of political authority between executive, legislative and judicial agencies. Here, we need to focus on the first two.

As in other parliamentary regimes, so too in Italy, the Cabinet or 'Council of Ministers' (*Consiglio dei Ministri*) is responsible to the legislature and remains in office only as long as it enjoys the confidence of the latter. Unusually, the Cabinet must retain the confidence of both branches of the legislature (the Chamber of Deputies and the Senate) – which are themselves relatively unusual in that they possess identical legislative powers. This aside, Italian arrangements share most of the characteristic features of parliamentary regimes elsewhere: ministers are individually and collectively responsible to Parliament and the executive is 'bicephalic' – in other words, there is a head of state (with the title of 'President' in the Italian case) in addition to the head of government (the Prime Minister).

The President's supreme function is to mediate and regulate interaction among the main political actors with the aim of ensuring that political processes are carried on without threatening national integration, and this can be seen both in the way the President is elected and in the President's formal powers. Thus, presidents are elected by an assembly that includes the members of the two branches of the legislature plus representatives of Italy's regions in order to broaden, beyond Parliament, the base on which presidential legitimacy rests. Election requires the support of two thirds of the members of the assembly at the first three rounds of voting to ensure, as far as possible, that the winning candidate enjoys the support of forces extending beyond those of the government of the day. The 2006 election of the current president, Giorgio Napolitano, therefore represented something of an unusual case: his support was confined to the governing majority and his election came at the fourth round. Presidential terms last for seven years in order to free the incumbent from any form of dependence on those who elected him (presidents have all been men so far): since parliamentary terms cannot exceed five years, presidents can never be re-elected by the same assembly that elected them previously.

The President's formal powers – to appoint the Prime Minister and other members of the Cabinet; to dissolve and convoke Parliament; to promulgate laws – are deliberately left unspecified so that they can be deployed to mediate political interaction flexibly. For example, when parties commanding a majority in Parliament have a clear preference, presidents have little choice in Cabinet appointments, bearing in mind that executives must retain the confidence of Parliament. On the other hand, when, as in the period between 1992 and 1996, the parties have lacked the authority to determine the composition of governments, effective governance requires that presidential discretion be greater – as has in fact been the case (see the chapter by Pasquino).

The 'perfectly bicameral' nature of the legislature has an obvious impact on the electoral system: identical authority and tasks means that the Chamber and Senate have to be elected in accordance with very similar electoral laws for each house. Electoral laws that diverged too radically might result in houses with very different political complexions. This almost happened in 2006 when the centre left that emerged victorious in the April election had a small majority of votes and a comfortable majority of seats in the Chamber, but was behind in terms of votes and had a majority of only two seats in the Senate. Contrasting majorities between the chambers would have serious consequences for the possibility of stable and effective governance. Theoretically, such contrasting majorities could come about even if the electoral systems for the two branches of the legislature were identical; for article 58 of the Constitution restricts elections to the Senate to those aged 25 and over (the voting age for the Chamber is 18).[4]

Space does not permit going into all the technical details of the electoral law,[5] but in essence, for elections to the Chamber of Deputies, the distribution of seats takes place in three arenas – a domestic arena; a constituency for Italians resident abroad (assigned 12 seats) and the single-member college of Valle d'Aosta – of which by far the most important is the first. Here, where 617 of the 630 seats are distributed, parties present lists of candidates in each of 26 multi-member constituencies, voters being required to make a single choice among the lists with which they are presented. Lists can either be fielded by parties independently, or as part of a coalition with others. Seats are distributed between the lists proportionally except that to be eligible to participate in such distribution, lists must obtain at least 4 per cent of the national total of valid votes cast if they are being fielded independently or as part of a coalition whose combined total turns out to be less than ten per cent. If they are part of a coalition whose combined total is ten per cent or more, then they must obtain at least 2 per cent of the national valid vote total or be the most-voted list of those below this proportion. If an initial proportional distribution of seats results in the most popular list or coalition receiving less than 340 seats, then it is assigned as many seats as are necessary to bring it up to that figure, this so-called *premio di maggioranza* (or 'majority premium') thus ensuring, for the list or coalition concerned, an overall majority. The remaining seats are distributed proportionally among the other lists and coalitions. Important to note is that for the purposes of assignment of the majority premium, the votes of all lists count, even those of lists below the vote thresholds. Second, for voters, the system potentially reduces the costs of political defection since – unlike in the British system where failure to support Labour is highly likely to assist the Conservatives and vice versa – the choice of party and coalition is combined into a single choice, allowing voters to continue to support a coalition even while switching to another party.

Arrangements for the Senate are similar, but with the important differences that in the domestic arena (where 308 of the 315 seats are distributed: 1 going to Valle d'Aosta and 6 to the 'overseas' constituency): (1) seats are assigned to regions (in accordance with their populations) rather than to constituencies; (2) seat distribution (including assignment of the *premio di maggioranza*) takes place region by region (that is, seat assignment depends on lists' and coalitions' regional, not their national totals); (3) in each region (except Molise and Trentino Alto-Adige which have their own systems) the *premio* consists in the number of seats, awarded to the largest coalition or list, that is necessary to bring it up to 55 per cent of the seats assigned to the region; (4) in order to be eligible to participate in the distribution of seats, lists have to have attracted, if fielded independently or as part of a coalition whose combined regional vote total turns out to be less than 20 per cent, at least eight per cent of the valid votes cast in the region concerned. If fielded as part of a coalition whose combined vote is above 20 per cent, then it must have attracted at least three per cent of the region's valid vote total.

As important for an understanding of the election as the institutional context, obviously, is knowledge of the basic characteristics of the party system, to which we now turn. These have been in a state of continuous evolution since the early 1990s.

The nature of the party system

That is to say, the election took place against the background of a series of long-term political changes establishing fragmented bipolarity as the predominant feature of the party system. In essence, the collapse of the Berlin Wall in 1989; the organisational disintegration of the then governing parties, and electoral-system change in 1993 had brought a party-system transformation away from the traditional 'polarised pluralist' (Sartori, 1976) pattern. This had been based on the permanence in office of the centre-placed Democrazia Cristiana (Christian Democrats, DC) as the mainstay of every conceivable governing coalition, and the continuous exclusion from office both of the Right and of the main party of opposition, the Communist Party (PCI), a situation that had rendered alternation in government impossible.

The 1989 events had undermined the assumptions on which this system had been based by bringing with them a transformation of the PCI into a non-communist party with a new name (Democratic Party of the Left (PDS); later, Left Democrats, DS). Thereby, they had subverted the appeal of the DC whose electoral influence centred on its claim to be the main bulwark against communism; and by subverting the DC they had removed the previously insurmountable obstacle in the way of the Right finding allies in a coalition to stop the Left.

The governing parties' organisational disintegration had been linked to 1989 insofar as it came as the consequence of a massive corruption scandal precipitated by the investigations of public prosecutors aware that moves against the illegal funding activities of the parties no longer risked assisting a Communist Party that had made the so-called moral question one of its own great battle cries.

Finally, a scandalised public had enabled reformers to win a referendum on a proposal to change the electoral law which, it was hoped, would bring an improvement in the quality of Italian government by facilitating the emergence of two coalitions competing for overall majorities of seats. Though such coalitions did emerge, they were fragmented owing to the fluidity of the party-system context in which the electoral-law change was introduced. Parties were aware that the largely single-member, simple plurality system ushered in, in 1993, gave even, and especially, the smaller of them considerable blackmail power in negotiations leading to the formation of electoral alliances. Parties were also aware that if cohesion was required in the electoral arena, then subsequently, in the parliamentary arena, barriers in the way of divisions and splitting were much lower because they would in any case be courted in coalition negotiations leading up to the *next* election.

Thus it was that by the first election of the new millennium, Italian politics had seen the emergence of two coalitions which seemed to have become permanent, but at the same time, fluid, features of the political landscape. The coalition of the centre right was led by the media magnate, Silvio Berlusconi, who had made his debut as professional politician in 1994 with the launch of a party, Forza Italia (FI), designed to further his personal political ambitions by bringing together the parties on the right of the political spectrum. FI did two things. First, its appeal was sufficiently great to enable it to play the role of 'coalition maker' and that is to enable it, because of its relative size, to impose a degree of cohesion and discipline on allies by dictating the terms on which coalition negotiations were to take place. Second, however, since FI's image and appeal was very much bound up with the charismatic qualities and populist appeal of Berlusconi himself, its ability to play this role was heavily dependent on the entrepreneur's own popularity. Otherwise, there was little to help the coalition cohere, its components – the secessionist NL, former Christian Democrats in the UDC and former fascists in the National Alliance (AN), besides a range of micro-formations and FI itself – being united by little more than opposition to the centre left. Consequently, whenever Berlusconi's popularity had shown signs of weakening, the diversity of the parties' ideologies, sizes, geographical strongholds and the interests they sought to represent (Diamanti and Lello, 2005: 9) had encouraged them to break ranks. They were aware that the political costs were not high – that voters were unwilling to switch between the two main *coalitions*, but increasingly willing to shift among the parties *within* the coalition with which they identified (Natale, 2002) – and this had encouraged them to keep in sharp relief, the profile of their separate identities: Representing conflicting socio-political interests, they were under pressure to shore up support among their core supporters. Finally, having embraced the 'personalisation' of politics that had developed in Italy as elsewhere, they had multiplied the tensions within and between themselves by transforming what were once contests between *parties* into face-offs between *individual leaders* (Diamanti and Lello, 2005: 10–12).

Many of the same features were at work within the coalition of the centre left, with the added factor of instability that its leader lacked a party. Essentially, the coalition had come together around the economics professor Romano Prodi, whose leadership, from the mid-1990s, had always been at the mercy of the constituent parties' interlocking vetoes. In particular, though recognised as the leader of the centre-left government from 1996, Prodi never completely acquired the undisputed status of leader of the coalition, and the notion that 'the premiership is not the leadership' (Pasquino, 2001: 29) became even more firmly established after the fall of the government and the advent of the subsequent centre left governments under Massimo D'Alema and Giuliano Amato in 1998 and 2000 respectively (Newell, 2003: 86–87). Francesco Rutelli, Prodi's successor during the period of the professor's stint as President of the European Commission, found that – his position having been legitimated not by any bottom-up process of selection, but by means of an agreement in 2000 by the coalition's leaders as to who should be Berlusconi's competitor – he necessarily remained 'exposed to the leaders' changing and conflicting views as to the value of his stewardship' (Newell, 2003: 80). Finally, primary elections in October 2005 strengthened the position of Prodi, back from the Commission, by demonstrating the sheer weight of the popular support he was able to mobilise and by thus considerably strengthening the project for coalition unity that he represented. However, they were unable fully to make up for the lack of bargaining power that came from lack of a party, ensuring that, in coalition negotiations leading to the 2006 election and beyond, Prodi's role as leader would never rise above that of mediator.

In summary, then, the 2008 election was a competition for seats in the Chamber of Deputies and the Senate, on the basis of proportional electoral systems with majority premiums; and it took place against the background of the emergence, since the early 1990s, of two – fragmented and ideologically heterogeneous and therefore un-cohesive – coalitions, one of the centre right, the other of the centre left each competing for overall majorities. Legislatures last for a maximum of five years; so the next question we have to address is: Why did the election take place in April 2008, just two years after the previous election?

The collapse of the Prodi government

Answering this question requires us to focus on the effects of three factors in particular: the electoral law; the characteristics of the 2006 centre-left government and the circumstances in which it took office; the attempts at reform that precipitated the government's fall.

As far as the first of these is concerned, the important point to note is that the electoral law was introduced in December 2005, by the centre right Berlusconi government which had won in 2001, with a double intent.

That is, unpopular and fearful of losing the elections that had to be held by the spring of 2006 at the latest, the Government calculated that it stood a better chance of retaining office with a shift from the largely single-member, simple plurality system of 1993 to a proportional system. The reason was that the 1993 system required coalesced parties to agree, through mutual stand-down arrangements, common coalition candidates to field in each constituency. Yet previous elections had shown that it was relatively difficult to persuade centre-right supporters who might be willing to vote for a candidate drawn from their *own* party, to continue to turn out for the coalition even when its chosen candidate was drawn from one of its *other* parties. The new law – which, as we have seen, allows voters to support a coalition *without* having to vote for a party other than their most preferred party – eliminated this problem. Second, even if the change turned out not to be enough to allow the centre right actually to *win*, it held out the prospect that it would make governing very difficult in the event of victory for the rival centre left. There were – bearing in mind that the centre left is the more heterogeneous of the two coalitions – three reasons for this. First, in the circumstances of 2006, the law encouraged the formation of the broadest coalitions possible bearing in mind that – as we have seen – every vote counted for the purposes of assignment of the majority premium, even those of parties below the thresholds. Thus it was that Romano Prodi, as the centre left's prime-ministerial candidate, came to be supported by no fewer than 18 electoral lists (Donovan, 2008: table 6.1). Second, for this very same reason, the law was likely to encourage further fragmentation of the political offering by lowering the costs, for both parties and voters, of 'exit' as compared to the costs of 'voice' and 'loyalty': in a situation in which virtually every party was part of one or the other of the two main coalitions, rationality no longer enjoined, as with the previous system, casting a vote for one of the two 'best placed' candidates. Third, therefore, it was likely to encourage parties, after the election, to cultivate their own electoral niches by distinguishing themselves from their allies and thus turning their backs on 'responsible' behaviour.

So, as Floridia (2008: 318) has pointed out, while it might be tempting to conclude that an unashamedly partisan electoral reform turned against its authors since Berlusconi lost the 2006 elections anyway, this is not so. The government that took office was staffed, roughly from left to right, by Communist Refoundation (RC), the Party of Italian Communists (PdCI), the Greens, the DS, the Socialists, the Radicals, the Margherita ('the Daisy'), IdV and the Democratic Union for Europe (UDEUR), each one of which contributed to instability by virtue of the fact that it was indispensable for the survival of the government in office. And although the victory of the centre left was unambiguous – it was 130,322 votes ahead of the centre right[6] – the narrowness of its lead – 24,755 votes – in the arena that counted for the purposes of assignment of the majority premium in the Chamber served to sustain the argument that the election had bequeathed a country split down the middle,[7] in turn making possible a range of attacks on its legitimacy. In the first place it enabled Berlusconi to make a series of insinuations about presumed irregularities – eventually revealed to be without foundation – in the way the votes had been counted, suggesting that their correction would be sufficient to overturn the result in his favour. Second, it served to sustain the argument that, as the Government had the support of only half the country at the very most, none of its measures could be deemed legitimate unless they were passed with the agreement of the opposition.

Needless to say, arguments that the centre left's claim to office was illegitimate acquired even greater force as the Government passed its 'honeymoon' period and its popularity began to decline. Then, as Berlusconi sought doggedly to topple the Government through constant calls for fresh elections as the only possible solution to Italy's problems (see the chapter by Albertazzi and McDonnell) the arguments nourished a vicious circle of growing instability and growing unpopularity whose dynamic amounted to the following. In the first place, vote-seeking parties, if they are to maximise their support, are obliged 'to compete for media exposure and communication space...[But] attracting media attention requires provocation, division and confrontation' (Paolucci and Newell, 2008: 289). Therefore, because it had to manage a coalition composed of large numbers of parties each driven to keep salient its own distinctiveness even as part of an alliance, the Prodi government found it more difficult than most to keep control over the processes of communication and to use them as a tool in the battle to control the political agenda. Therefore, the Government found it unusually difficult to engage in that 'permanent campaigning' – using support mobilisation as a key resource for governing, while using governing as an instrument to build and sustain support – that is essential for survival in mediated democracies. Unable to control the political agenda to ensure its survival, the Government was, consequently, able to do little to counteract the tendency of the media, in their constant search for the newsworthy, to highlight feuds and divisions and so to frame the government as 'catastrophic' (Roncarolo and Belluati, 2008). In doing so, willingly or otherwise, the media necessarily gave credence to the opposition's portrayal of the Government – so fuelling the downward trajectory in its poll ratings, shortly after it took office. And the more the Government was *portrayed* as litigious and unstable, the more likely it was *actually* to be so as the parties, first, argued about how to retrieve the position and then came to be driven by a logic of *si salvi chi può*.

When this situation came to be combined with objective economic difficulties, enabling the state of the country to be framed as one of irreversible decline and depression (see the chapters by Capriati and Campus), the climate of opinion thus created made easier the abandonment of the Government by UDEUR leader, Clemente Mastella, whose actions, in January 2008, were precipitated by the point at which debate on reform of the electoral law had by then reached.

The arrival in office of a government whose precariousness seemed to owe so much to the nature of the electoral law, ensured that the latter would continue to be a high-profile matter of debate. Consequently, the period after the February 2007 crisis (when Prime Minister Prodi resigned temporarily following the Government's Senate defeat on an important foreign-policy motion) witnessed the emergence of 'CO.R.EL 2008'. This was a cross-party grouping of intellectuals and persons in public life, seeking, in accordance with article 75 of the Constitution, to gather the 500,000 signatures required to make possible a request that the Constitutional Court approve a referendum – in this case on proposals to abolish parts of the electoral law. Of these, the two most important sought (a) to remove the option available to parties to field lists as part of a coalition with other parties, and (b) to strike down those clauses allowing attribution of the majority premium to the largest coalition. The result would thus be to reserve the premium to the largest single list, and automatically to raise the vote thresholds for all lists to 4 per cent in the Chamber and 8 per cent in the Senate. The promoters' expectations were thus that the reform would drive party actors to pursue the formation of single large groupings, bringing disappearance of the distinction between coalitions and their constituent parties, in effect reducing fragmentation by considerably raising the political costs of defection for both parties and voters.

Clearly driven by the intention of putting pressure on the parties in Parliament to introduce incisive reform as the price of avoiding the referendum, the initiative undermined the Government because of the dilemma it created for the larger parties of the centre left. On the one hand, they could not officially support the referendum campaigners (even though they were the most obvious likely gainers from the initiative) without risking the defection of their smaller allies (as the likely losers). On the other hand, they could only effectively head off the referendum through reform that, by also reducing fragmentation, was at least as likely to undermine the loyalty of the smaller parties. Either way, then, it seemed that the smaller parties were facing a threat from which the only escape might be the end of the Government: if bringing it down led to dissolution of Parliament, then the referendum would automatically be suspended until a year after the resulting elections – whose outcome, it could be supposed, might be such as to remove the threat of the referendum altogether; for any referenda in train do not take place at all if rendered redundant by changes in the law on which citizens would otherwise be called to vote. So, as Mastella's withdrawal from Government took place a few days after the Constitutional Court's verdict that the referendum's questions were constitutionally permissible, he appeared to be being driven by a determination to resist the implications of the Court's decision; and, following an unsuccessful attempt on the part of Senate president, Franco Marini, to form an alternative government, fresh elections were called for 13–14 April.

This, then, throws a spotlight on the final issue that needs to be addressed in setting the scene for the subsequent chapters – namely, the characteristics of the coalitions among which voters were called upon to choose at the election – for these were heavily influenced by the emergence of a new party in 2007 – the PD – which also contributed to the Prodi government's fall.

The choices presented to voters

The PD was the result of a merger of former Christian Democrats in the Margherita, and former communists in the DS. A seemingly unlikely combination, it represented a puzzle whose solution appeared to lie in four sets of circumstances. First, there was widespread awareness of the need for a large party that would play, within the centre left, that same role of 'coalition maker' that Berlusconi and FI were able to play on the centre right, and there had been several efforts in the direction of such a party going back at least to Prodi's call for a single list of the so-called Ulivo (Olive-tree) parties for the European Parliament elections of 2004 (see the chapter by Favretto). Second, therefore, it is likely that with the passage of time, the various efforts had become subject to factors of path dependency, making it less costly for political actors to persist with them than to give up. One of the factors was the groundswell of support for the project that had accumulated among centre-left supporters – as was demonstrated by the overwhelming endorsement they gave in the 2005 primaries to Romano Prodi (whose own special project the PD clearly was) and in the 2006 elections when the combined Ulivo list, presented for the Chamber by the DS and the Margherita, had a clear advantage (at 31.3 per cent) over the lists of its constituent parties (at 27.7 per cent) for the Senate. Third, the size of the ideological obstacles in the way of merger between ex-communist and Catholic activists is likely to have been reduced by a political context in which abnegation of Communism on the one side had made room for adherence to a rather indistinct and eclectic set of reformist values – shared on the other side by the heirs to a political outlook – that of the left of the old DC – that already had a tradition of seeking accommodation with the Communists (Berselli, 2007: 45). Finally, the power of potential losers from the project within the two main founding parties is likely to have been neutralised by the steps taken (through the October 2007 election of the leader and constituent assembly, open to everyone) to give those without any prior involvement with either party the opportunity to be involved in the foundation process on the same terms as those with such involvement.

The reason why the project undermined the Prodi government is that the party's emergence was accompanied by a declaration by Walter Veltroni, the man who would shortly be elected its leader, that governments had hitherto been too heterogeneous to be able to act incisively with regard to the country's structural problems; that for this reason, the PD would 'move beyond the idea that what counts is to win elections, that is, to beat the opposing line-up by fielding the broadest coalition possible regardless of its actual capacity to govern the country' (Veltroni, 2007: 20); that therefore at the next election the PD would run alone, whatever the electoral law.

This weakened the Government in two ways. First, it made clear to the governing coalition's smaller components that that they could not count on their larger partner to assure them representation in a future parliament. Second, once this point had been established, it seemed to heighten the prospects of electoral reform to the small parties' detriment (since it made it more likely that the PD would be willing to pursue reform by colluding with FI, bearing in mind that a reform designed to reduce fragmentation could only come about *if* the larger forces of centre-left and centre right in Parliament were willing to reach a cross-coalition agreement at the expense of their respective smaller allies). Thus, once the Constitutional Court had given the go-ahead for the referendum, the smaller centre left parties seemed faced with a simple choice: either to allow the Government to continue and risk, in the spring, a referendum outcome unfavourable to them, or else to attempt to avert this risk by bringing the Government down. The centrist components which in fact toppled the Government were those whose placement on the political spectrum made it likely that if they could not, in the ensuing elections, find allies in their 'own' coalition, then they could assure their survival by passing over to the other side (as some, though not all, successfully did) – especially as by far and away the most probable outcome of the elections was that Berlusconi would win.

This likelihood initially made Veltroni's decision to run alone seem irrational. Its logic was that fighting the elections on the basis of the coalition that had presented itself in 2006, and therefore, having to defend a government that despite everything was deeply unpopular, was not a winning proposition.[8] On the other hand, an independent stance would give Veltroni bargaining power that Prodi never had, enabling him to offer to the very small parties, the so-called micro-formations, an arrangement that would be confined to places on *his* lists and on *his* terms, failing which these formations might risk electoral annihilation. Running alone would allow him to present the PD as something new, rather than a re-edition of the past; to take his distance from the Prodi government, and thus encourage 'prospective voting' rather than voting based on the outgoing government's record. An independent stance would squeeze the vote of rivals, especially on the left, whose supporters would be forced to decide between a vote for their *most* preferred choice and a *voto utile* for the formation most likely to defeat the prospect of their *least* preferred outcome.[9] Finally, even if, as seemed likely, the PD failed to win, running alone had the advantage that, since the thresholds are higher for non-aligned than for aligned lists, the seats not assigned to the winning coalition would have to be shared with fewer lists (Floridia, 2008).

The initial move by Veltroni, then set off, in the days following his announcement, a sequence of actions and reactions on the part of the other main political actors that showed how the construction of the electoral offer for 2008 could be explained as a game of strategic interdependence given the framework of constraints imposed by the electoral system.

The second move in order of time, then, came from the parties of La Sinistra L'Arcobaleno (Rainbow Left, SA) list – which brought together the Sinistra Democratica (Democratic Left, SD), RC, the PdCI and the Greens, and whose emergence had been a direct consequence of the emergence of the PD. This event had provoked the break away, from the DS, of the SD. Since it saw in the merger of the DS and the Margherita the simultaneous disappearance – uniquely in Europe – of Italy's main party of socialism and the left, the SD had as the fundamental objective giving life to it in the first place, the unification of the parties of the Italian left in a single organisation. Its view of the significance of the PD's appearance is one that was shared by RC which, as the largest of the groupings to the left of the PD – and of those groupings, alone capable of surmounting the vote thresholds – saw in the SA an opportunity to establish for itself a position of leadership over the Italian left as a whole. The PdCI and the Greens, which had already come together for the purposes of the 2006 election, saw in the new SA an opportunity to escape the consequences of any new electoral law that might penalise smaller groupings running independently.

In the end, then, divorce between Veltroni and SA leader, Fausto Bertinotti, was consensual (Meli, 2008: 8). In the first place, both needed to mark a break with the experience of the Prodi coalition – Bertinotti in order to escape the dilemma the experience had necessarily created for his party (RC) in attempting to be *di lotta e di governo* (Albertazzi, McDonnell and Newell, 2007). In the second place, that decision, once it had been taken, automatically gave RC enormous power vis-à-vis its allies, over whom it could establish hegemony: like the PD, it too could, because of the electoral-law thresholds, now reject a coalition, insisting instead on a single list which would, of course, be drawn up on its terms.

Even more dramatic were the consequences of Veltroni's initial move for the centre right. Here it swiftly became apparent to Berlusconi's advisors that if Veltroni was going to fight the election as the leader of a new formation, one turning its back on 'the idea that what counts is … to beat the opposing line-up by fielding the broadest coalition possible', then the entrepreneur could hardly counter this by himself cobbling together a coalition of several lists. The question then was, what coalition *was* to be constructed and on what basis? It was a question whose answer reflects the same logic as that at work elsewhere in the party system. That is, once fresh elections had been announced, the belief that the probable winner would be Berlusconi immediately strengthened his position as leader of the centre right, putting him in a similar position of power vis-à-vis his own potential allies as the one in which Veltroni found himself vis-à-vis *his* potential allies. This then enabled him to insist on the idea of a single list, the 'Popolo dell Libertà', bringing together FI and AN, and whichever of the remaining centre right parties could be persuaded to join it.

Since Berlusconi had already begun to push the PdL the previous autumn as a prospective new unified party of the centre right, AN leader, Gianfranco Fini, was more than willing to embrace Berlusconi's idea given that he, of all potential contenders, would be the best placed to assume the leadership after Berlusconi. NL leader, Umberto Bossi, was in a different position, less vulnerable than AN, to the threat of re-isolation on the far right and with a reservoir of support whose geographical distribution was highly concentrated. With the power, therefore, to split the centre right vote in the north, perhaps delivering the Senate to the PD if the contest were close, he was able to obtain a coalition agreement declining the invitation to renounce his party's separate identity within a single list. Third, the micro-formations on the other hand – those such as Lamberto Dini's Liberal Democratici, Gianfranco Rotondi's DC and so on – were in no position to resist this and quickly fell into line (Buzzanca, 2008: 2).[10] That left the UDC and la Destra (bringing together a number of AN dissidents and groupings of the far right), which were in a rather different position to the one occupied by the micro-formations in that they were more than just 'virtual' or 'personal' parties, and had identities and genuine political traditions to defend. Faced with the choice between the threat of liquidation or defence of their autonomy, albeit in unfavourable circumstances, they chose the latter (Di Caro, 2008: 2).

Finally, Veltroni somewhat blurred the clarity of his decision to 'run alone', by agreeing to reach a coalition arrangement with Antonio di Pietro's Italia dei Valori (IdV) and to accommodate a small number of Radicals within the PD's lists. In the case of IdV, the decision was driven by poll evidence which suggested that di Pietro's party might be decisive with regard to the outcome for the Senate contest in a number of regions, and that it would bring with it the support of those voters driven above all else by the anti-political sentiments widespread in the Italian electorate (Vecchi, 2008: 13). In the case of the Radicals, the reasoning was that their involvement would reassure voters with left-wing sympathies that the new PD would not concede too much to those in the party whose sympathies are strongly driven by religious values and who therefore take strongly conservative positions on ethical and civil liberties issues. Tables I.1 and I.2 show how radically the nature of the electoral supply offered to voters on 13 and 14 April differed from the supply offered two years previously.

Table I.1 Coalitions, lists and component parties competing in the Chamber of Deputies elections 2006 and 2008

2006			2008		
Coalitions	**Lists**	**Component parties**	**Coalitions**	**Lists**	**Component parties**
l'Unione	L'Ulivo	DS	Sinistra Arcobaleno	Sinistra Arcobaleno	Communist Refoundation
		Margherita			PdCI
		Movimento Repubblicani Europei			Greens
	Communist Refoundation				Sinistra Democratica
	La Rosa nel pugno	Socialists	Coalition led by Walter Veltroni	Partito Democratico	Partito Democratico
		Radicals			Radicals
	PdCI	PdCI		Italia dei Valori	Italia dei Valori
	Italia dei Valori	Italia dei Valori	Partito Socialista	Partito Socialista	Partito Socialista
	Greens	Greens	Unione di Centro	UDC	UDC
	UDEUR	UDEUR			Rosa Bianca
	Pensioners' Party	Pensioners' Party			De Mita
	SVP	SVP	Coalition led by Silvio Berlusconi	Popolo dell Libertà	Forza Italia
	Other Unione lists				National Alliance
Casa delle Libertà	Forza Italia				DC
	National Alliance				Liberal Democratici
	UDC				Azione Sociale
	Northern League-MPA	Northern League			New PSI

Continued

Table I.1   Continued

2006			2008		
Coalitions	**Lists**	**Component parties**	**Coalitions**	**Lists**	**Component parties**
		MPA			Partito Repubblicano Italiano
	DC-New PSI	DC			Pensioners' Party
		New PSI		Northern League	Northern League
	Alternativa Sociale			MPA	MPA
	Fiamma Tricolore		La Destra	La Destra	La Destra
	Other CdL lists				Fiamma Tricolore
Others			Others		

Table I.2   Coalitions, lists and component parties competing in the Senate elections 2006 and 2008

2006			2008		
Coalitions	**Lists**	**Component parties**	**Coalitions**	**Lists**	**Component parties**
l'Unione	DS	DS	Sinistra Arcobaleno	Sinistra Arcobaleno	Communist Refoundation
	Margherita	Margherita			PdCI
	Movimento Repubblicani Europei	Movimento Repubblicani Europei			Greens
	Communist Refoundation				Sinistra Democratica
	La Rosa nel pugno	Socialists	Coalition led by Walter Veltroni	Partito Democratico	Partito Democratico
		Radicals			Radicals
	Together with the Unione	PdCI		Italia dei Valori	Italia dei Valori
		Greens			

Continued

Table I.2 Continued

| | 2006 | | | 2008 | |
| | | Component | | | Component |
Coalitions	Lists	parties	Coalitions	Lists	parties
	Partito dei Socialisti (Craxi)	Partito dei Socialisti (Craxi)			
	Italia dei Valori	Italia dei Valori	Partito Socialista	Partito Socialista	Partito Socialista
	Greens	Greens	Unione di Centro	UDC	UDC
	UDEUR	UDEUR			Rosa Bianca
	Pensioners' Party	Pensioners' Party			De Mita
	SVP	SVP	Coalition led by Silvio Berlusconi	Popolo dell Libertà	Forza Italia
	Other Unione lists				National Alliance
Casa delle Libertà	Forza Italia				DC
	National Alliance				Liberal Democratici
	UDC				Azione Sociale
	Northern League-MPA	Northern League			New PSI
		MPA			Partito Repubblicano Italiano
	DC-New PSI	DC			Pensioners' Party
		New PSI		Northern League	Northern League
	Alternativa Sociale			MPA	MPA
	Fiamma Tricolore		La Destra	La Destra	La Destra
	Casa delle Libertà				Fiamma Tricolore
	Other CdL lists				
Others			Others		

Conclusion and plan of the book

In this introductory chapter we have sought to present the basic factual information that will allow the reader to appreciate the subsequent chapters' analyses of

- the political, economic and international contexts in which the election took place;
- the processes whereby the choices presented to voters were constructed;
- the nature of the election campaign itself;
- the outcome of the election in terms of the distribution of the vote, the profile of the new legislature and the formation of the new government.

Each of these issues are analysed in detail in the 12 chapters and four sections that follow.

Yet we have sought to introduce these issues, not only by providing basic factual information, but also by offering an *interpretation* of the essential characteristics of the political institutions impinging most directly on the election and its aftermath; of the party system; of the political dynamics responsible for the end of the XV legislature and actors' decisions about the political products to offer voters at the 2008 elections. Any interpretation is – to recall a point made at the start of our opening contribution (by Alfio Mastroapolo) – inevitably 'skewed', insofar as it must highlight some features of a situation at the expense of others. For this reason the reader will find, in the chapters that follow, *other* interpretations that to a greater or lesser degree contrast with the one offered here. But the essential point about an interpretation is that however skewed it is, if it is expressed with sufficient clarity, it enables the reader to *make sense* of a reality whose complexity places a barrier in the way of its immediate comprehension.

For this reason, interpretations are inescapable necessities when it comes to providing accounts of political and other phenomena. From that point of view, this book has been conceived very much as a guide to enable the reader intellectually to engage with the 2008 election and its significance. And with that in mind, this chapter has, to draw an analogy, sought to introduce the guide by providing the essential instructions for its use. It is now up to readers to explore for themselves, in the chapters that follow, the fascinating terrain to which this material is devoted.

Notes

1. I have explained why I think this view of the 2006 outcome is misleading in Newell (2006a, 2006b, 2008a, 2008b). From the point of view of the centre left it was an interpretation of the election that was doubly unfortunate; for besides being inaccurate, it necessarily gave sustenance to that view of the outcome the centre right sought to push, in the election's aftermath, as part of its campaign to deprive of legitimacy the incoming government's claim to office: see below.

2. As the country is a parliamentary democracy, politics since the war had of course always been based on the assumption that at any given moment certain parties were part of the governing coalition and the remainder part of the 'opposition'. However, in a context of high fragmentation, the legislative behaviour of the parliamentary groups had often belied such simple conceptualisations. Most proposals that made it on to the statute book did so thanks to ample majorities drawn from across the governing/opposition divide (Capano and Giuliani, 2001; Newell, 2006c); and there was no formal recognition in Parliament's standing orders of an official opposition.
3. World Bank data taken from http://siteresources.worldbank.org/DATASTATISTICS/Resources/GDP.pdf
4. It also stipulates (in article 59) that, besides being themselves entitled, at the end of their terms, to a senatorial seat for life, presidents have the right to nominate five life senators. These are to be nominated from among individuals who have distinguished themselves in the 'social, scientific, artistic and literary fields'.
5. An especially clear and detailed exposition of the law is given in Chiaramonte (2008).
6. Though modest, such a lead was by no means unusual by international standards. The Israeli Knesset contest of 1981 saw Menachem Begin's Likud party beat Labour by just 10,405 votes or 0.5 percent of the total. The United States presidential contest in 2000 was decided by just 537 votes in the state of Florida. The German federal election in 2005 saw the CDU/CSU emerge ahead of the SPD by just 1 per cent of the vote. The fact that the centre left trailed the centre right in the Senate (by 176,454 votes) could be argued to suggest little other than a preference for the centre right among that segment of the electorate that is above the age of 25.
7. An odd argument, since *most* elections split countries in two more or less equal components and this one was hardly likely to split the country into three.
8. As opinion polls confirmed. See, for example, Gualerzi (2008).
9. At least in the Chamber. For the Senate contest, the situation would vary, depending on the region of residence of the voter concerned.
10. Mastella, having contributed decisively to the fall of the Prodi government, claimed in March that with the benefit of hindsight he would think ten times over before doing something similar again (Zuccolini, 2008: 11) – not surprisingly: in the political situation that emerged following the Government's fall, his bargaining power collapsed. As negotiations with Berlusconi became increasingly difficult, he was abandoned by his followers and his party rapidly disintegrated. Mastella being unable to find a home for himself or his few remaining followers anywhere, it was claimed that he was betrayed by a Berlusconi who had promised him a number of places in his lists and then reneged on the promise in the face of polls suggesting that it would lose him votes (Milella, 2008: 9). In the end, therefore, Mastella was forced to acknowledge complete defeat, announcing that neither he nor his party would contest the election at all. Mastella's must, surely, count as one of the most spectacular and picturesque of political miscalculations in the history of post-war Italian politics.

References

Albertazzi, D., McDonnell, D. and Newell, J.L. (2007) '*Di lotta e di governo*: The Lega Nord and Rifondazione Comunista in coalition', paper presented to the panel, 'Outsider parties in Western Europe: the opposition in government? I', at the

57th Annual Conference of the UK Political Studies Association, 11–13 April, University of Bath.

Berselli, E. (2007) 'Destra e sinistra: Con chi e come fondersi', *la Repubblica*, 10 April, p. 45.

Buzzanca, S. (2008) 'Berlusconi-Fini, via al Pdl ultimatum a Casini: dentro o fuori', *la Repubblica*, 9 February, p. 2.

Capano, G. and Giuliani, M. (2001) 'Governing without suviving? An Italian paradox: law-making in Italy 1987–2001', *Journal of Legislative Studies* 4: 13–36.

Chiaramonte, A. (2008) 'How Prodi's Unione won by a handful of votes', pp. 203–222 in J.L. Newell (ed.), *The Italian General Election of 2006: Romano Prodi's Victory*, Manchester and New York: Manchester University Press.

Diamanti, I and Lello, E. (2005) 'The Casa delle Liberta`: a house of cards?', *Modern Italy* 10(1): 9–35.

Di Caro, P. (2008) 'Berlusconi: FI e An unite. E dà l'ultimatum all'Udc', *Corrierie della Sera* 9 February.

Donovan, M. (2008) 'The processes of alliance formation', pp. 115–135 in J.L. Newell (ed.), *The Italian General Election of 2006: Romano Prodi's Victory*, Manchester and New York: Manchester University Press.

Floridia, A. (2008) 'Gulliver unbound. Possible electoral reforms and the 2008 Italian election: toward an end to "fragmented bipolarity?"', *Modern Italy* 13(3): 317–332.

Gualerzi, V. (2008) 'Pd, sondaggio promuove Veltroni sconfitta contenuta se corre da solo', *la Repubblica*, 29 January, http://www.repubblica.it/2008/01/sezioni/politica/sondaggi-2008/primo-dopocrisi/primo-dopo-crisi.html

Itanes [Italian National Election Study] (2006) *Dov'è la vittoria?*, Bologna: il Mulino.

Meli, M.T. (2008) 'Bertinotti: giusto dividerci ora. E Walter vola nei sondaggi', *Corriere della Sera*, 7 February, p. 8.

Milella, L. (2008) 'La resa di Mastella: "Non mi presento"', *la Repubblica*, 7 March.

Natale, P. (2002) 'Una fedeltà leggera: i movimenti di voto nella II Repubblica', pp. 283–317 in R. D'Alimonte, and S. Bartolini (eds), *Maggioritario finalmente?*, Bologna: Il Mulino.

Newell, J.L. (ed.) (2002) *The Italian General Election of 2001: Berlusconi's Victory*, Manchester and New York: Manchester University Press.

Newell, J.L. (2003) 'The opposition role of the centre left party', pp. 78–94 in Jean Blondel and P. Segatti (eds), *Italian Politics: The Second Berlusconi Government*, New York and Oxford: Berghahn.

Newell, J.L. (2006a) 'The Italian General Election of 2006 and the Social Construction of Reality', *Italian Politics and Society: Review of the Conference Group on Italian Politics and Society*, no. 63, Fall/Winter 2006, pp. 15–32.

Newell, J.L. (2006b) 'The Italian Election of 2006: Myths and Realities', *West European Politics* 29(4): 802–813.

Newell, J.L. (2006c) 'Characterising the Italian parliament: legislative change in longitudinal perspective', *Journal of Legislative Studies* 12(3–4): 386–403.

Newell, J.L. (2008a) 'Introduction: An ambiguous outcome?', pp. 1–12 in J.L. Newell (ed.), *The Italian General Election of 2006: Romano Prodi's Victory*, Manchester and New York: Manchester University Press.

Newell, J.L. (2008b) 'Conclusion: not an ambiguous outcome (even though of uncertain consequences)', pp. 245–259 in J.L. Newell (ed.), *The Italian General Election of 2006: Romano Prodi's Victory*, Manchester and New York: Manchester University Press.

Newell, J.L. (ed.) (2008c) *The Italian General Election of 2006: Romano Prodi's Victory*, Manchester and New York: Manchester University Press.

Paolucci, C. and Newell, J.L. (2008) 'The Prodi Government of 2006 and 2007', *Modern Italy* 13(3): 283–291.

Pasquino, G. (2001) *Critica della sinistra italiana*, Rome and Bari: Laterza.

Roncarolo, F. and Belluati, M. (2008) 'Surfing and trying to keep afloat. The political communication process in a highly fragmented coalition led by a "great mediator"', *Modern Italy* 13(3): 333–348.

Sartori, G. (1976) *Parties and Party-Systems: A Framework for Analysis*, Cambridge: Cambridge University Press.

Vecchi, G.G. (2008) '«Di Pietro nel Pd? Certi deliri non mi riguardano»', *Corriere della Sera*, 15 February.

Veltroni, W. (2007) *La Nuova Stagione*, Milan: Rizzoli.

Walston, J. (2008) 'La politica estera: il difficile perseguimento di un ruolo influente', pp. 151–171 in M. Donovan and P. Onofri (eds), *Politica in Italia: I fatti dell'anno e le interpretazioni*, 2008 edition, Bologna: il Mulino.

Zuccolini, R. (2008) 'Mastella e il no a Romano «Ora ci penserei 10 volte»', *Corriere della Sera*, 14 March.

Part I
The Context

1
The Political Context: 2006–2008

Alfio Mastropaolo

The purpose of this chapter is to place the election in the context of political developments since 2006 and thereby to provide an interpretation of its outcome. The first section considers the behaviour of voters and of the parties that sought to represent them. The second explains why a crisis overtook the centre left Prodi government after less than two years, bringing with it the early dissolution of Parliament. The third advances some hypotheses to explain Berlusconi's victory and the defeat of the centre left, which in many ways looked like a case of 'voluntary surrender', without any particular resistance being offered. As is frequently the case in the social sciences, this chapter is a description informed by a particular interpretation. Like all interpretations, it is necessarily subjective, and it will be up to the reader to determine whether or not the author has organised his facts convincingly; and whether his interpretation is more or less persuasive than others.

The never-ending returns of Italian democracy

Italians can be accused of many faults, but not of being unfaithful voters. As taxpayers they leave much to be desired. They profess themselves to be Catholics but very rarely go to Mass. They have no particular respect for the Highway Code. They lie, sometimes bare-facedly, when they are interviewed for pre-election polls or for exit polls. And yet, in the secrecy of the polling booth, where no one can see them, they always vote the same way. Between one election and the next, only a very small minority crosses the line dividing right and left (or 'centre right' and 'centre left' as we could somewhat hypocritically say in deference to a vocabulary implying that the centre is better than the wings).

Prior to the 1994 elections when it became majoritarian, Italian democracy was consensual in nature. A large centre party formed alliances with parties to its immediate left and right, while the remaining left- and right-wing parties made up the opposition. This state of affairs lasted for almost half a century until the 1990s party-system transformation. Then, parties divided into two, positioning themselves as part either of the left-wing or of the right-wing grouping. What electoral mobility there has been, has taken place within the two groupings. If they do not want to shift from one party to another within the same grouping, then if anything, rather than consider parties belonging to the other grouping, they resolve the situation by abstaining.

Since Italians love to confuse the pollsters, election results always hold surprises (Feltrin, Natale and Fabrizio, 2006; Newell, 2006). On the eve of the 2006 elections, opinion polls appeared to confirm the unpopularity of the Berlusconi government and to suggest a climate of opinion highly favourable to the return of Prodi. The climate was so favourable to the centre left, and the discontent with the five years of centre-right government apparently so great, that commentators were amazed by the very limited success of the coalition led by Prodi, reading into Berlusconi's apparent electoral comeback, an ability to perform miracles. In 2008 there was a similar misunderstanding, when opinion polls suggested another striking advance by Berlusconi and the centre right. After the elections, if we do some sums, we discover that the electorate remained where it had been two years previously (Feltrin and Natale, 2008).

The distribution of seats in Parliament heavily penalised the centre left; the small parties disappeared, and the seats obtained by the Lega Nord (Northern League, NL) and Antonio Di Pietro's party, Italia dei Valori (Italy of Values, IdV), roughly doubled. However, this does not mean that the election result represents a great advance for the right and a great retreat of the left. Nor was there a massive betrayal of the left by the working class, as some post-election interpretations have tried to show. The only real change is the substantial growth of two protest parties, the NL and IdV, which shows that the electorate on both sides of the left-right divide feels discontented.

However, in 2008 voters did not move more than they had done in 2006, just as in 2006 they had not moved very far from where they were in 2001. At more or less every election the gap separating the two main coalitions is about one million votes. Of the total of over 40 million votes cast, that is less than 2.5 per cent. Some will object that net differences mask gross movements – which are mostly self-cancelling and of course larger. But analyses of vote flows suggest that straight switches from left to right and vice versa remain relatively rare (Feltrin and Natale, 2008).

One realisation of this type generates another: it is not the electors who decide the results of elections in Italy, but rather, as occurs in many other systems, the configuration of party 'products' that is offered in the electoral marketplace. Before going into this issue, however, there is another that deserves mention. Not only is Italy a country split in two electorally, but the dividing line does not pass exactly down the middle of the electorate. That is, Italy is predominantly a moderate and conservative country. Perhaps it is not the only one. In any case, the sum of those who vote for the right-wing and those who vote for centre right has, since 1948, always been higher than the sum of centre-left and left-wing voters. In the immediate post-war period, parties of socialist and communist extraction, plus the Republican Party, accounted for just over 40 per cent, and so it remained until the 1970s. The gap with the right then narrowed, the reasons for this being linked to Italy's transformation from a predominantly backward peasant country into a modern industrial nation. The practice of religion declined; Catholics lost their deference towards Church leaders; customs changed. In 1974, a sizeable majority confirmed, in a referendum, the recently introduced law on divorce, and women began demanding equal rights with men. The left-wing parties were ready to represent and spearhead these changes.

The narrowing of the electoral gap convinced the Communist Party (PCI) in the second half of the 1980s to support the transition in the nature of Italian democracy from consensual to majoritarian, through a reform of the electoral law. Then, parts of the left – the Socialist Party, the Social Democrats and the Republican Party – were allied with the Christian Democrats and had joined in governing the country. The assumption was that if the party system took on a new bipolar structure, then the left-wing parties would form a coalition together. In combination, they would beat the Christian Democrats, giving the country the advantages of alternation in government.

It was not only the PCI that favoured a development of this type: for a range of political actors who believed that the Christian Democrats' domination condemned them to play secondary roles, bipolarism appeared to provide an opportunity to increase their political influence. For others – those belonging to so-called civil society – bipolarism, and the expectation that leadership of the country would alternate, would raise the standards of conduct of those in public life by giving the electors – rather than the parties – the power directly to determine the political composition of the executive. Thus would it also make leaders more responsive to the electorate.

Finally, the change having produced results that few considered satisfactory, a more mature line of reasoning emerged. As elsewhere, in Italy too, democracy has been overtaken by changes that have taken place on an international scale. Some have talked of the 'presidentialisation' of European politics (Poguntke and Webb, 2005); it might be more appropriate to speak of 'Americanisation'. This process has at least three fundamental aspects. The first is the upgrading of the premier's role, effectively introducing a form of direct election. The second is the personalisation of leadership (McAllister, 2007). The third is the transformation of parties from mass associations, rooted in society and in the localities, into political enterprises whose aims are confined strictly to maximising electoral support and their hold on public office (Katz and Mair, 2002; van Biezen, 2004).

The factors responsible for the Americanisation of politics were at least three: First, the transformation of European societies consequent upon the 'crisis of Fordism' that caused the great class aggregations to disintegrate, replaced by a society that was much more fragmented and heterogeneous: culturally, politically and in other ways (Pizzorno, 2007). The second factor consists of the media, and especially the advent of television as the fundamental tool of political communication. The third is an overriding cultural offensive (in which political science imported from the other side of the Atlantic played an important role) aimed at accrediting the democratic superiority of the bipolar, two-party, Anglo-Saxon model.[1]

However, it is undeniable that, in Italy, the most significant role was played by the defects of Italian democracy: its slow decision-making processes; its inefficiencies; the frequent cases of bribery and corruption; the difficulty of controlling the public debt (Hine, 1993). The rhetorical exaggeration of these issues, the over-dramatisation of problems, the spread of anti-political discourse – in other words discourse critical of politics as such – and the consequent mobilisation of widespread resentment among citizens, were the weapons with which the offensive was fought (Mastropaolo, 2000). In the two years from 1992 to 1994, that offensive came to a head when a new electoral law was introduced and public prosecutors charged numerous members of the political class with corruption (Reyner, 2005).

The initial hopes of those who wanted this change were that the Christian Democrats and the PCI would become the two aggregating poles of a bipolar democracy. However, things went very differently. The Christian Democrats broke up within two years, the old parties disappeared, and the PCI was forced to undergo a radical transformation when the Berlin Wall fell, bringing down with it not only the party's communist symbolism, but also its more robust standing as a social democratic party, now fully acclimatised to a democratic regime. Finally, the vacuum left by the disintegration of the Christian Democrats and their traditional partners was filled when Berlusconi came onto the scene, not only in possession of the necessary know-how and financial resources to profit from the new rules of the game, but also ready and willing to promote the definitive Americanisation of the political-electoral market. This development has not yet been reflected in any significant constitutional change, as has happened almost everywhere else. But it has been reflected in the introduction of majoritarian electoral laws at both national and local levels. And it has also been reflected in political habits: Italian politics have become highly personalised and, as mentioned, the parties have changed from being mass associations to being political enterprises that are voter and office maximisers.

Looking back at these events, what appears surprising is the extent to which the left-wing political forces, and in particular the PCI and its successors, underestimated the moderate-conservative outlook of the Italian electorate. The 1980s in many ways brought with them a reversal of the climate of the 1970s. Once the social and political changes of the previous decade had been consolidated, the pursuit of private economic interests once again took centre stage. As is well known, Italy is a country with a large independent middle class: it is the country of the self-employed (Sylos Labini, 1974, 1986). This made it highly receptive to the neo-liberal model that was imposed upon it in the 1980s. In its turn the Catholic Church, thanks to the papacy of John Paul II, began to regain credibility, not least because secular culture and politics were unable to counter it with any adequate alternative. This advance has been a lasting one, helping to provide the conditions in which, from 1994 onwards, Berlusconi – corresponding perfectly to the figure of a strong leader for which, throughout the 1980s, calls had been coming from a number of quarters (Briquet, 2005) – would thrive. The political product he offered blended traditional values, liberalism and a massive dose of populism.

The casual way in which even the left favoured this transformation, misreading the mood of the electorate, still remains a cause for amazement. In any case, as long as the popular attitudes we have mentioned predominated, the centre right was always going to win. And yet the centre right does not always win because, unlike other systems in which the political product on offer is rather stable, in Italy it varies considerably, in the sense that the coalition choices of the two sides often change from one election to the next. These choices are therefore decisive in the outcome of elections. In brief: if the centre right remains united, generally speaking it wins. The left can profit from the centre right's governing failures but only on condition that it remains united, if possible including some fragments of the centre right.

This proposition is supported by the past 15 years of Italian electoral history. At the 1994 elections, Berlusconi 'entered the field'. He forged a coalition agreement between Alleanza Nazionale (National Alliance, AN), the NL and Forza Italia (FI), the party he had founded on the eve of the election. He also included, in the lists presented by FI, the most moderate segments of the ex-Christian Democrats, under the leadership of Pierferdinando Casini. On the opposite side were the ex-communists of the Democratic Party of the Left, Rifondazione Comunista (Communist Refoundation, RC) and some smaller parties, including ex-Christian Democrats. A third segment of the ex-Christian Democrats declared that they wanted to locate themselves in the centre and decided to run alone. The centre right won the election by a small margin and, thanks to the new electoral law and to some centrist members of Parliament who sided with him, Berlusconi formed his first government.

That government lasted for only eight months, due to the defection of the NL. In 1996 new elections were held and were marked by two novelties: the NL decided to stand alone, and attempts to found an independent centre coalition were abandoned, bringing many Christian Democrats into the centre left fold. This time it was the centre left led by Prodi, which won, though with a small majority. The lead rapidly dissipated in internal conflict within the coalition. Prodi must be given credit for having taken significant steps towards balancing the budget, which was to enable Italy to be among the first to enter the Euro Club. To do so he had to take measures the unpopularity of which was revealed first by opinion-poll respondents and then by the electorate. RC dissociated itself from the Government and underwent a split. A new executive was created, led by a new premier, with a new parliamentary majority, including some who had abandoned the centre right, but the Government's popularity did not improve. It lost the regional elections of 2000, again changing premier. The centre left also lost the general elections of 2001, when it decided to stand divided and was led by a prime-ministerial candidate drawn from among none of the three who had led the Cabinet, thus effectively disowning the outgoing government and its performance. By contrast, the centre right rediscovered the unity it had lost five years previously, the NL changed tack, and they won the elections by a large margin.

In accordance with the law of constant repetition that dominates Italian politics, 2006 presented a scenario similar to that of 1996. This time, while Berlusconi paid for the unpopularity of his record in government, the centre left stood united, again under Prodi's leadership, and won the elections. In truth, in the run up to the vote the polls had predicted a huge victory, also showing widespread discontent with the performance of the centre right. But when the votes were counted it was discovered that the electors had lied to the pollsters. For his part, Berlusconi conducted an unexpectedly combative election campaign, which left voters less convinced of the inevitability of a centre right defeat, and may have convinced some centre right electors not to abstain. The centre left thus obtained the same proportion of votes as the centre right, and had a very slight lead in terms of seats in the Senate (Briquet and Mastropaolo, 2008b).

An essential part was played by the new electoral law, introduced by the centre right a few weeks before the end of the legislature. If Berlusconi had thought victory possible, he would not have changed the rules of the game. He would have kept the old law, which distributed three-quarters of the seats on the basis of the single-member, simple plurality system the remaining quarter proportionally. Fearing defeat, Berlusconi sought to reduce the scale of the likely left-wing victory and complicate life for its representatives after the vote. Because it is thought that single-member constituencies give an advantage to the centre left, which has stronger local roots, the new law strongly nationalises the vote, reintroducing the proportional system, but assigning a majority premium to the coalition that wins most votes. In contrast to the proportional system in force until the early 1990s, it makes no provision for allowing voters to cast preference votes among the individual candidates presented by their preferred parties. In effect, the vote becomes a choice between the two best-placed candidates for the premiership. In the lower house, assignment of the premium depends on parties' and coalitions' national vote totals so the seat advantage for the centre left was comfortable. In the Senate the premium is distributed region by region, and the lead was only a couple of seats. In any case, the rule that the centre left can win only if it remains united was confirmed.

The 2008 elections were a re-run of the 2001 elections. After two years of bitter internal conflict, the centre left decided to stand divided; by contrast, the centre right was united and again won the elections. Like all good remakes, there were a number of variations. The centre left stood divided, but the centre right (reassured by the splits in the centre left and by the favourable poll predictions) also decided to separate. For starters, the new Partito Democratico (Democratic Party, PD) – which under the leadership of Walter Veltroni brought together two parties, the Left Democrats and the Margherita (the Daisy), which had stood separately at the previous elections – decided to challenge Berlusconi alone. It would accept a coalition agreement only with Antonio Di Pietro's IdV, and gave a few seats, through the provision of secure places on its own lists, to the Radical Party.

In his turn, and reassured by this decision, Berlusconi decided to throw out the most undisciplined partner in his coalition, the ex-Christian Democrats (UDC) led by Casini. We should not forget that the majority premium is given to the side that has obtained the most votes. Based on the 2006 results, the electoral capital of the PD and IdV came to around 32–35 per cent. By contrast, the electoral capital of the grouping led by Berlusconi could be presumed to be considerably more than 40 per cent. The UDC's five per cent was thus superfluous and indeed, it was apparent that if Berlusconi were to win the election, the votes obtained by the UDC would serve appreciably to reduce the number of seats awarded to the Democratic Party. The last of the novelties is that FI formed a single list in alliance with AN – the Popolo della Libertà (People of Freedom, PdL). This is not yet a new party, but promises to become one. The NL on the contrary was allowed to run alongside the PdL as a fully autonomous coalition partner.

It is very probable that had the PD again come to an agreement with the radical left, Berlusconi would not have gone without the contribution of the UDC under Casini, who would have demanded and obtained large benefits in exchange. In this case, though, the far left parties (RC, the Greens, the Party of Italian Communists) would not have been eliminated from the political scene. It is equally certain that the centre-right majority would have obtained far fewer seats than it actually did, while the presence of a former Christian Democrat like Casini in the majority would have had a considerable moderating effect, as it did between 2001 and 2006.

This gives a strong foundation to the suspicion that Berlusconi and Veltroni made an agreement before the elections, to seek to expel the small parties from Parliament. It remains to be understood why such an agreement should ever have been reached, given that, in making the decision, Veltroni ensured that his opponent obtained a striking success in terms of seats. There are many possible answers. The most probable one undoubtedly revolves around the conflicts that divided the centre left between 2006 and 2008. But we will come back to that later.

The tragedy of the Prodi government

If the 2008 elections were a remake of 2001, those of 2006 were a remake of the 1996 elections. Similarly, the Government's record during the 2006–2008 legislature was an accelerated remake of the 1996–2001 legislature: there were more or less the same conflicts within the majority, and the legislative achievements were even more modest than those of the previous government – with the additional difficulty that, by reducing the centre left majority, the electoral law approved *in extremis* by the centre right proved to be the trap it had been designed to be.

As had been the case in 1996, the coalition was a sort of *Union sacrée* against Berlusconi. It included not only centre-left parties, but also two ex-allies of Berlusconi: the Democratic Union for Europe (Unione Democratici per l'Europa, UDEUR) under Clemente Mastella, and Berlusconi's former Treasury Minister, Lamberto Dini. It combined Catholics and lay politicians, communists, ex-communists and post-communists, culturally closer to the Third Way than to the social democratic tradition, together with socialists and self-declared liberals alongside IdV. Led by an ex-public prosecutor who had entered politics by raising the issue of corruption in public life and giving stirring anti-political speeches, IdV is a party that it is difficult to regard as belonging genuinely on the centre left.

At over 200 pages, the electoral programme of the centre-left Unione was thus a lengthy and woolly document, which laboriously tried to reconcile the demands of the coalition's mixed components. That life for the new majority would be highly complicated was immediately confirmed by the birth-pains of the new executive, which was the largest to have taken office in the previous 20 years. Each coalition partner wanted to maintain its distinctness, helping to complicate the situation. The far left could not allow itself be eclipsed by the moderate left or the centre, and vice versa.

This is not to say that Prodi had no clear ideas or any political agenda of his own: that he did is shown by his choice of key ministers (Briquet and Mastropaolo, 2008a), which represented Italy's most illustrious political and cultural tendencies. Prodi himself represented the Catholic-democratic tradition. The Treasury Minister, Tommaso Padoa-Schioppa, was an expression of the *grand commis* of state-run corporations in the 1950s; of liberal-democratic background, from the 1970s he worked at the Bank of Italy. Lastly, Pierluigi Bersani and Vincenzo Visco, responsible for economic development, and finance, respectively embodied the PCI's tradition of efficient administration, which for 40 years had made a name for itself in local government. This was more or less the same team as in 1996, with Padoa-Schioppa (ex-manager of the Bank of Italy) in place of Carlo Azeglio Ciampi, who had been Governor of the Bank of Italy before he entered politics.

These men were united by their commitment to a political and economic strategy involving a thoroughgoing reform of Italian capitalism and of its operating procedures (Barca, 2006). Embarked upon by the Amato and Ciampi governments following the 1992 crisis but interrupted by Berlusconi's victory in 1994, the strategy was tenaciously revived after 1996. Over the following five years, its most salient features were: the adoption of the Euro (to impose external restraints that would put Italian industry under pressure to perform more efficiently) and a huge privatisation programme (to expand and reinvigorate the entrepreneurial class). The results had been rather modest. The lira was successfully consigned to history, but privatisation produced results that were frequently disastrous, the low prices paid by purchasers impoverishing the country's industrial fabric (Florio, 2004).

With few variations, the second Prodi government advanced the same plan for modernisation in 2006 as it had the first time, although this time it had an extremely difficult inheritance. As well as the modest results it had achieved previously, there were the failures of the Berlusconi governments between 2001 and 2006. Some of the responsibility lies with the difficult economic situation after 11 September. However, the Government had pursued a chaotic blend of neo-liberal and consensus policies with very disappointing results (Ricolfi, 2005). The introduction of the Euro had caused a large increase in real prices, much larger than that recorded by the official rate of inflation, with a corresponding impoverishment of families. Neither investment nor consumption had grown, and the industrial system was in a depressing state of decline. The crisis at Fiat, which had seen the Government simply stand by, was certainly the most visible demonstration of this, while promises to initiate large-scale infrastructural projects had not been kept. If electors had been rational, and if they had not enjoyed fooling the pollsters, then in the light of data on GDP and the distribution of income, the defeat of Berlusconi in 2006 would have been every bit as overwhelming as polls were predicting.

In line with its cultural reference points, the Prodi government immediately put in place a rigorous policy to balance the budget by reducing public spending and imposing fiscal discipline. As a result it immediately made a name for itself by successfully addressing one of the country's most intractable problems, the very high propensity of taxpayers to evade taxes. The problem was that the resulting substantial increase in revenue (which in truth must partly be attributed also to a more favourable economic situation) was not enough to satisfy anybody. The large companies obtained only timid measures to support industry. The trade unions failed to obtain pay rises for employees. The result was that both groups remained dissatisfied, to Berlusconi's obvious gratification. The Prodi government had also begun a vast programme of liberalisation affecting taxi drivers, pharmacies, banks and notaries. During the subsequent 20 months, though, the Government's proposals ran aground in Parliament and the measure was highly diluted, with the effect of causing disappointment and resentment not only among the interest groups involved, but also those – the general public – who were in favour of liberalisation. Indeed, with a majority of only two in the Senate, and racked by internal divisions, what the Government could do was limited. Measures to redistribute income in favour of the less well-off were blocked by the moderate wing. The attempt to introduce regulations to protect homosexual couples failed due to the opposition of the Catholics (noisily supported by the Church). In foreign affairs, the verdict on the Prodi government is only slightly better.

In short, for two years the Prodi government struggled to survive in a political atmosphere saturated with Berlusconi's invective, while most of the press, unhappy with the demands made by the radical left, even though these chiefly went unmet, rapidly dissociated itself from it. The atmosphere was worsened by the protests of some of the occupational associations, first and foremost the taxi drivers, and by the public mood as expressed in polls, which quickly became very negative. Lastly, in the second half of 2007, the international economic situation changed for the worse with a devaluation of the dollar, the sub-prime mortgage crisis and spiralling oil prices. So retrospectively the 2006–2008 legislature may be remembered as little more than a long election campaign, carried out energetically by the centre right and by Berlusconi personally. Berlusconi ignored the dissociation of his allies (who were convinced that despite everything, the Prodi government would last, and who wanted to rid themselves of the encumbrance of Berlusconi's leadership) and doggedly pursued his plan to bring about the early dissolution of the legislature (see Chapter 5 by Albertazzi and McDonnell). If the latter had reached its natural conclusion in 2011 he would have been too old to lead the centre right again.

The post-election honeymoon

The reasons for the early end to the legislature will no doubt be debated at length. The most obvious one is that it started very badly, with too heterogeneous and too weak a majority for the complicated constitutional architecture of Italy's political system to be able to sustain. However, as we shall now explain, the paradox is that it was Prodi himself who lit the fuse that was to ignite the dynamite beneath his and his ministers' seats.

The political project Prodi sought to pursue when he stood for the premiership the first time was the bringing together of all the most significant forces sharing a reformist outlook. After the disintegration or metamorphosis of the traditional parties, the intention was to create one large Democratic Party, which would be able to preside over and stabilise the left of the political spectrum, overcoming outdated divisions. Initially launched in 1994, the project had encountered insuperable obstacles in the form of parties that already had their own consolidated political machinery, with strong and heterogeneous national and local leadership groups. And the parties were enormously varied. There were Catholic and secular parties, the former reinvigorated and spurred on by the Church's political activism. There were parties that identified themselves with the European social democratic tradition and belonged to the European Socialist Party. There were ex-Christian Democrats, closer to the European Popular Party. There were advocates of the Third Way and exponents of Catholic solidarity. Nor were regional diversities of secondary importance. There were those who supported an American-style democracy, tending towards presidentialism, together with fond supporters of the parliamentary model enshrined by the 1948 Constitution, who were against any abrupt revision.

It was no accident then that the project remained on hold for almost 15 years, only to be revived when the difficulties of the Prodi government became clear (Lazar, 2008). Obviously, Prodi could not oppose it, although it was immediately clear that he would be unable to lead the new party: both because opinion polls showed a marked decline in his popularity, and because his competitors did not intend to offer him any further position of prominence. Nevertheless it was also clear that, once a leader had been chosen for the party, objectively speaking for Prodi he would be a competitor to be feared.

And this is exactly what happened. Primaries were called; party members were asked to indicate their preferred leader, and the telegenic Walter Veltroni – the ex-communist who has openly distanced himself from the tradition of the PCI and whose political icons are the Kennedys – was chosen. Given the Government's unpopularity and Veltroni's need to establish, for the party, an image of novelty, his first problem was that he had to distance himself from the Government. And despite all the official denials, this worked in favour of the calling of early elections.

However, there was a brake, real or presumed, on early elections: the electoral system. The man who had designed the system – NL ex-minister Roberto Calderoli – had himself described it as 'muck'. Veltroni thus engaged in negotiations with the opposition aimed at producing a new electoral law – one which, as Veltroni said right from the start, would reduce the party system's fragmentation. Probably his goal was a law that on one hand would eliminate the small 'personal' parties – those based on the charisma of single individuals – and on the other hand would strengthen the role of the UDC so that Casini could dissociate himself from Berlusconi. This would enable Veltroni to free himself from the radical left wing.

But the main effect of this engagement with the opposition parties, ignoring the majority parties, was to destabilise Prodi's coalition. Once plans for reform were on the table, Dini and Mastella openly took their distance. Meanwhile, the radical left, made nervous by Veltroni's opening towards the centre and the threat of new electoral laws; concerned by opinion polls unfavourable to the Government and its record, and spurred on by the need to confirm its own identity, became more strident and began to join in the challenges to the Government.

The Prodi government fell after a vote of no confidence, on 24 January 2008. From that moment, Berlusconi broke off all discussion on the electoral law, Veltroni's attempts to persuade Casini's UDC to constitute an emergency executive to introduce a new law failed, and all that remained for President Napolitano to do was to sign the decree dissolving Parliament and calling new elections, which he did on 8 February.

There is no doubt that the 722 days of the Prodi government's existence were very difficult for it. Its friends made its life difficult, surely, but its enemies were absolutely merciless. On no occasion – except once or twice on foreign affairs – did the opposition take into account the interests of the country. Even when faced with serious emergencies, it continued its no-holds-barred war, which it began as soon as the ballot boxes had closed, claiming that the elections had been rigged. With the agreement of FI (which demanded handsome compensation for the crime of electoral fraud) Parliament approved a general amnesty at the beginning of July, aimed at alleviating dramatic overcrowding in the country's prisons. Immediately afterwards it accused the Government of not caring about citizens' security. The legislature concluded with the Government ruthlessly pinned to the monstrous mountain of rubbish that had accumulated in Campania. Little did it matter that the problem was ten years old or that the Berlusconi government had done nothing significant during five years to tackle the emergency. When it exploded, Berlusconi unreservedly thrust all responsibility onto Prodi's government and he succeeded perfectly. The same may be said for the case of Alitalia. The disastrous state of Italy's flagship air carrier was long-standing, and Prodi inherited the situation from Berlusconi. Instead of supporting attempts at privatisation and measures to balance the company's books, the opposition unconditionally supported the role of international hub for Malpensa Airport, although it was unsustainable financially and logistically, and during the 2008 election campaign went so far as to cause negotiations for the sale of Alitalia to Air France to fail, promising an unlikely intervention by Italian businessmen.

Prodi also had to deal with the anti-political attitudes widespread among crucial sectors of the population. In that respect, nothing had changed since the previous legislature, but for some unfathomable reason a lethal wave of discontent over the privileges and costs of politicians swept the public. Exploited by the opposition – even though, when in government, it had increased those very privileges and costs – this wave of discontent was encouraged by a well known comedian, Beppe Grillo, who assumed the role of chief defender of public morality and even organised a street demonstration with the support of the NL and Di Pietro's party. That Italian politicians enjoy disgraceful privileges, and cost the taxpayer immense amounts of money is undeniable (although the Catholic Church costs much more). But the striking thing is that the mobilisation took as its main target the Prodi government and its majority, and that the latter reacted clumsily, underestimating the danger. To minimise the significance of the protest by labelling it 'anti-political' and 'populist' was an imprudent move, when some cost-cutting measures might have had more success. On the other hand, attempts to introduce such measures would almost certainly have been undermined by the weakness of the parliamentary majority and no-one succeeded in laying at the opposition's door its sizeable slice of the responsibility.

Prodi also made a number of gaffes. These were nothing as compared to those of his predecessor who, while a gaffe-maker of the first order and a very mediocre humorist, as a political entrepreneur has shown himself to be made of excellent stuff. There is not much to be said about his election campaign. It had none of the fire of his 2006 campaign, and it was, indeed, conducted in a low key. But this did not prevent him from drawing on all of the themes that are currently typical of the mainstream European right, which now has no scruples about exploiting the fears surrounding immigration, to be restricted at all costs, that have been aroused by the new populist right. To this, Berlusconi added proposals to reduce the tax burden, to introduce fiscal federalism, to limit further the rights of wage-earners, and to restrict jobs in the public sector. Elsewhere in this book, the election campaign will be analysed in detail, together with the results of the election. Here one point stands out clearly: Berlusconi's success was not based on any progress made by his own party – which occurred in a very limited form only in some parts of Southern Italy – but rather on the advance of the NL which, together with the success of Di Pietro, confirms the existence of a widespread democratic malaise, and also bears witness to the diffidence of a part of the centre-right electorate towards the leader of the coalition.

It is worth asking whether Berlusconi and his majority have any strategic plan to guide their actions in office. Judging by the initial acts of the new government, it would appear that such a plan does not exist. Berlusconi often demonstrates an ability to combine the calculation of electoral advantage with a solid practical spirit – which pushes him to sympathise with the radicalism of the right-wing politicians of the NL (for example on immigration) while adopting a more cautious stance, satisfying them on a symbolic level only (aware, as he is, that Italy needs immigrants and that in any case it would not be easy to remove them). The Government's moves concerning questions of public spending and public administration have reflected a neo-liberalism of a sort of 'sorcerer's apprentice' variety. Meanwhile the premier's concern to exploit his position to further his personal affairs remains uppermost. However, this limited do-it-yourself style of programming does not rule out the possibility that some broader strategic plan may also exist.

If Berlusconi himself is without any such plan, it may lie in a book written a few months ago by one of his most important ministers, Giulio Tremonti (2008), who is in charge of the economy. Here he attempts to weld together three highly heterogeneous elements. The first is the egoistic and uninhibited individualism of Berlusconi, based on a casual ostentation of wealth and privilege, aimed at allowing even the poorer classes to share in them, though only vicariously. The second element is the provincial right wing, which is anti-globalisation and unenthusiastic about Europe. The third is the 'reactionary moralism' demanded by the Church hierarchy (Cousin and Vitale, 2007: 111–112).

The title of Tremonti's book already says a lot about it: *La paura e la speranza* ('The fear and the hope'). In it, the author offers a rigorous, critical analysis of globalisation. Far from being the Promised Land, globalisation and the many crises it has triggered – from financial crises to the energy crisis – risk precipitating a terrible catastrophe. In this scenario, the fundamentalist neo-liberalism of the EU renders Europe one of the most defenceless players. Having no foreign policy, no industrial or commercial policy, no energy policy, no social policy, no employment policy, Europe is also culturally defenceless. Having given up the benefits of statism in exchange for a complex and uncertain style of political leadership, Europe thus has only one chance to save itself: to rediscover the unifying – community-wide – principle of its Judeo-Christian cultural roots, closing ranks to defend itself against the economic, political and cultural dangers coming from outside. This leads to a further proposal that the authorities of the European Union take responsibility for managing the economy, so as to re-launch investment in strategic sectors, bypassing the requirement, erroneously portrayed as sacred, to contain the level of public debt. According to Tremonti, the reaction to neo-liberalism should thus be a mixture of post-Keynesianism and EC withdrawal. We will see in the years to come how much progress such a strategy actually succeeds in making. Effectively, though it is not without realistic suggestions, and undoubtedly wrong-foots the left, it above all calls to mind the attempts made by the Congress of Vienna to eradicate the inheritance of the French Revolution.

Let us now come to Veltroni to try to answer the question posed earlier. Why, leaving aside the agreement with Di Pietro's IdV, did Veltroni decide to run alone? The answer he himself has given is a simple one. The Prodi government fell not because of the defection of its centrist partners, but because of the extreme and unrealistic demands made by the radical left, driven by communist nostalgia unmindful of the country's need for modernisation. One might as well, therefore, seek alternative allies, if not today, then tomorrow.

There is of course some truth in this answer. There actually was conflict between the Democratic Party and the radical left-wing parties and, in some cases – such as policies to protect the environment – the action of the radical left really did have a paralysing effect. The conflict over employment and job security was also acute, as it was over welfare policies. However, aside from the substance of the conflicts, what was more significant was their amplification by the more moderate segments of the Democratic Party, by the press and by business. The irresponsibility of the radical left was a theme that was obsessively repeated for 18 months. By contrast, whereas it went as far in some more extreme *milieux* to theorise the uselessness of sacrificing itself to the defence of Prodi, the radical left showed itself prepared to give ground in terms of policies. It is no accident then that the far left also made no effort to dissuade Veltroni from his intentions. Though proposed by Veltroni, the separation was a consensual one.

But Veltroni's decision may have been driven by more deep-seated factors. One is very probably psychological. As heir to the moderate wing of the PCI, Veltroni saw in the electoral law an opportunity to settle old scores both with the wing that was determined to remain communist and with an old rival of the PCI, the Socialist Party. Unable to defeat his principal adversary, Veltroni thus preferred to use the elections to free himself from his secondary competitors, those who had the most power to block any compromise he might want to enter into with Berlusconi, with whom he shares some degree of community of outlook about the future of the Republic's institutions. More than once, the leader of the Democratic Party has said he is in favour of a presidential regime.

Be that as it may, the election campaign was one of the most boring in Italy's post-war history. Veltroni produced a very lean programme, fully in agreement with the Third Way: there was no mention of inequality or poverty; little mention of job insecurity; considerable mention of privatisation and liberalisation. Not only that, Veltroni also abandoned those themes that had been so dear to the old *Union Sacré* against Berlusconi. Not a word was said about his rival's excessive media presence, or his conflict of interests, or the doubtful standards of conduct suggested by Berlusconi's numerous court cases – neutralised by regulations tailored to his personal needs and introduced by his own government – as well as various lesser charges. Veltroni never once even named his adversary during the election campaign and, if anything, was concerned to shape the parliamentary representation of his party to his own advantage.

Having saved a small group of prominent people, Veltroni exploited the electoral law, which forces voters to accept the candidates selected by their preferred party's leaders, to swell the ranks of the PD's parliamentarians with men and women faithful to him, who were also very young and without previous political experience. The rhetoric of rejuvenation thus succeeded in further rejuvenating what was already the youngest parliament among those of the great Western democracies. Persuaded he would be defeated, Veltroni invested in the future. It remains to be seen what will happen. For the moment, the big names in the PD have been annihilated by the defeat Berlusconi has inflicted upon them and by the one they have suffered at the hands of Veltroni. For his part, Prodi has left the scene while the party has been highly Americanised.

Conclusion

Since electors do not change their decisions, or they change them rarely, in 2008 the political class again decided to change. More or less as happened in 1994, it changed the product on offer, and changed the rules, or rather, how they are applied, which amounts to the same thing. Thereby, the long-standing dream of drastically simplifying the party system has finally been realised. Apart from IdV, the 'personal' parties have disappeared. Dini has contented himself with a seat among the ranks of the centre right. Mastella, who also betrayed Prodi, saw the reward for that betrayal denied him, becoming the symbol of political immorality. Furthermore, the most radical formations, of both left and right, have been eliminated from Parliament. Italy does not yet have a two-party system, but it is getting very close. In any case, from the cultural standpoint politics is now less heterogeneous. We will see whether appearances, as so often happens, are misleading, or whether this time they correspond to the substance.

It is perhaps this that explains the apparent change in the political climate that took place for a few weeks after the elections, Berlusconi's ferocious polemic against Prodi – and the harsh polemic against Berlusconi's habit of exploiting public office to advance his own personal interests – seeming for a while to belong to a distant past (Diamanti, 2008). Subsequently, this climate of appeasement, though unaffected by Government measures against immigrants, evaporated as Parliament began to approve legislation restricting the investigative powers of the judiciary and sheltering the head of government from the impact of the legal proceedings currently under way against him. By contrast, the climate that has been created within so-called civil society does not appear destined to disappear at any time soon. On the contrary, the climate has recently got quite a lot nastier and become uncivil. It has been reflected in the burning of gypsy encampments in Naples; their obstruction in Veneto, where protesters have prevented them from being built; the NL's promises of a militia to maintain security and provide defence against immigrants. On 25 April, shortly after the elections, Grillo had already brought together new crowds of people irate about politics. In Rome, fascist gangs beating people up and hunting down students and homosexuals have reappeared; not to mention smaller scale, less obtrusive episodes such as bullying in schools – which the public was not used to seeing, but that sometimes circulate on YouTube and often end up in the crime pages of the newspapers – without anyone connecting them to politics.

In all of this, the centre right feels at home, while the centre left is silent. The Democratic Party has issued reminders that immigrants are useful for business and in caring for families, and has defined measures to curtail illegal immigration, planned by the Government, as 'impractical' – while failing to criticise them in terms of concepts like pity, solidarity and humanity, as though it were unaware of the inequalities dividing Italian society.[2] For his part, the leader of the People of Freedom group in the Senate has legitimated the act of NL militants bursting into gypsy encampments being built in Venice and destined for gypsies of Italian nationality, by saying that houses for Italians should be built first. The truth is that the right has preached hate against its political adversaries, against the State and the tax authorities, against immigrants, against those who are different and against Southern Italy, for years. In Parliament it has behaved in ways that are unacceptable in a civilised country – going so far as to open champagne in the Chamber of Deputies the day the Prodi government fell – while the centre left has failed to offer any contrasting message.

Since the PD believes itself to be a potential governing party, it feels its style of opposition should be restrained. Those are also the styles that opinion polls say the public wants. Opinion polls are the voice of the sovereign people, and the sovereign people must not be contradicted. What little solidarity remains in Italy is monopolised by the Church, but the Church exercises it with numerous reservations. We are left with the results of a prolonged campaign to poison civil society that a facade of good manners is unlikely to counteract – the less so because, for its part, civil society is already rather sick.

Notes

1. A history of the spread of American political science to Europe has not been written. A valuable contribution, whose focus is confined to the British case, has been made by Adcock, Bevir and Stimson (2007).
2. According to the daily newspaper *la Repubblica* (11 June 2008), in the very wealthy Veneto area the gap between rich and poor is larger than anywhere else in Europe (Visetti, 2008).

References

Adcock, E., Bevir, M. and Stimson, S. (2007) *Modern Political Science*, Princeton: Princeton University Press.
Barca, F. (2006) *Italia frenata. Paradossi e lezioni della politica per lo sviluppo*, Rome: Donzelli.
Briquet, J.L. (2005) 'Leçons d'une crise: l'affirmation de la droite italienne', pp. 229–250 in F. Matonti, (ed.), *La démobilisation politique*, Paris: La Dispute.

Briquet, J.L. and Mastropaolo, A. (eds) (2008a) *Italian Politics: The Center-Left's Poisoned Victory*, New York and Oxford: Berghahn.

Briquet, J.L. and Mastropaolo, A. (2008b) 'Introduction', pp. 37–58 in J.L. Briquet, and A. Mastropaolo (eds), *Italian Politics: The Center-Left's Poisoned Victory*, New York and Oxford: Berghahn.

Cousin, T. and Vitale, T. (2007) 'De Portorotondo à Wolfenboro. Vertus et faux-semblants de la comparaison Sarkozy-Berlusconi', *Mouvements* 52: 105–113.

Diamanti, I. (2008) 'Politica educata e società incivile', *la Repubblica*, 7 June, www.repubblica.it/2008/06/sezioni/politica/bussola-diamanti-7-giu/bussola-diamanti-7-giu/bussola-diamanti-7-giu.html

Feltrin, P. and Natale, P. (2008) 'Elezioni politiche 2008. Primi risultati e primi scenari', *Polena* 1: 143–167.

Feltrin, P., Natale, P. and Fabrizio, D. (2006) 'La sorpresa di aprile. Una prima analisi delle elezioni politiche 2006 in Italia', *Polena* 1: 145–169.

Florio, M. (2004) 'Le privatizzazioni come mito riformista', *Meridiana* 50(51): 133–160.

Hine, D. (1993) *Governing Italy: the Politics of Bargained Pluralism*, Oxford: Clarendon Press.

Katz, R.S. and Mair, P. (2002) 'The ascendancy of the party in public office: party organizational change in twentieth-century democracies', pp. 113–136 in R. Gunther, J.R. Montero and J.J. Linz (eds), *Political Parties: Old Concepts and New Challenges*, Oxford: Oxford University Press.

Lazar, M. (2008) 'La nascita del partito democratico', pp. 67–86 in M. Donovan and P. Onofri (eds), *Politica in Italia. I fatti dell'anno e le interpretazioni. Edizione 2008*, Bologna: Il Mulino.

Mastropaolo, A. (2000) *Antipolitica. Alle origini della crisi italiana*, Naples: L'Ancora.

McAllister, I. (2007) 'The personalization of politics', pp. 571–588 in R.J. Dalton and H.-D. Klingemann (eds), *The Oxford Handbook of Political Behaviour*, Oxford: Oxford University Press.

Newell, J.L. (2006) 'The Italian election of 2006: myths and realities', *West European Politics* 29(4): 802–813.

Pizzorno, A. (2001) 'Natura della disuguaglianza. Potere politico e potere privato nella società in via di globalizzazione', *Stato e mercato* 2: 201–236.

Poguntke, T. and Webb, P. (2005) *The Presidentialization of Politics. A Comparative Study of Modern Democracies*, Oxford: Oxford University Press.

Reyner, H. (2005) *Les scandales politiques – L'opération mains propres en Italie*, Houdiard: Paris.

Ricolfi, L. (2005) *Dossier Italia: a che punto è il contratto con gli italiani*, Bologna: Il Mulino.

Sylos Labini, P. (1974) *Saggio sulle classi sociali*, Rome and Bari: Laterza.

Sylos Labini, P. (1986) *Le classi sociali negli anni '80*, Rome and Bari: Laterza.

Tremonti, G. (2008) *La paura e la speranza. Europa: la crisi globale che si avvicina e la via per superarla*, Milan: Mondadori.

van Biezen, I. (2004) 'Political parties as public utilities', *Party Politics* 6(10): 701–722.

Visetti, G. (2008) 'Il Veneto della ricchezza nasconde i suoi poveri', *la Repubblica*, 11 June.

2
The Economic Context

Michele Capriati

Introduction

Normally, in western democracies, governments concentrate the less popular economic-recovery measures on the first two years of their periods in Office.[1] This enables them to husband the resources required for expansion policies, for the period towards the end of their mandate – enabling them to go into the subsequent election campaign with a healthy economy, and in this way to maximise their electoral support. A government which is in office for only two years and inherits a large budget deficit is therefore forced to take upon itself only the 'dirty work' without benefiting from the advantages of the second part of the story. That this does not pay from an electoral point of view is also due to the fact that voters find it rather difficult to understand why deficit reductions are important or why the level of public debt is significant. Moreover, when prices go up, mortgages become increasingly expensive, and consumption goes down. These are some of the reasons why the 2008 election campaign was very unusual. Long-standing unresolved problems became entwined with more recent uncertainties, and with the great expectations of the less well-off, with the bitter disappointment of the more fortunate and with the resistance of those enjoying exclusive privileges.

In this chapter I will provide an overview of the economic context, which directly or indirectly affected voters' decisions. In the first two sections I will focus on the short- and long-term changes in the economic situation in general, and in the performance of the Italian economy. In the third section I will analyse in greater depth the principal economic-policy measures taken by the outgoing government and in the fourth I will focus on the most important economic proposals outlined in the major coalitions' manifestos. In the last section I will make some closing remarks about the victory of the right-wing coalition led by Silvio Berlusconi.

Between stagflation and income inequality

The 2008 election campaign was marked by a widespread sense of uncertainty. A problem that seemed to have been resolved after the crisis of the 1970s again presented itself: stagflation, or the presence of both economic stagnation and inflation. Since August 2007 the world economy has been affected by the crisis of the US sub-prime mortgage sector, which has contributed to a progressive slowdown in economic growth. In fact, following this event, the United States and to a degree the European banks reduced the amount of credit available for mortgages, thus affecting the property market. The main stock-market indices showed a downward trend, while US unemployment rates began to rise. This took place in spite of the expansive monetary policies implemented by the Federal Reserve, which reduced the fed funds reference rate from 5.25 per cent in September 2007 to 3.00 per cent at the beginning of 2008. Concerned about the inflationary push, the European Central Bank has kept the rate at 4.00 per cent since June 2007.[2]

The remarkable development of the major emerging countries (China, India and Russia) helped to push oil prices up from an average of $65 a barrel in 2006 to $133 a barrel in May 2008. Food prices went up following increases in demand from the newly industrialised countries and also because of transport costs and the use of certain types of grains in the production of bio-fuels (Targetti, 2008). Since the end of 2007, these trends have generated growing inflationary pressures.

The significant increase in crude-oil and base food prices was due not only to the imbalance between supply and demand caused by the sudden increase in consumption in the major Asian countries, which had found suppliers largely unprepared, but also to significant speculative activities in the international market (the *Economist*, 2008; Rampini, 2008; Targetti, 2008). In Europe, thanks to the strength of the euro, price rises in the raw-materials markets have been significantly lower than elsewhere. Nevertheless, together with other European countries, Italy runs the risk of stagflation, which, thanks to appropriate monetary policies and less adverse trends in the raw materials markets, has not occurred since the 1970s.

Another element of uncertainty that weighed heavily on the election campaign and its outcome was growing hardship among wage-earning and salaried employees, as well as pensioners. The reasons lie in long-term processes common to all industrialised countries, which as a result have seen increased profit shares and reduced incomes from employment.[3] According to a recent study published by the Bank of International Settlements (Ellis and Smith, 2007), in 1983 the share of Italian GDP accruing to profits and to paid employment was 23 and over 75 per cent respectively. Since the mid-1980s, the share associated with capital remuneration has risen. But the real jump took place in the mid-1990s: profits reached 29 per cent in 1994 and more than 31 per cent in 1995, rising to a peak of 33 per cent in 2001. In 2005 they still stood at 31 per cent of GDP, almost a third. That year, employees earned just over 68 per cent of the national income, eight percentage points less than the 76 per cent of 20 years earlier.[4]

The upshot was that the conditions generated by long-term processes, together with economic trends that are leading the national economy to a mixture of high inflation and zero growth, created a particular climate during the election campaign, which prevented either a rational discussion of economic performance in recent years or the expression of unbiased opinions about the achievements of the government in office, particularly with regard to the budget deficit and the public debt.

The macroeconomic scenario

Production and prices

The years 2006 and 2007 marked a significant turnaround as compared to the previous five-year period, which had been characterised by substantial stagnation (Capriati, 2008). Real GDP grew by 1.8 per cent and 1.5 per cent in 2006 and 2007 respectively. This was about one percentage point below the average value recorded for the countries of the European Monetary Union (see Table 2.1), but, as mentioned, was higher than the average recorded in the previous five-year period, that is 0.6 per cent. The forecast for 2008 indicates a new check on growth with percentage values below one (0.6 per cent). This slowdown, which has its origins in the world economic trends mentioned above, is one that was common to all the industrialised countries; but in Italy it has given rise to economic stagnation of significant proportions.

In the 2006–2007 period, growth was stimulated by exports, which rose by more than 5 per cent, and by investments, particularly in 2006, when

Table 2.1   Real GDP growth rate in the main world regions

	2005	2006	2007	2008*
Italy	0.6	1.8	1.5	0.6
United States	3.1	2.9	2.2	1.3
Japan	1.9	2.4	2.1	1.4
EMU	1.6	2.7	2.6	1.7
France	1.9	2.2	2.2	1.7
Germany	0.8	2.9	2.5	1.6
United Kingdom	1.8	2.9	3.1	1.7
Spain	3.6	3.9	3.8	2.7
The rest of the world except for the EU	5.5	5.6	5.4	4.5

Note: * Forecast
Source: Own eleboration of data from IMF, OECD and EU

they rose by 2.5 per cent (see Figure 2.1). In 2007, growth was also stimulated by domestic consumption, which increased by 1.5 per cent. It can therefore be affirmed that in the 2006–2007 period, despite a strong euro, the Italian economy more or less kept pace with the general trend in world growth, dragging investment and, in part, domestic consumption along with it. On the other hand, the slow-down in international trade that began at the end of 2007 slowed down the national economy.

As regards the prices of consumer goods, Italy has, in most recent years, maintained levels equal to the average values recorded for the countries of the European Monetary Union, with a stable inflation rate of about 2.2 per cent (see Table 2.2). Economic forecasts for next year predict an increase in the rate of inflation of more than one percentage point.

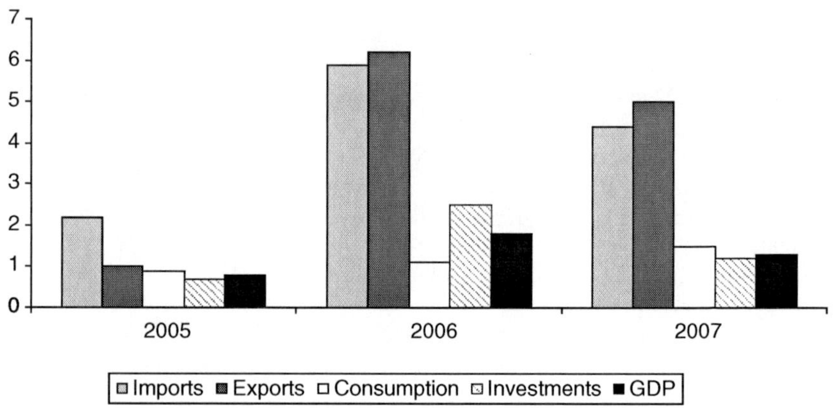

Figure 2.1 GDP, consumption, investments, imports and exports (% variation over the previous year)

Source: Own elaboration on ISTAT data

Table 2.2 Harmonised consumer price indices (% variation over the previous year)

	2005	2006	2007	2008*
Italy	2.2	2.2	2	3.3
Germany	1.9	1.8	2.3	3.1
France	1.9	1.9	1.6	3.3
Spain	3.4	3.6	2.8	4.5
Euro Zone	2.2	2.2	2.1	3.4

Note: * First quarter
Source: Own elaboration of Eurostat data

Trade balance

Due to the considerable increases in oil prices, Italy's trade balance deteriorated sharply between 2004 and 2006, in which year it showed a deficit of €10.2 billion. If we distinguish energy from non-energy products (see Figure 2.2), the negative impact of the former on the balance of payments is quite evident. In fact, between 2003 and 2006, the balance for non-energy products remained substantially unchanged, whereas, after 2004, the balance for energy products rapidly deteriorated, dragging the overall balance downwards to a negative value in 2006. In 2007, the balance of payments improved by €2.9 billion, reversing the deficit of the previous year. This occurred as a result of the improvement in the trade balance both in non-energy products, where the surplus rose from €37.5 billion in 2006 to €47.7 billion in 2007, and in energy products, where the deficit declined by €3 billion, going from €47.7 billion in 2006 to €44.7 billion in 2007. The deficit in energy has, nevertheless, been increasing since the end of 2007 owing to further major increases in oil prices.[5]

Despite the slowdown in world trade at the end of 2007 and the euro's appreciation, export growth was high, over 10 per cent a year. Imports, on the other hand, increased by 14.8 per cent in 2006, and by only 6.0 per cent in 2007. The latter result is entirely due to the euro's appreciation. Export growth was achieved in European and non-European markets alike. Particularly significant is the trade surplus between 2005 and 2007 in the production of machines and mechanical equipment (€10.3 billion) and, to a lesser extent, in the production of electrical instruments and precision tools (€2.1 billion), vehicles (€2.1 billion), and refined oil products (€2.0 billion).

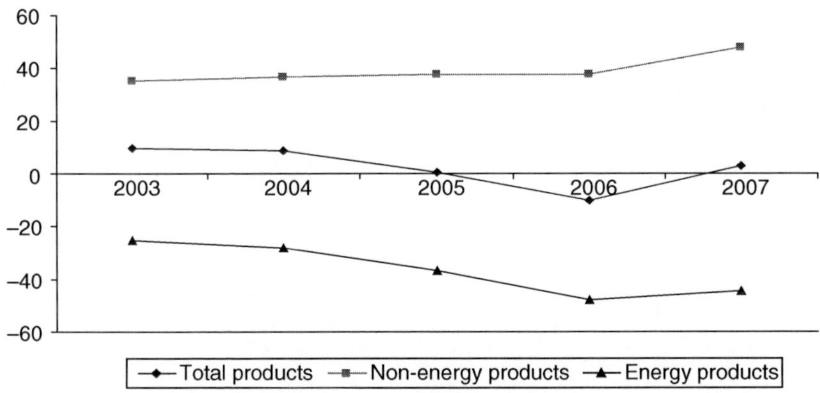

Figure 2.2   Foreign trade balance in goods (millions of euro)

Source: Own elaboration on ISTAT data

Labour market

In the 2006–2007 period, employment continued to rise (see Figure 2.3). It was sustained by increased production, which, as we have just seen, was higher than that of the previous five-year period, and was facilitated by moderation in wage demands. Employment rose by 600,000 units, while the number unemployed decreased by 380,000 units.[6]

This growth mostly affected women, whose employment rate increased by 1.3 per cent, compared to the 0.8 per cent recorded for males and for foreign residents. For the latter group employment increased by 332,000 units, equal to 55 per cent of the total increase recorded in the two-year period. The incidence of this group on the overall employment figures rose to 6.4 per cent (from 5.9 in 2006). The number of foreign workers is particularly large in the regions of the centre-north, in the hotel and catering sectors, as well as in the building industry and family services, where they take the lowest-paid jobs. Owing to these trends, the unemployment rate, following quite a consistent trend that began in 1999, fell to 6.0 per cent (see Figure 2.4), and returned to the levels of the early 1980s. Rates, however, continue to vary across regions; and in fact, at the end of 2007 the employment rate in the south was 11.8 per cent, whereas in the centre-north it was 4.4 per cent.

Public accounts

With regard to the national budget, the trend of the previous five-year period, characterised by an increase in the budget deficit and in the public debt, was reversed (see Figure 2.5). The budget deficit went from 4.3 per cent of GDP in 2005 to 3.4 per cent a year later and to 1.9 per cent in 2007. Hence it was much lower than the 3 per cent limit allowed for by the Stability and Growth Pact.

Figure 2.3 Number of employed and unemployed in Italy (seasonally adjusted absolute values, 000s)

Source: Own elaboration on ISTAT data

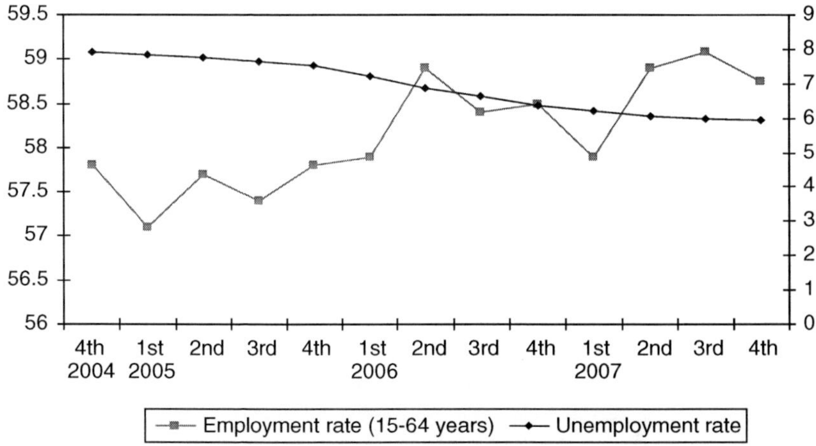

Figure 2.4   Unemployment and employment rates in Italy

Source: Own elaboration on ISTAT data

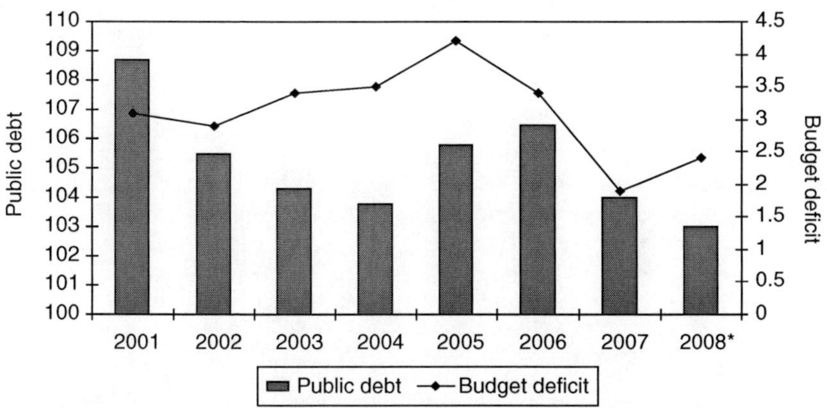

Figure 2.5   Budget deficit and public debt (% of GDP)

Note: * forecast

Source: Own elaboration on ISTAT data

Over the same period of time, the average budget deficit recorded in the countries of the euro zone decreased steadily, bringing those countries very close to balancing their budgets (see Table 2.3). This result was due to the virtuous behaviour of almost all member states, some of which, such as Spain, Holland, Finland and Ireland, managed to achieve a budget surplus. Despite all the efforts that have been made, Italy's deficit is still one of the largest among the countries of the euro zone after Greece, France and Portugal.

Table 2.3   Budget deficit and public debt in the countries of the euro zone (% of GDP)

Country	Budget deficit				Public debt			
	2004	2005	2006	2007	2004	2005	2006	2007
Germany	3.8	3.4	1.6	0	65.6	67.8	67.6	65
France	3.6	2.9	2.4	2.7	64.9	66.4	63.6	64.2
Italy	3.5	4.2	3.4	1.9	103.8	105.8	106.5	104
Spain	0.3	−1	−1.8	−2.2	46.2	43	39.7	36.2
Holland	1.7	0.3	−0.5	−0.4	52.4	52.3	47.9	45.4
Belgium	0	2.3	−0.3	0.2	94.2	92.1	88.2	84.9
Austria	3.7	1.5	1.5	0.5	63.8	63.5	61.8	59.1
Greece	7.4	5.1	2.6	2.8	98.6	98	95.3	94.5
Ireland	−1.4	−1.6	−3	−0.3	29.5	27.4	25.1	25.4
Finland	−2.4	−2.9	−4.1	−5.3	44.1	41.3	39.2	35.4
Portugal	3.4	6.1	3.9	2.6	58.3	63.6	64.7	63.6
Luxenbourg	1.2	0.1	−1.3	−2.9	6.3	6.1	6.6	6.8
Slovenia	2.3	1.5	1.2	0.1	27.6	27.5	27.2	24.1
Cyprus	4.1	2.4	1.2	−3.3	70.2	69.1	64.8	59.8
Malta	4.6	3	2.5	1.8	72.6	70.4	64.2	62.6
Euro zone	2.9	2.5	1.3	0.6	69.6	70.2	68.5	66.4

Source: Bank of Italy

Italy is now the only country of the euro zone to have a public debt larger than GDP: 104 per cent in 2007.[7] The percentage is, however, now again following the downward trend that started in 1994 and was interrupted during the two-year period, 2005–2006.[8] However, the size of the public debt remains much larger than the average in the euro zone (66.4 per cent), and it continues to create considerable difficulties for the management of public expenditure. In fact, in 2007, 5 per cent of GDP, equal to €75 billion euros, was paid out to the holders of state securities. This amount of money does not all stay in Italy, though, but some goes abroad since half of the securities are owned by foreign investors. Owing to its huge public debt, Italy has to earmark one tenth of public money for interest payments, hence reducing the resources that can be allocated to the improvement of public services.

Government actions

Public finances

The most important results of the Prodi government were achieved in the area of reorganisation of the public finances. As we saw earlier, the deficit inherited from the previous Berlusconi government amounted to 4.2 per cent of GDP in 2005. This exceeded the limit set by the terms of European Monetary Union, and led the European Commission in 2005 to initiate infringement proceedings under the excessive deficit provisions.[9] The budget deficit for 2006 was 3.4 per cent and for 2007 1.9 per cent (see Table 2.4). These results were obtained as a consequence of an increase in revenues of 1.7 per cent in 2006 and 1.3 per cent the year after. At the same time, primary expenditure (net of interest) remained essentially the same with an increase of 0.8 per cent in 2006 and a reduction of 0.6 per cent the year after. This permitted an increase in the primary surplus (that is, the difference between revenue and expenditure net of interest on the public debt), which went from 0.3 per cent of GDP in 2005 to 1.3 and 3.1 per cent in the following two years respectively. This, as we saw earlier, allowed the public debt to be brought back onto a downward path.

A major contributory factor to the increase in revenue came from the successes achieved in the fight against tax evasion. It is estimated (MEF, 2008) that during the 2006–2007 period, the variation in revenues that cannot be attributed to the trade cycle or to measures of fiscal policy is more than one per cent of GDP (over €20 billion). This increase can be attributed mainly to the fight against tax evasion and to the spontaneous compliance of taxpayers. This beneficial effect on revenues seems to have been the result of action that was the exact opposite of the action taken by the governments of the 2001–2006 period, when tax amnesties and explicit invitations to tax evasion and avoidance by the Prime Minister (Capriati, 2008), led to a reduction in tax revenues, which in turn led to the trade deficit mentioned earlier on.

The outgoing government's commitment to financial rigor also led to important results in the area of expenditure. This was significantly reduced by adopting a 'bottom-up approach' involving the agreement of the regions and local authorities to a *patto di stabilità interno* (internal stability pact) and a *patto per la salute* (health pact) which sought to control expenditure through a system of incentives and penalties for non-compliance.

Table 2.4   Principal budget indicators for Italy (% of GDP)

	2001	2002	2003	2004	2005	2006	2007	2008*
Revenue	45.0	44.5	45.1	44.5	44.2	45.9	47.2	46.9
Expenditure	48.1	47.4	48.6	48.0	48.4	49.3	49.1	49.4
of which:								
interest payments	*6.3*	*5.5*	*5.1*	*4.7*	*4.5*	*4.6*	*5.0*	*5.0*
Primary expenditure	41.8	41.9	43.5	43.3	43.9	44.7	44.1	44.4
Primary surplus	3.2	2.7	1.6	1.2	0.3	1.3	3.1	2.6
Net deficit	3.1	2.9	3.5	3.5	4.2	3.4	1.9	2.4
Debt	108.8	105.7	104.4	103.8	105.8	106.5	104.0	103.0

Note: * Forecast
Source: ISTAT and Ministry of Finance and Economics

In addition, the Prodi government introduced in 2007 a tax reform designed to amend the two reform laws passed by the Berlusconi government in 2003 and 2005. The resulting three changes to the Imposta sul Reddito delle Persone Fisiche (Personal Income Tax, IRPEF) had a contradictory effect, as observed by Baldini and Bosi (2007). This study shows that the 'first module' favoured those on middle and low incomes, while the 'second module' benefited in particular those in the higher tax brackets – with a clearly regressive impact. In contrast, the measures contained in the 2007 finance law favoured those on middle and low incomes and to a very small extent the poor, while reducing the fiscal benefits available to those on high incomes. The latter reform, however, did not restore the status quo ante, as the reduction in benefits for those on high incomes did not compensate for previous gains. With the 'second module', families in the top 10 per cent of income earners benefited from an increase of more than one per cent, that is about €1,200 a year, while as a result of the 2007 reform law they gave half this amount back. In other words, in 2007 the rich paid less IRPEF than in 2004.

The two modules introduced by the Berlusconi government had cost about €13 billion in total, while the reform introduced by the Prodi government cost no more than a couple of billion euros (even less, according to official estimates).

Liberalisation

The Prodi government implemented two important measures, the so-called Bersani Laws, aiming to increase liberalisation in various sectors in order to assist consumers and extend consumer protection. The measures concerning insurance policies and car insurance eliminated most of the contractual obligations that disadvantaged consumers vis-à-vis insurance companies; improved the transparency of insurance premiums and information about the insured, and reduced contract cancellation costs. In the banking sector, the measures taken focused on reducing the costs of closing an account and re-mortgaging. Moreover, a *fondo di garanzia* (guarantee fund) was established for savers and investors. As regards consumer protection, the government introduced 'class actions', through which consumer associations and committees representing the public interest could claim compensation for damage caused by businesses. Strong protests were staged by taxi drivers against the Government's decision to let municipalities hold special competitions for the recruitment of additional drivers and issue new licences in order to increase supply and reduce taxi fares, mainly in big cities. Very well received, by consumers at least, was the law stipulating that telephone, TV and electronic communication operators could not impose fixed charges on prepaid cards in addition to telephone or service charges. Liberalisation concerned various professions and businesses; in particular the sale of drugs over the counter was allowed in special supermarket departments with the assistance of pharmacists.

According to the Government (PCM, 2008) the impact of these measures, aimed at protecting the citizen/consumer, was significant. It was estimated that Italian families would save between €2.4 and €2.8 billion a year. In 2007 the prices of over-the-counter drugs fell by more than 5.0 per cent, those of mobile phones by 14.6 per cent. The abolition of recharging costs on mobile phone cards led to a saving of about €1.9 billion every year. The elimination of notary fees for the signature authentication required when changes of car ownership take place brought a saving of about €40 euros for every deed (it is worth pointing out that the volume of car sales amounts to €6 billion a year). As for mortgages, the elimination of early repayment charges led to a saving of 2–3 per cent on the residual debt, and the elimination of re-mortgage fees affected about 50,000 people.

Welfare, employment and social cohesion

In the field of welfare, the Prodi government implemented a series of measures designed to increase the protection against a range of risks threatening income loss. Thus, families with children in the middle-to-low income brackets were supported by increases in child allowances. A special plan was introduced in order to increase the number of nurseries, mainly in the South. Protection against loss of income due to old age was addressed through a number of pensions reforms (below).

In the field of employment, the Government reinforced the existing protection available to temporary workers, and through tax relief and tax credits, it encouraged businesses to increase the numbers employed on permanent contracts. The Government re-introduced the principle that employment is normally permanent, stipulating that contracts of over 36 months' duration with the same employer were to be considered permanent contracts. Unemployment benefits were increased and could be claimed for a longer period: up to eight months. A specific package of measures concerned job security: it involved tidying up regulations and imposing more severe sanctions on non-compliant businesses.

A series of interventions were generated through application of the welfare protocol signed by employers' and employees' representatives on 23 July 2007. The Government abolished the Maroni reform introduced by the previous Berlusconi government in 2004, which had provided for an increase, from 1 January 2008, in the minimum retirement age to 60 in the private and public sectors, and to 61 for those registered with the Istituto Nazionale della Previdenza Sociale (National Social Security Institute, INPS) as being self-employed. The protocol replaced that law with a gradual, sustainable increase in the retirement age, which took into consideration the peculiarities of unusually demanding jobs.[10] Moreover, the Government increased very low pensions, which had been excluded from previous measures, and introduced new safeguards for professional categories with temporary contracts.

As part of the wider reform of supplementary benefits, the Government brought forward to 2007 payment of the Trattamento di Fine Rapporto (Severance Pay, TFR)[11] to those employees without a pension fund. This money could be used as additional liquid assets by the employer until it was paid off. Through the Government's welfare reform, firms with more than 50 employees had to allocate the TFR quotas to a fund managed by INPS on behalf of the state. The fund is used to finance specific interventions in the areas of infrastructure, transport and investment.

Competitiveness and the Mezzogiorno

As provided for by the centre left's 2006 election manifesto, the so-called cuneo fiscale (tax wedge)[12] was reduced through tax concessions and reductions for businesses. The Imposta sul Reddito delle Società (Company Income Tax, IRES) was reduced from 33.0 to 27.5 per cent, and the tax credit for investment in research and innovation was raised.

Specifically aimed at the Mezzogiorno were two important tax relief measures, one for new investments the other for new permanent jobs. The Fondo Aree Sottosviluppate (Fund for Underdeveloped Areas) was set up to finance national regional policy measures for the 2007–2013 period, and the Quadro Strategico Nazionale per la Politica Regionale di Sviluppo 2007–2013 (National Strategic Framework for Regional Development Policy 2007–2013) was introduced to facilitate the utilisation of European regional development funds. Particularly significant was the Fondo per le Aree Sottoutilizzate (Fund for Underused Areas), which – pursuant to the Government's Quadro Strategico Nazionale for 2007–2013, which earmarked €118 billion for the following seven years – allocated €63 billion up to 2015. Besides these, numerous additional funds were set up to deal with issues ranging from competitiveness and development, to business finance and investment in scientific and technological research.

Election manifestos

In the 2008 election campaign, unlike those of 2001 and 2006, there was little by way of conflict over alternative programmes; and in fact, for the conscientious voter, there were no fewer than 16 programmes to read, each advanced by as many premier candidates. It is very difficult to give a full account of such a great variety of proposals. I will therefore focus on the programmes put forward by the two main coalitions and on three specific areas which seem to be particularly relevant: fiscal policy, the labour market, fiscal federalism.

Fiscal policy

The tax proposals put forward by the Partito Democratico (Democratic Party, PD) (2008) were based on reductions in IRPEF of one percentage point every year for three years. These were to be financed by extending and strengthening the fight against tax evasion that had been begun by the outgoing government. It was explicitly stated that no tax amnesties would be granted. To assist the lowest wage earners, the manifesto proposed to lighten the tax burden upon them through an increase in tax allowances.

For families, the programme proposed the introduction of a universal tax allowance of €2,500 for the first child, with additional allowances, the size of which would vary according to household income, for further children. Moreover, women's domestic care work was to be recognised through a tax credit, graded according to income and number of children, which in effect considered domestic care as an income production cost.

Repeating the declarations made in previous election campaigns, the programme of the Popolo dell Libertà (People of Freedom, PdL) (2008) called for a reduction in the tax burden to below 40 per cent (from 43.3 per cent in 2007) and a reduction in the maximum rate of IRPEF to 33 per cent. A second proposal was the introduction of a family tax rate to replace the child tax allowance, so that IRPEF would be based on household income rather than the incomes of the individual household members. In effect, total household income remaining equal, the average rate of IRPEF would decrease with increases in the number of household members. Consistent with their traditional proposals, the centre right again proposed to abolish the inheritance and endowment taxes, which had been re-introduced by the Prodi government only for the largest estates,[13] and the total abolition of the Imposta Comunale sugli Immobili (local property tax, ICI) for first-time buyers. This measure would make municipalities more dependent for finance on the state and, as ICI had already been significantly reduced by the Prodi government, it would mainly benefit the owners of larger properties. Moreover, the PdL's manifesto proposed the gradual abolition of the Imposta Regionale sulle Attività Produttive (Regional Business Tax, IRAP); an experimental period of no taxation for new businesses and professional activities by young people, and overtime tax abatement.

The effect of the PD's proposal to reduce rates of IRPEF by one percentage point across the board would have been to reduce the burden on all tax payers, while reduction of the highest rate of IRPEF to 33 per cent, proposed by the PdL, benefits high-income earners only.[14] The abolition of IRAP had already been proposed by the PdL in the 2006 election campaign. It is difficult to implement because it involves a conspicuous loss of revenue (€39 billion euros) and because IRAP is the main source of regional fiscal autonomy.

Labour market

The three pillars of the PD's labour-market policy concerned women, security of employment and the low paid. Various measures were devoted to women including tax incentives designed to encourage female recruitment (as outlined above) and the promotion of family services; a law on equal opportunities; more nurseries and flexitime in the public services. In the area of security of employment, the underlying principle was to sustain work flexibility with state intervention in training, and employment policies which avoid sustaining or enhancing job insecurity. Temporary contracts were to become more expensive for employers and were not to exceed two years. The state was to facilitate long-term employment for young people through measures and incentives that would make it better value for money. A third important theme concerned the wages of low paid workers where the PD proposed a guaranteed minimum wage of €1,000–1,100 per month for contracts not covered by national agreements. There was to be a significant reduction in the fiscal pressure on wage increases negotiated with employers, business groups or local and regional business consortia.

The manifesto of the PdL focused on the themes of full employment and the elimination of job insecurity. To this end it proposed to put into effect the labour-market reform, law no. 30/2003, known as the 'Biagi law', passed by the previous Berlusconi government, and to harmonise supply and demand in the labour market. As regards fiscal reforms, it promised to lift the tax on overtime, productivity bonuses and incentives, and, gradually, also on the thirteenth-month salary.

By lifting taxes on wage increases negotiated with the employer, the PD aimed to encourage workers' and employers' representatives to rely less on national collective bargaining and more on company-level and local pay negotiations. At present the latter concern only large companies and 40 per cent of wage-earners, almost all in central and northern Italy. The incentives proposed by the PD would have increased regional pay differences.[15] They would not, however, have required the State to intervene in collective bargaining, where it would be quite sufficient, in fact, for workers and employers to agree to a reform of the system of pay negotiations. Besides, the PD's proposal would have excluded all the employees of small businesses, where there are no unions, and where company-level and local pay negotiations do not take place.

The PdL's proposal to lift the tax on overtime is fairly easy to apply and benefits most those who put in a lot of it. However, it creates an incentive to use existing employees more intensively rather than create new jobs. Italy has a great need to increase the number of employed, especially women and young people, in the South. Since in many families the male is the breadwinner, the proposal would have the effect of increasing his working hours, while decreasing women's job prospects.

As regards the labour market, on the whole, the election manifestos of the two main political parties were not radically different. Both were concerned with pay issues, both proposing to reduce the taxation on wages. If the PD proposed to lift the tax on the pay rises negotiated with employers, while the PdL proposed, instead, to lift the tax on overtime, in both cases those who would have benefited were employees with secure jobs: male workers, employed in large companies in the centre-north of Italy.

Fiscal federalism

In the 2008 election the theme of fiscal federalism was addressed only in a limited way by the parties, with the sole exception – for obvious reasons – of the Lega Nord (Northern League, NL). Though the issue was not salient in the campaign, the electoral success of the NL, together with continuing pressures for constitutional reform, will make fiscal federalism an important theme in the current legislature. The NL proposed dividing the national territory into three macro-regions, giving regions total fiscal autonomy, and leaving up to 90 per cent of tax revenues in the local territories that had generated them. At least 75 per cent of these resources were to be used for public works and infrastructure, while the rest would be available for improvements to public services.

Fiscal federalism was one of the seven missions of the PdL's manifesto, even though it was one of the least discussed. In this part of the programme the PdL committed itself to a reform of article 119 of the Constitution that had been proposed by the Lombardy Regional Council in 2007. This envisaged allocating to the regions 15 per cent of the taxable base of IRPEF, 80 per cent of VAT revenue, all the excise duties on petrol, and the taxes on tobacco and cigarettes as well as games.

The PD's programme proposed that 'two thirds of the country be freed from the involvement of central government in financing their activities and that state intervention be limited to ensuring conditions of equality for the regions with the lowest per-capita incomes and those historically disadvantaged by the distribution of public resources' (PD, 2008: 5). This implied that the regions in the centre and the north could become totally self-sufficient, whereas southern regions would have to continue to rely on additional resources transferred by the state. Moreover, it was proposed that any public services additional to 'the basic services defined by the Constitution' and guaranteed by the state, be financed by local taxation. The model proposed by the PD thus emphasised the regions' financial autonomy and was willing to contemplate a high level of local variation in the provision of public services.

The proposals of the principal formations thus converged in envisaging a high level of local financial autonomy coupled with the decentralisation of service provision. More specifically, there seems to be a clear consensus on the constitutional reform proposed by Lombardy's regional council. It is no coincidence that the PD's regional councillors abstained when the proposal was voted on by the council. Some observers (e.g., Petrini, 2008) have emphasised that the proposal would entail a huge transfer of resources – one that far outweighs the number and significance of the functions it would be possible to transfer from the state, according to current legislation – and would therefore deprive central government of the resources required for its own general activities and for territorial equalisation.

How the economy helped the right

In the 2008 election campaign economic issues had a different role compared to the role they had in the campaigns of 2001 and 2006. Political leaders did not announce any major new objectives – such as the creation of 'a million jobs' or 'the abolition of ICI' in the case of the centre right; or 'reduction of the fiscal wedge' in the case of the centre left. Apart from the similar proposals on overtime tax abatement (for the centre right) and productivity bonuses (for the centre left) the remaining economic proposals put forward by the main coalitions followed in the footsteps of previous election manifestos and government actions. The themes that had the greatest impact on the electorate were security and immigration.

The individual economic proposals thus do not seem to have shifted support from one coalition to the other. This does not rule out the (highly likely) possibility that the economic context affected the election results in a more general, though nonetheless profound, way this time around. In fact, as argued above, since the summer of 2007 the rapid worsening of economic conditions has created serious difficulties for large swathes of the population. Despite the steady growth of GDP, financial instability and growing inflation changed voters' expectations, and hence the credibility of the political alignments that took to the field. Long-standing, unsolved problems and negative immediate-term trends became closely intertwined, thus generating a widespread sense of frustration.

Income inequality; loss of competitiveness; loss of purchasing power; restrictions on public spending caused by a large public debt: all these gave rise to considerable uncertainty over the economic future. Pessimistic economic expectations together with uncertainty and fear of foreigners (aroused mainly by the media) created contradictory feelings that would benefit the alliance that was able to advance radical and simple solutions, while showing the greater unity behind its leader (Berlusconi).

More often than not, successful management of these socio-economic changes lies beyond the power of the single state, and in any case requires careful reading of the transformations under way. Yet the changes brought about by globalisation were not the subject of much debate between the alignments among which voters were required to choose. Or rather, the centre-left coalition was not able to give an adequate, convincing answer to growing competition from the Far East, the immigration flows from the poorest countries of the world, the progressive impoverishment of wage-earners, and the enormous increases in profits and unearned incomes. On the other hand, the right-wing coalition emphasised the external threat and the need for a defensive answer to the unruliness of the financial market, international trade and immigration flows (Tremonti, 2008).

The lack of adequate answers by previous governments to these problems led to exasperation amongst a considerable number of voters, even those who traditionally supported the centre left, such as wage-earners and pensioners from the regions in the centre of the country. This leads us to think that changes in support at the election will have been deeper and less transient than similar changes at previous elections. The initial actions of the fourth Berlusconi government fulfilled promises made during the election campaign, and contained a novelty. The abatement of taxes on overtime and the abolition of ICI for first-time buyers have been accomplished. The novelty concerns the introduction by the Finance Minister, Giulio Tremonti, of a 'Robin Hood Tax' intended to increase taxation on the profits of oil companies so as to finance a reduction in taxation on the lowest incomes. Besides its uncertain impact, this initiative seems to have been taken more for reasons of propaganda than for its actual likely impact, thus reinforcing a tendency already displayed by previous centre-right governments.[16] And for a country that has a pressing need for effective, permanent solutions, this is not a good start.

Notes

1. This is known as the political or electoral business cycle. There have been numerous contributions on the subject, one of the first being the one by Nordhaus (1975).
2. For a summary of the trends that have affected the international financial markets see Bank of Italy (2008).
3. One of the reasons for this change is the entry into the world economy of one and a half billion workers from the emerging countries, which has increased fourfold the workforce available to global capitalism, particularly multinationals, thus decreasing the collective bargaining power of the workforce in developed countries. The other reason is technological progress, which accelerates the replacement of machinery and techniques, as well as quickening the pace of organisational change, hence supplanting workers and their skills more and more easily, while reducing their bargaining power and wages. In Italy the collective bargaining system established by the 1992–1993 agreements and the labour market reforms introduced in 1997 also had a role to play. The former weakened workers' bargaining power and their ability to regain the purchasing power worn away by inflation; the latter encouraged the spread of flexible, and therefore less expensive, job contracts. For the weight of incomes from employment in Italy see Capriati (2005).
4. To have an idea of the significance of this change it is worth considering that today 8 per cent of GDP is equal to €120 billion. If the distribution between profits and incomes from employment were the same as twenty years ago, then Italian employees would each earn €5,200 more a year on average. However, contrary to conventional thinking, the changed distribution has not generated more investment, since over the past decade the investment rate has been very low on the whole, particularly in Italy.

5. On 3 January 2008 the price of crude oil broke the threshold of €100 a barrel, whereas only three months previously, in early October 2007, it had been $70 a barrel.
6. The difference between the two figures is due to the 'non-work force' category, largely made up of women.
7. Beside Italy, Greece and Belgium also had public debts larger than GDP at the time when the single currency was introduced.
8. In 1994 public debt was at its highest level, 124.3 per cent. Thereafter it declined steadily to 103.8 per cent in 2004.
9. On 9 May 2008, as the Prime Minister, Romano Prodi, handed power over to the new Berlusconi government, the EC officially announced the end of the infringement procedure started in 2005.
10. Shift workers; workers who carry out repetitive tasks; drivers of heavy public-transport vehicles.
11. The TFR gives all workers whose contracts of employment come to an end the right to receive payment approximately equal to one month's salary for every year of employment.
12. This is equal to the difference between the cost of employing labour and the net salaries accruing to that labour. It therefore includes the taxes, welfare contributions, insurance and social-security contributions that are paid by employers and employees.
13. The inheritance tax is already applied only to estates of over €1 million for each spouse and for each heir apparent.
14. It would have benefited in particular incomes above €75,000 and excluded those below €28,000. The personal income tax rates currently above 33 per cent are in fact: 43 per cent for incomes above €75,000, 41 per cent for incomes between €55,000 and €75,000, and 38 per cent for incomes between €28,000 and €55,000.
15. This reform would have entailed re-introduction of the so-called *gabbie salariali* (literally, 'wage cages'), a form of regional wage differentiation which existed before 1969 and was abolished that year after fierce protests by the trade unions.
16. In fact, increases in oil prices depend on phenomena which the Italian government is unable to influence, i.e. the state of world demand and financial phenomena linked to the oil futures markets. If the 'Robin Hood Tax' is implemented as a tax on profits, then it should be borne in mind that a large portion of these are generated outside the national territory during the production phase, rather than during the phases of distribution and sale. On the other hand, any form of taxation on production can be transferred to consumers through price increases, especially when demand is inelastic, as it is in the case of energy products.

References

Baldini, M. and Bosi, P. (2007) *L'equità in tre riforme*, www.lavoce.info, 25 January.

Bank of Italy (2008) *Relazione annuale sul 2007*, Rome: Bank of Italy.

Capriati, M. (2005) 'The Italian economy, 2001–03', *Modern Italy* 10(1): 37–57.

Capriati, M. (2008) 'The economic context', pp. 33–57 in J.L. Newell (ed.), *The Italian General Election of 2006: Romano Prodi's Victory*, Manchester and New York: Manchester University Press.

Economist (2008) 'Double, double, oil and trouble', 31 May.

Ellis, L. and Smith, K. (2007) 'The global upward trend in the profit share', BIS Working Papers, no. 231, July.

MEF [Ministero dell'Economia e delle Finanze] (2008) *Relazione Unificata sull'Economia e la Finanza Pubblica*, Rome, 20 March.

Nordhaus, W. (1975) 'The political business cycle', *Review of Economic Studies* 42: 169–190.

PCM [Presidenza del Consiglio dei Ministri] (2008) *Il Governo Prodi. Rapporto Conclusivo sull'attuazione del Programma del Governo*, Rome. www.attuazione.it.

PD [Partito Democratico] (2008) 'Adesso una Italia nuova. Si può fare', www.partito democratico.it

Pdl [Popolo delle libertà] (2008) 'Sette missioni per il futuro dell'Italia', www.votab erlusconi.it.

Petrini, R. (2008) 'Il fisco di Bossi fa ricco il Nord', *la Repubblica*, 15 May.

Rampini, F. (2008) 'Il casino del greggio virtuale. Così i signori della speculazione manipolano il mercato dell'energia', *la Repubblica*, 9 June.

Targetti, F. (2008) 'Agflazione, fame nel mondo e carovita', www.nelmerito.com.

Tremonti, G. (2008) *La paura e la speranza. Europa: la crisi globale che si avvicina e la via per superarla*, Milan: Mondadori.

3
The EU and International Contexts

Giovanna Antonia Fois

Introduction

Foreign policy did not have a high profile during the election campaign, which was much more intensely focused on internal problems. As in other policy areas, so too here, significant programmatic differences between the two coalitions were not in evidence and such differences as there were, were not, on the whole, the subject of sharp campaign clashes. Thus, as Michele Capriati (Chapter 2) suggests as was true of economic policy, so too in the case of foreign policy, it would hardly be possible to suggest that specific proposals were responsible for any significant shift in the distribution of support from one coalition to another. However, even though Italian citizens are not especially well informed on average, they show growing levels of interest in, and attention to, foreign policy (especially economic aspects linked to immigration, energy supply and exports).[1] Moreover, aside from specific issues, the foreign-policy context may have affected the outcome in a more general way. There are at least five reasons for thinking that this may well have been the case.

First, in a globalised and interdependent world, domestic- and foreign-policy choices are so interwoven that it is hardly possible to distinguish the two in a way that would in fact allow an easy assessment of their relative impact. For example, immigration and security, which *were* salient in the campaign and were heavily exploited by the centre right, are well known for their influence on internal matters. In addition, internal matters, like the problem of garbage in Campania, were exploited, as much by the foreign as by the domestic media, to show how deep was the crisis of the central State – implying a loss of power and prestige of the Italian government in external forums.

Second, therefore, foreign policy issues can also be expected to influence voters through the contribution they make to enhancing or diminishing the general reputations of politicians and governments. If the election campaign was mainly focused on internal issues, some of these were discussed by the foreign press as signs of Italy's decline. In the case both of the rotting garbage, the riots and fires on the streets of Naples, and of the Alitalia crisis, the Government was portrayed as unable to propose or organise effective solutions – as incapable, therefore, of taking important decisions in the future. And the case of the garbage in Naples had real, major, consequences at the European Union level, with the Environment Commissioner, Stavros Dimas, demanding compliance with European law, and threatening Italy with fines to force compliance with EU waste management rules.[2]

Third, there are well-known rhetorical – or perhaps better put: 'meta-political' – differences (that is differences on fundamental values) between parties of the centre left and centre right that are driven especially by different foreign-policy choices. Though, since the end of the Cold War, the choice between one of two geo-political camps has ceased to be an issue in domestic politics, foreign policy-driven 'meta-political' values have remained relevant for the competing elites. In recent legislatures, for instance, the centre left has often pointed a finger at the centre right's supposed Euro-scepticism. On the other side, for the extreme left parties, the dichotomy between peace and war has been very deeply felt, and it twice put at risk the stability of the Prodi government.

Fourth, then, though the fall of the Government at the beginning of 2008 was essentially the consequence of internal factors (especially the approaching date of the referendum on the electoral law), the first major governmental crisis, in 2007, leading to the temporary resignation of Romano Prodi, concerned foreign and defence policy. The Government was outvoted in the Senate twice within the space of a few days. The first time, it happened on a motion concerning enlargement of the US military airport at Vicenza. The second time a foreign-policy debate ended in a statement by Foreign Minister, Massimo D'Alema, not supported by the majority of the Senate. The motion presented by the parties of the Unione was rejected by two votes.

Fifth, therefore, with an uncertain majority in the Senate and such a large number of parties in the coalition that had emerged victorious from the 2006 general election, debates on beliefs and ideology were everlasting. Indeed, the dissimilarity in attitudes and values among the parties of the coalition appeared manifold, since the electoral system and the precarious stability of the majority encouraged parties to differentiate themselves and to push their differences to the limit of political crisis. Thus, on several issues, the most salient political debates took place *inside* the governing majority rather than *between* Government and Opposition. Under these circumstances, one of the ways in which Prodi sought a clearer profile and greater cohesiveness for his coalition was by seeking to emphasise the idea of sharp discontinuity between his own and the preceding Berlusconi government, especially in the area of foreign policy, where meta-political disagreements were so in evidence. In this way, he could present the continuation of his own government as the only viable alternative to a return of Silvio Berlusconi.

The differences that were emphasised concerned, in particular, the intervention in Iraq, discussed further, below. Prodi highlighted that his government had reverted to the traditional multilateralism characteristic of Italian foreign policy, in accordance with the spirit of the Italian Constitution,[3] against the bilateralism of the previous government, which, it was claimed, always acted in uncritical agreement with the Bush administration. Multilateralism was considered an opportunity to seek a new, more autonomous, international role and a higher profile for Italy through activism in international organisations and participation in international missions. Thus, in August 2006 Italy agreed to lead the international mission in the Lebanon following the month-long conflict between Israel and Hezbollah; on 16 October 2006, the country was voted by a large majority as a non-permanent member of the Security Council of the United Nations; in December 2007, Italy's representatives obtained the agreement of the UN General Assembly (by 104 to 54 votes, with 29 abstentions) to a call for a moratorium on the death penalty.

So, whatever its difficulties in other respects, the Prodi government was not without foreign-policy successes. Prodi and his cabinet tried to improve efficiency and coordination in specifying and representing Italian interests. Much effort was devoted to improving the country's performance in international organisations in order to challenge accusations that the multilateralism of Italian political elites was mostly symbolic. Efforts were also made to create and to reorganise structures needed for the implementation of measures required by the EU and other international organisations. In particular, coordination among the various branches of the public administration in the so-called ascending phase of the development of European Community law was improved. Thus, the so-called *vincolo esterno* (external constraint) remained central to domestic policy-making, even when action to comply with European commitments risked being unpopular – as was the case with the stringent fiscal measures adopted in the financial bills of 2006 and 2007, which however, were necessary to avoid further application of the excessive deficit procedure provided for by the Stability and Growth Pact.

In short, the foreign-policy arena provided a not insignificant backdrop and set of constraints that were implicit in much of the debate that took place during the election campaign. With the aim, therefore, of enhancing an appreciation of some of the specific features of these constraints, the remainder of this chapter is devoted to an account of the major foreign-policy themes that unfolded during the life of the outgoing government. The following section thus considers the vicissitudes of the governing coalition in the area of policy towards the Middle East and Afghanistan; the section after, the way in which the life of the Government was affected by the EU agenda. The fourth and fifth sections consider Kosovo and immigration, two foreign-policy issues that would rise to a position close to the top of the political agenda just about the time that the Government's final crisis and the calling of fresh elections was taking place. The sixth section offers an account of elite-level policy makers' views of the challenges, opportunities and constraints currently facing Italian foreign policy. The last section concludes.

Iraq and Afghanistan, Lebanon and the Middle East

In many respects, things began promisingly for the Government. In the election of 2006, Iraq had been an issue on which each coalition had sought discontinuity with respect to the policy the government had pursued to that point, each side supporting the withdrawal of Italian troops, albeit with some differences concerning the schedule of that withdrawal. In his first speech to the Senate, Prime Minister Prodi stated that the war and occupation in Iraq were critical errors 'that have not solved – but have complicated – the problem of security'.[4] In June 2006, Foreign Minister D'Alema went to Washington to explain that the withdrawal of Italian troops was planned to begin in the summer and to end in the autumn. He emphasised, however, that the Italian government did not intend to overlook its responsibilities to aid and assist civilians, being willing actively to support democracy and development in Iraq. In this he revealed the two fundamental objectives underlying the Government's foreign policy: on the one hand to mark a discontinuity with the excessive Atlanticism of the previous government, while on the other, providing tangible signs of its recognition that the end of the Cold-War certainties required the country to assume greater responsibility for its own security through the assumption of international responsibilities that would raise its prestige and influence. Starting from September 2006 Italian troops progressively handed over, to the trained Iraqi security forces, control of the territory for which they had been responsible, thus ending their 'Antica Babilonia' mission.

At the same time, the Italian government offered to lead the UN peace-keeping mission in Lebanon: besides being an important opportunity for Italy to demonstrate its commitment to peace and security in the Middle East (it offered to send 3,000 troops: more than any other country)[5] the mission necessarily involved a significant degree of military and diplomatic cooperation with France, which was also playing a leading role. Observers thus saw in the Italian decision the perception of an opportunity to facilitate a broader EU role in the area and thus to make progress towards a common EU security policy (Bordonaro, 2006). The military conflict between the paramilitary forces of Hezbollah, and the Israeli military forces in Lebanon and northern Israel, which began on 12 July 2006, continued until 14 August with the United Nations-brokered ceasefire, and formally ended on 8 September, when Israel lifted its naval blockade. On 11 August, the United Nations Security Council unanimously approved UNSC Resolution 1701, with the consent of both the Lebanese and Israeli governments, calling for the disarmament of Hezbollah, the withdrawal of Israel from Lebanon, and for the deployment of Lebanese soldiers and an enlarged United Nations Interim Force in Lebanon (UNIFIL) force in southern Lebanon.[6]

If Italy's international profile has been significantly enhanced by its role in the UNIFIL peacekeeping in Lebanon, in Afghanistan, its contribution has been judged in less unanimously positive terms (Walston, 2008: 157) – largely because the withdrawal from Iraq became gradually linked to the situation in Afghanistan. In spite of the fact that Foreign Minister D'Alema emphasised the profound difference between the two missions and that any claims that there were links between the two issues would not be admissible, Italy's NATO partners expected a strengthening of the Italian presence in Afghanistan in view of the withdrawal from Iraq – while the radical left was becoming increasingly critical of and outspoken about the mission. The issue became more and more urgent as discussions on renewed funding for Italy's contingent there gradually moved to the top of the agenda. The Government's divisions were fully revealed when, on 25 January 2007, three ministers, one from the Green party (Alfonso Pecoraro Scanio) and two from the communist groups (Paolo Ferrero of Rifondazione Comunista (Communist Refoundation, RC) and Alessandro Bianchi of the Partito dei Comunisti Italiani (Party of Italian Communists, PdCI)) left a Cabinet meeting early in order to avoid having to put their signatures to the government decree providing for a re-financing of international missions.

On 3 February 2007, the ambassadors of six countries (Australia, Canada, the Netherlands, Romania, Britain and the United States), Italy's partners in Afghanistan, published an open letter asking for unity in order to intensify security as a condition of peace and economic development, and to improve the strategy for total reconstruction, urging Italy to renew its efforts in Afghanistan. The initiative of the six ambassadors was defined as inappropriate by Foreign Minister D'Alema, who retorted that if they wanted to represent their countries' interests, then there were more suitable forums in which to raise the question (Walston, 2008: 158).

However, the letter gave the opposition the opportunity to exploit the divisions in the Prodi coalition, stressing that while there was little doubt that the centre left would find an apparent solution to its divisions on Afghanistan, it would be a solution destined to silence the disagreements for a few days only, but then to come apart since it could do no more than paper over the fundamental differences between those who believed in traditional pro-Atlantic policy stands, and those who were always driven by anti-Americanism. Moreover, the opposition emphasised the uncertainty and inconsistency in government action and the way in which it produced international isolation and perceptions that Italy was unreliable as a partner. Former Foreign Minister, Gianfranco Fini, said he could not understand how D'Alema could consider unconventional a letter asking the Italian government to honour an international commitment. According to Fini, what was to be considered unconventional was, rather, the irritated and embarrassed answer of the Italian government (*la Repubblica*, 2007a).

On 16 January 2007, the Government also split on the issue of expansion of the United States base in Vicenza. The purpose of the project was to expand the 'Dal Molin' airport – which would thus become the most important European base servicing the US military deployment in Europe, the Middle East and Africa, housing the entire 173rd air brigade. Defence Minister, Arturo Parisi, spoke in favour of the base's expansion, arguing that it was in the spirit of friendship between Italy and the United States and would be a natural extension of the current US military presence in Vicenza. The centrist Catholic Union of Christian Democrats and Centre Democrats (Unione dei Democratici Christiani e dei Democratici di Centro, UDC), and the Radicals, were convinced that the expansion should go ahead in order to prevent damage to Italian-American relations. However, there were repeated demonstrations against the expansion supported by several other parties belonging to the coalition. In the debate that took place in the Senate, there were several defections of senators of the majority coalition (1 February 2007) with the Government being supported by the opposition. Berlusconi blamed the extreme left for making demands that were 'jeopardising relations between Italy and the United States', arguing that the Government had come to the end of its life.

On 21 February, Foreign Minister D'Alema went to the Senate to defend the general outlines of the Government's foreign policy in a debate on a motion which would not have been subject to special criticism had not the opposition, the radical left and D'Alema himself not chosen to invest it with the significance of a 'test' for the entire government (Walston, 2008: 151). D'Alema emphasised that the Government's approach was in line with Italian traditions in this area, and in line with the Unione programme, and that it took account of the strategic interests of the country. He emphasised that article 11 of the Italian Constitution – on the repudiation of a war as means of resolving international disputes – was the basis of the Government's foreign policy, at the same time stressing the prominent role of Italy in peace-keeping and conflict-prevention in several areas. Participation in the mission in Afghanistan (and in particular the country's leading position in the United Nations Assistance Mission in Afghanistan, UNAMA) was to be confirmed as a way of promoting stability and guaranteeing peace and security. It was stressed that this mission, being authorised by the UN, differed from the intervention in Iraq, evidence that the foreign policy being pursued in the current legislature differed profoundly with respect to the foreign policy-choices of the previous government, which, in opting for a conservative, American unilateralism, had been responsible for sending troops to Iraq in the first place. D'Alema asked for a strong show of political support in order to allow the country to face the subsequent complex challenges,[7] but despite his appeal two senators, Fernando Rossi and Franco Turigliatto, 'dissidents' of the extreme left, abstained along with some of the life senators, with the result that the motion of the Unione was rejected.[8]

Prodi resigned, but after consultations, the President of the Republic, Giorgio Napolitano, asked him to return to Parliament to seek a vote of confidence. In outlining the reasons for his action, Napolitano explained he was satisfied that Prodi's coalition was ready unanimously to support its Prime Minister in order to complete the passage of needed reforms and to approve a new electoral law.

Somewhat paradoxically, in view of the February debacle, the period after was characterised by at least some developments that were rather positive for Italian foreign policy (Walston, 2008: 153). First, on 20 March 2007, D'Alema went to New York for the UN meeting on the renewal of UNAMA's mandate, and to explain why Italy felt it essential that there be an Afghan peace conference involving all the neighbouring countries and the international community generally. This was a proposal that was supported, among other European partners, by the German Chancellor Angela Merkel. The outcome was that Italy managed to acquire a quantity of diplomatic prestige with the tripartite conference (involving the UN Secretary-General, Ban Ki-Moon, the Afghan president, Hamid Karzai and Italy) on the rule of law in Afghanistan that took place in Rome at the beginning of July in order to define a strategy for the functioning of justice. The conference had been cited by UNSC Resolution 1746 which in March had renewed UNAMA's mandate and had invited the Afghan Government, with the assistance of the international community, 'to continue to work towards the establishment of a fair and transparent justice system...in order to strengthen the rule of law throughout the country'.[9] D'Alema announced an additional appropriation of €10 million for 2007 for reconstruction of the judicial system, as a fundamental step in the fight against corruption and the illegal drugs trade (*l'Unità*, 2007).

Second, the Government was able, widely supported by public opinion (Coticchia and Giacomello, 2006: 727; MAE, 2008: 88–104), to draw on its role in the Lebanon to construct for Italy the solid image of peacekeeper in areas of crisis and thus to make very concrete contributions to the progress of peace in the Middle East itself. In particular, as a country that had developed expertise in military policing in theatres such as Kosovo and Iraq and as one that wanted to compensate for the Iraq withdrawal with the assumption of alternative responsibilities in the region, Italy was especially well placed for the crucial task of winning the confidence of Israel. At the same time, D'Alema's sympathies for the radical Palestinians – in this reflecting a traditional theme in Italian foreign policy – gave the country credit with the other party to the dispute as well. The Italian soldiers were thus able to act more as diplomats than as combatants (Walston, 2008: 154).

Again, however, in pursuit of its objectives, the Government was not free of consequential domestic difficulties. In essence, it wanted to draw back from the strongly pro-American and pro-Israel foreign policy of the previous government in favour of a more balanced approach that involved the rebuilding of ties with the Arab world along with ties with the government of Israel. But pro-Palestinian versus pro-Israeli attitudes had been a meta-political issue dividing Government and Opposition since the start of the new millennium. Italian governments' foreign policy had traditionally expressed strong pro-Arab sympathies, a tendency that had managed to unite parties across the spectrum – from the far right (by virtue of the interest shown in fascist ideologies by Arab and Islamic opponents of British and French colonial rule) through the Catholic centre (influenced by Vatican opposition to the Zionist movement) to the left (whose anti-colonialist sympathies led to support for bodies such as the Palestine Liberation Organisation) (Romano, 2002). But this changed, to a certain extent, during the 2001–2006 legislature, when Berlusconi and Foreign Minister Fini adopted an attitude more in line with the approach of the Bush administration. Attitudes towards Israel had also been an issue during the election campaign of 2006, when the coalition of the centre left was strongly criticised for the supposed tepidness of its support for Israel. The centre right thus attacked the partial change of direction of the centre-left government and the pro-Palestinian statements of Foreign Minister D'Alema. A lively debate followed when, in July 2007, D'Alema stated that Hamas was a real political organisation with significant popular support and that it should not be encouraged to draw near to Al Qaeda. Fini replied that Hamas was on the list of the EU's terrorist organisations, since it refused to recognise Israel or to repudiate violence (*Corriere della Sera*, 2007a; 2007b). Prodi weighed into the debate by arguing that Hamas was a reality that could not be ignored and whose evolution toward peaceful action should be encouraged in transparent and open ways (*la Repubblica*, 2007b). This point of view was reaffirmed when Tony Blair came to Italy as a special envoy of the Quartet on the Middle East (the United States, Russia, the EU and the UN) to discuss the Bush proposal of organising a peace conference on the Middle East in the autumn.

Despite these difficulties, the fruits of Italy's efforts in the Middle East became apparent in the preparations leading up to the Bush-proposed conference, which was held in Annapolis, Maryland, on 27 November 2007. The significance of this conference was that it represented the first occasion on which a two-state solution was articulated as the mutually agreed upon outline of a solution to the Israeli-Palestinian conflict. Europe and Italy played a crucial role in assuring the participation of a broad swathe of Arab countries. None of the sensitive problems – the Palestinian state, borders, settlements, refugees, the status of Jerusalem, water – were excluded from the discussions. The parties committed themselves to make every effort to conclude an agreement before the end of 2008 – giving Foreign Minister D'Alema an opening to announce that Italy and Europe would assure a follow-up to the conference in order to facilitate the achievement of this deadline (*la Repubblica*, 2007c).

If, then, there was going to be a foreign policy-issue raised during the 2008 campaign, it was, given its profile, likely to be the Italian mission in Lebanon. Such was the case. Antonio Martino, who had been Berlusconi's defence minister from 2001 to 2006, complained, a month before polling day, that the UN peacekeeping force did not have the power to be effective; the Italian troops in Lebanon were not only unhelpful, but at risk. On the other hand, Italy should deploy combat troops in Afghanistan, responding positively to NATO requests for more troops and resources and should send military instructors to Iraq. Consequently, if, as he hoped would be the case, he once more became Defence Minister, he would 'drastically reduce [the Italian] presence in Lebanon, if not eliminate it altogether, and send troops to Afghanistan and Iraq, where they [were] needed.' (*la Repubblica*, 2008a).

Not surprisingly, this intervention threw the centre right temporarily off balance. For Massimo D'Alema, to bring foreign policy into the campaign 'in such an instrumental way' was simply 'an error'; for without continuity – without, that is, avoiding the impression that positions assumed by the country internationally might be thrown into question every time there was an election – Italy's entire credibility would be put at risk (*la Repubblica*, 2008b). Thus it was that Berlusconi was forced to intervene – which he did, while desperately trying to avoid the impression of an outright repudiation of what he and Martino agreed to describe as opinions expressed in a personal capacity. With regard to Afghanistan, the ex-minister's position merely echoed the United Nations' own request to countries to augment the sizes of their military contingents. With regard to Iraq, it was not additional troops that were being proposed, but mere military instructors. With regard to Lebanon, the centre right had voted for the Italian mission, but they did not agree with the rules of engagement, which they would change if they formed a government – to which D'Alema replied: 'It is the UN that decided the rules of engagement, not Berlusconi' (*il Sole 24 Ore*, 2008).

The EU context and energy

While Berlusconi's government privileged the relationship with the United States, Prodi put the EU at the heart of his Government's concerns – perhaps not surprisingly: the EU agenda had a particular resonance both for him, given his experience as President of the European Commission, and for the Minister for European policies, Emma Bonino, given her experience as a former EU commissioner. This led the Government to seek to distinguish itself from its predecessor in two specific ways.

The first concerned Italy's poor performance in the implementation of EU laws. The large number of infringements of which it was periodically accused, were taken by scholars and the country's EU partners as tangible evidence of the rhetorical nature of the Europeanism of Italy's elites (Cotta, Isernia and Verzichelli, 2005). Indeed infringement of EU law has been higher than for other, more Euro-sceptical countries such as the United Kingdom and has been due mainly to the complexity of the procedures according to which EU directives are typically implemented and the lack of coordination between the central State and the Regions. Consequently, reforms designed to improve efficiency and coordination, both in the ascending and descending phases of European law-making, were a fundamental tool of the EU strategy of Prodi's government. As far as the ascending phase is concerned, management of the most important European issues was brought under the control of the Prime Minister together with the Minister for European affairs. The other structure at central level with responsibility for following the development of EU legislative initiatives is the Permanent Network for the EU (*Rete permanente UE*). The tasks of coordination were assigned to an Inter-ministerial Committee for European Community Affairs (Comitato interministeriale per gli affari comunitari europei, CIACE). The committee has responsibility for defining the Italian position on matters on the EU agenda, especially in relation to legislative initiatives. Meetings of this body are open to participation by the Regions and local authorities wherever the European initiative in question concerns matters affecting their interests, for example the Lisbon Strategy and the Sustainable Development Strategy. In order to prevent the initiation of infringement procedures a special body (*Struttura di missione per le procedure di infrazione*) was created with the remit of ensuring the proper application of EC law. Thanks to these bodies Italy's transposition deficit has fallen from 2.7 to 1.3 per cent – a percentage in line with the EU average (1.2 per cent). In January 2008, open infringements amounted to 198 (the lowest number for the previous five years), while the figure was still 275 in May 2006.

In the second place, the Prodi government sought to boost the traditional role of Italy as a promoter of the widening and deepening of integration. Though the European reforms were in deep crisis after the negative outcomes of the 2005 referenda on the European constitution, the Italian government actively supported the continued progress of European integration, promoting a compromise solution on the new European treaty, which was intended to preserve the results of the Constitutional treaty, and in particular the structural mechanisms allowing a more efficient functioning of the decision-making process.

The Italian government supported enlargement of the EU to include Serbia and continued the action of the previous government in favour of the accession of Turkey, trying to pursue an open-door policy, notwithstanding the existence of several critical unresolved issues, such as human rights, reform of the penal code, the status of the Kurdish minority and Cyprus. Both bilateral and multi-lateral strategies were pursued. Turkey being one of Italy's most important commercial partners, the Government created a committee on Turkey (the 'Tavolo Turchia'), involving various branches of the public administration, along with a range of social and economic actors, in order to intensify economic cooperation.

Activism at the EU level was ultimately rooted in the conviction that multilateral frameworks offered opportunities to cope with problems that cannot be dealt with by the single state on its own and that are solvable only through coordinated international action. This is particularly true for energy and the environment which have a strong influence on economic development and citizens' welfare. The problem of assuring adequate energy supplies and independence from external energy providers has been a key issue, and so featured in the election campaign when some candidates, for example Pierferdinando Casini and Silvio Berlusconi, promoted the idea of heavy investment in nuclear energy.

Over 80 per cent of the world's total energy requirements are currently met by natural gas, carbons and oil, and this situation will remain unchanged for at least a decade according to the International Energy Agency. With the exception of the biomass category (e.g., wood) which amounts to 10 per cent, renewable sources, like solar energy or wind, account for less than 1 per cent. Nuclear energy covers 6 per cent of the requirements. The Italian situation is little different – with two notable exceptions, namely, the amount of energy that comes from renewable sources (which is less than in other EU countries) and the absence of nuclear energy (as the result of a popular referendum in 1987). Italy, even more than other EU countries, has, in recent years, developed a strategy that gives it a heavy reliance on gas. More than 40 per cent of Italian energy needs are met from it; and moreover 80 per cent of Italian gas imports come from a restricted number of suppliers – Russia, Algeria, Libya and Norway (in line with the EU).

An Italian priority is, thus, a diversification of gas supplies to be facilitated by building new infrastructures, notably liquefied natural gas terminals as well as pipelines. Italian foreign policy has also focused on a harmonisation of the EU's national markets, as this will promote competition, finally resulting in a genuinely single EU market, while the Italian government has signed international agreements to build pipelines,[10] and new liquefied natural gas terminals are planned to make possible gas imports from countries like Qatar, Niger and Venezuela.

The Prodi government considered nuclear energy less important for two main reasons: first, the so-called fourth generation of nuclear plants are still under development, and second, traditionally, there has been public resistance to this energy source. Nevertheless, it did consider the construction of nuclear plants and following this line Italy joined the Global Nuclear Energy Partnership in 2007, even though the idea of a return to nuclear energy production was strongly opposed by the Green party.

Italy has difficulty in planning and implementing an energy policy since policy makers are aware of the way in which the country's landscape, climate and endowment of natural resources makes it likely that any new plant required for the distribution of energy from non-renewable sources will run into the resistance of local communities, animated by the so called 'nimby' (not in my back yard) problems and strengthened in their ability to resist by the wide variety of levels through which the governance of energy policy takes place in Italy.

Thus the Italian government needs to link decisions concerning energy to a form of *vincolo esterno* which, as happened in the case of Economic and Monetary Union, can help to overcome internal vetoes and trigger reforms. The action plan to combat climate change, 'An energy policy for Europe', adopted by the Spring European Council in 2007, could be interpreted as another *vincolo esterno* for Italy, since it imposes a series of binding targets, to be achieved by 2020, for reductions in greenhouse gas emissions, the production of energy from renewable sources and energy savings. On the other hand, European energy policy could be seen as an opportunity, since competitiveness would be positively affected by an effective policy designed to create technological advantages and to reduce the cost of renewable sources (Department for European Affairs, 2007).

In order to exploit the opportunity of a European energy policy the Italian government has called for clear and effective governance and harmonisation rules, avoiding distortions and favouring the spread of technologies. The creation of European agencies, rules or institutions regulating energy policy could ease the internal streamlining of the decision-making process and improve efficiency, fostering reform of the decision-making settlement between the central State and the Regions.

Kosovo

Kosovo had already been a problem for the centre left in 1999, when the government led by Massimo D'Alema had endorsed the NATO decision to intervene against Serbia and agreed to provide airports and logistical support to the NATO air force. Then, the goal had been to demonstrate the reliability of the centre-left government as a NATO ally. Massimo D'Alema in particular felt that as an ex-communist he had no alternative, in the face of US pressure in the crisis and more generally, but to give proof of his reliability as an 'Atlantic partner' (Croci, 2000: 118–119). The decision was conceived as a peacekeeping operation and approved after long and difficult negotiations among the parties of the coalition.

The independence of Kosovo from Serbia, declared by the Kosovar assembly on 27 February 2008 after the election had already been called, likewise created a problem for the Government. In the first place, there was the risk that, due to the multi-ethnic composition of the population (for instance the presence of Serbian minorities), the declaration would bring instability and violence. In the second place, Serbia could recognise the autonomy but not the independence of Kosovo, and neither could Russia, fearful of the potential consequences in terms of the creation of precedents for other nations seeking independence. Under these circumstances, both the UN and the EU found it difficult to reach an agreed position on the matter. Italy sought to promote a solution that would safeguard the independence of Kosovo and at the same time maintain good relationships with Serbia. But a compromise solution sought in the UN Security Council, where Italy encouraged dialogue between Pristina and Belgrade, failed because of the veto of Russia. The European Council of 18 February approved a platform leaving to each member state individually the decision as to whether to establish relationships with Kosovo. Several member states announced their recognition; others (like Greece, Spain, Slovakia, Bulgaria and Romania) preferred to postpone recognition, while Cyprus declared that it intended not to recognise Kosovo.

The Italian government decided to recognise the independence of Kosovo, the Council of Ministers approving the recognition with one dissenting voice – that of RC's Minister for Social Solidarity, Paolo Ferrero (2008). He considered that recognition would undermine the role of the UN (which officially opposed independence) in upholding international law, and destabilise power in the region (which was a terrain of conflict between the United States and Russia). Nevertheless, Italy decided to fall into line with the other large European states as the condition for maintaining its influence in the region. At the same time, the Italian government attempted to maintain its good relationship with the Serbian government, concerned as it was not to take any action that would hurt Italian companies with extensive trade and production contracts in the country. Several meetings were organised to shore up relations between Rome and Belgrade (with Prodi meeting the president of Serbia, Boris Tadić) and to give reassurances of Italy's continuing commitment to promoting the cause of Serbia as a candidate for membership of the EU. In any case, Foreign Minister D'Alema emphasised that recognition was essential to enable Italy to meet its responsibilities in the region, in particular to assure protection of the 2,600 soldiers already present and the more than 200 civil and military officials and judges which were being sent to the region as part of the European mission to ensure the rule of law and the prosecution of organised crime.

Though the election campaign had begun, the independence of Kosovo was not an issue of debate, both because there were no significant differences on the issue between the Partito Democratico (Democratic Party, PD) and the Popolo dell Libertà (People of Freedom, PdL) and because, notwithstanding its importance for the security of Italian trade and investments, (in)stability in the Balkans was not a salient issue for voters (MAE, 2008: 88–104).

Immigrants

What was a salient issue, and one that did figure in the election campaign, was public safety and the threat to it supposedly posed by immigrants. In November 2007, the murder, in Rome, of an Italian woman, Giovanna

Reggiani, by a Romanian immigrant aroused public indignation, and wide-spread expressions of hostility towards Romanians. Immigrant camps were repeatedly set on fire, while in several towns there were attacks against immigrants. Opposition to Romanian immigration came mainly from the centre right but it was Walter Veltroni, mayor of Rome, who said that 'before Romania joined the European Union, Rome was the safest city in the world'; that '75 per cent of the arrests made [the previous] year involved Romanians'; that 'prefects must have the power to expel EU citizens who have committed crimes against property and persons' (*la Repubblica*, 2007d).

So although the fears surrounding immigration were exploited mainly by the centre right, both majority and opposition spokespersons dealt with the problem in emotional rather than rational terms, establishing a cause-and-effect relation between security on the one hand, and immigration from Eastern Europe on the other. The measures proposed by the centre right were a modification of EU rules on the free circulation of people, and expulsions of immigrants. Meanwhile, far from devising policies aimed at facilitating the inclusion of immigrants, or managing illegal immigration, the Government and local authorities failed to draw on European funds available for such purposes and the only measure taken was to set up settlements whose results were in most cases degradation and segregation. One of the consequences was to fan popular hostility towards the Roma and Sinti population – whose members were frequently confused with Romanian citizens and who had settled in Italy long before Romania joined the EU. Official figures showed that the Roma and Sinti amounted to less than 0.3 per cent of the population, one of the lowest proportions in Europe, and that the crime rate was no higher among immigrants than among Italian citizens.

The Government reacted to the attack on Giovanna Reggiani, and the resulting public outcry, by approving a decree allowing prefects to expel immigrants, including EU citizens, if considered a danger to public security. Officials in Brussels maintained that Italy appeared to be within the terms of a European directive allowing member states to expel citizens of other EU countries on these grounds or else if the persons involved were a threat to public health or had insufficient means for their maintenance. Franco Frattini, EU Commission vice-president for Justice, Freedom and Security, said: 'The countries of the European Union must be lands of welcome, especially for citizens of other EU states. But we have to be tough on those who commit offences. Italy must not become a safe haven for criminals, a place where the rule of law is not respected' (Hooper, 2007).

The Government's anti-immigrant turn created tensions with the Romanian government, which issued notes of protest. Romanian Prime Minister, Calin Popescu Tariceanu, said his government would do everything it could, but that it could not take legal Romanians back home by force. Steps were taken to ensure the maintenance of cordial relations with Romania and to deal with the issue through cooperation. Clemente

Mastella, Minister of Justice, concluded an agreement with the Romanian Minister of Justice, Tudor Alexandru Chiuariu, establishing mechanisms for more effective coordination between the countries' judicial systems and the possibility for Romanians convicted of crimes in Italy to serve their sentences in Romania.

In spite of the Government's initiatives, during the election campaign the supposed link between immigration and lack of security acquired a heightened salience and was one of the main arguments exploited by the centre right to show the ineffectiveness of the centre-left government, unable to punish crime, and weak toward immigrants. Immigration was also represented as a symbol of the dangers deriving from enlargement of the EU in the direction of Eastern Europe.

Ideas and attitudes on foreign policy

As the foregoing sections have shown, the international dimension has, in complex and changing ways, become increasingly interwoven with the domestic arena – creating a series of risks and opportunities that have offered matters for reflection to Italian political elites, matters that have been addressed in different ways by government and opposition. Among the most significant contributions to the debate are those of the *Gruppo di riflessione strategica* (Strategic thought group), created in 2007 at the Foreign Ministry, and the book by the current Minister for the Economy, Giulio Tremonti (2008), *La paura e la speranza* (The Fear and the Hope). A description of these contributions offers a convenient way of setting out the underlying contrasts in the approaches to foreign policy of centre left and centre right.

The setting up of the *Gruppo di riflessione strategica* involved the Foreign Ministry in calling upon academic, economic and social actors to reflect on the major challenges, constraints and opportunities which Italy has to face in the international context and to suggest some operational proposals for the medium and long term. The group issued a document (MAE, 2008), 'Rapporto 2020: Le scelte di politica estera' (The 2020 Report: Choices in foreign policy) whose authors argue that action in the international arena should not be confined to the simple defence of Italian positions regardless, but rather, should be driven by the search for consensus on concrete actions. In this vein, the report argues that more efficient multi-lateral governance in international organisations like NATO, the UN and the EU is the tool to increase Italian influence. This also requires greater efficiency on the internal level. In particular, domestic stability and coordination among the different governmental, administrative and parliamentary bodies concerned with action in Europe is a necessary condition for influential and incisive action within EU institutions. Related to this, foreign policy has to be supported by better investment in terms of political and economic resources, especially because the international dimension now has a great impact on citizens' lives (through, for example, immigration and energy policies).

Closer and more robust forms of integration can prevent the decline of Europe, allowing the EU to become a global actor, in particular through a common defence policy. To encourage the construction of such a policy, the 2020 Report considers it essential to build a coalition that embodies the different geopolitical, social and historical traditions of the EU, through the creation of a contact group of six member states (Italy, France, Germany, Great Britain, Spain, Poland) with the purpose of coordinating action in the field of intelligence and voicing the position of the large countries in the Council and in the Parliament. This informal contact group would be a tool to eliminate divergences among the big countries, improving consistency in the EU's external action.

The Report also addresses the problem of competition from the large emerging markets such as China, India, Brazil and Russia, which should be met by strategies that are both bi-lateral and multi-lateral, promoting the openness of these markets and investments. The situation with Russia and China is potentially more conflictual due to the absence of a genuinely open market. To cope with the challenges of globalisation, a European commercial policy, safeguarding the productive system; the internationalisation of the Italian commercial system through a clear definition of Italian priorities in several geographical areas, and finally, a reform of the instruments protecting the internationalisation of the Italian entrepreneurial system, are the main tools to be deployed.

Tremonti's *Fear and Hope* warns of a decline of Europe, in terms of population and rates of economic growth, and of the dangers of globalisation, seeing the main threat to the well-being of the Italian economy as coming mainly from Asia. Chinese and Indian growth rates in particular have been responsible for rising prices and consequent losses of purchasing power. Moreover, Italian medium- and small-sized enterprises risk being excluded from international markets by unfair competition from China, with the risk of unemployment and cuts in wages. Globalisation should be managed by trying to restrain Chinese and Indian growth and competitiveness. Italy should promote at the EU level a sort of global government of the economy. The feeling of insecurity arising from immigration is due to a lack of management of the process of globalisation, for which liberal ideology is responsible.

In order to build the EU as a bulwark against Asia, European institutions need to be thoroughly reformed. Globalisation challenges national sovereignty, and European policy and policy-making needs to find a new basis of legitimacy. The democratic deficit has to be faced by giving to the European Parliament the right to make laws on matters that are already outside the competence of the member States. In order to exploit the power of the Euro, European bonds could support investment in infrastructural projects and industrial policies aimed at alleviating the constraints of the Stability and Growth Pact. There needs to be the creation of a new economic space between Europe and the United States harmonising antitrust and patent rules, as well as agricultural policy. An agreement on the rules of international trade, a new Bretton Woods, allowing the imposition of tariffs and sanctions on countries that do not follow the rules of fair competition would avoid the slow growth and decline of Europe and Italy. Fundamental to Europe's rejuvenation is a rediscovery of the roots of European identity, that is the values of family, authority and leadership, order, responsibility, and federalism – values that run in the opposite direction to those of 1968 and its mistakes. The European *demos* could arise only from an identity based on national attachments and on security.

In both views, the role of Europe is essential to tackling the negative effects of globalisation; but while the centre left assigns this role to an improvement and reform of institutions and decision-making processes (the 2020 Report bases its proposals on the traditional multi-level pillars of Italian foreign policy), in *The Fear and the Hope* Tremonti regards Europe as a fortress against unfair competition and a source of values and identity counter-posed to the non-Western world. The essential actor remains the nation State, promoter of attachment and values whose internal powers are enhanced and can influence the international context mainly by bilateral agreements.

Conclusion

The clear distinction between internal and external, national and international contexts faded in the 2008 election campaign. Problems like immigration, security and the environment enabled the centre right to exploit the weaknesses of the outgoing government due to its internal divisions and the ineffectiveness of decision-making processes. Indeed the few proposals made by Prodi's government in these three areas were adopted following events rather than by anticipating them, and they betrayed a lack of long- or medium-term strategies.

Though the Government was successful in a number of other international initiatives, particularly in multilateral contexts, its fragility was highlighted by Berlusconi to argue that Italy had lost influence internationally, in particular stressing the positions held by the extreme-left parties in foreign policy. These positions may have contributed to the electoral failure of the parties, insofar as they were perceived as contributing to government instability. On the one side, the Green party seemed to oppose every proposal that was advanced concerning the problem of waste management and disposal, as well as the construction of new energy plants in any area; on the other side, government positions on the participation of Italian troops in peacekeeping missions appeared constantly to be questioned by RC and the PdCI.

On certain fundamental values and choices (for example Europe, the NATO partnership, participation in peacekeeping missions, the importance of good relations with the United States) the differences among the major parties involved in the electoral competition, the PD and the PdL, appeared to be less deep than those between either, and the extreme parties on each side. The major differences between the two main parties in foreign policy concern means rather than ends; for, the PD wants to adopt an approach that would involve internal reforms being used to strengthen the country's position in the external arena,[11] whereas the PdL places greater reliance, on the one hand, on Western values and identity, and, on the other, on the personal relationships of its leader. The 'personalisation' of foreign policy had been one of the distinctive features of the previous Berlusconi government, so it seemed likely that another shift in the style of foreign policy would give the 2008 election the character of a watershed, as it already was in so many other respects.

Notes

1. As is demonstrated by the CIRCaP Report on public opinion and foreign policy (CIRCaP, University of Siena, 2008).
2. The Waste Framework Directive requires Member States to ensure that waste is recovered or disposed of without endangering human health, to prohibit the abandonment or uncontrolled disposal of waste, and to establish an integrated and adequate network of disposal installations. The Italian authorities had already been pressed to set up a long–term strategy to deal with the region's waste. In fact a waste management plan for Campania had been adopted in 1994 but never properly implemented.
3. Articles 10 and 11 set out a number of principles to which policy makers must adhere in the conduct of foreign policy. Besides the well-known repudiation of war as a means of resolving international disputes, these principles include: consenting, in conditions of parity with other states, to such limitations on Italy's sovereignty as may be necessary to assure justice and peace among nations; supporting and encouraging international organisations pursuing such ends.
4. Senato della Repubblica Comunicazioni del Presidente del Consiglio dei ministri, Resoconto stenografico della seduta n. 4 del 18 maggio 2006.
5. The decree was approved by the Government on 28 August 2006 and voted by Parliament on 20 October 2006, with the abstention of the Northern League.
6. UNIFIL has responsibility for: monitoring the cessation of hostilities; supporting the Lebanese Armed Forces as they deploy in the south of the country, and helping ensure humanitarian access to civilians and the voluntary and safe return of displaced persons.
7. XV Legislatura – Aula – Resoconto stenografico della seduta n. 112 del 21 febbraio 2007, Comunicazioni del Ministro degli affari esteri sulle linee di politica estera e conseguente discussione.
8. Let it be noted, in respect of the responsibility to be attributed to the far-left parties for the Government's instability, that Rossi had already left his party, the PdCI, while Turigliatto's party, RC, reacted to his abstention by expelling him.
9. Resolution 1746 (2007) adopted by the Security Council at its 5645th meeting on 23 March 2007.

10. The GALSI pipeline will transport gas from Algeria to Italy, passing through Sardinia, while the ITGI pipeline will transport gas from Azerbaijan to Italy passing through Turkey and Greece.
11. The structures that have been created to improve Italian performance in the EU are an example.

References

Bordonaro, F. (2006) 'Lebanon mission, chance to strengthen EU', *International Relations and Security Network*, http://www.isn.ethz.ch/news/sw/details.cfm?id=16656

Corriere della Sera (2007a) 'D'Alema: «Non regaliamo Hamas ad Al Qaeda»', 17 July, http://www.corriere.it/Primo_Piano/Politica/2007/07_Luglio/17/dalema_hamas_alqaeda.shtml

Corriere della Sera (2007b) 'Fini: «D'Alema irresponsabile su Hamas»', 18 July, http://www.corriere.it/Primo_Piano/Politica/2007/07_Luglio/17/fini_hamas.shtml

Coticchia, F. and Giacomello, G. (2006) 'Il ruolo internazionale delle forze armate italiane', *il Mulino* 55(4): 727–734.

Cotta, M., Isernia, P. and Verzichelli, L. (2005) *L'Europa in Italia*, Bologna: il Mulino.

Croci, O. (2000) 'Dovere, umanitarismo e interesse nazionale. L'Italia e l'intervento della Nato in Kosovo', pp. 109–130 in Mark Gilbert and Gianfranco Pasquino (eds), *Politica in Italia*, 2000 edition, Bologna: il Mulino.

Department for European Affairs (2007) 'Energy: issues and challenges for Europe and for Italy. Position paper of the Italian government', www.politichecomunitarie.it/file_download/318

Ferrero, P. (2008) 'Il mio dissenso sul Kosovo', 21 February, http://www.paoloferrero.it/?p=161

Hooper, J. (2007) 'Italian woman's murder prompts expulsion threat to Romanians', *The Guardian*, 2 November, http://www.guardian.co.uk/world/2007/nov/02/italy.international

il Sole 24 ore (2008) 'Berlusconi corregge Martino: in Libano nuove regole d'ingaggio', 15 March, http://www.ilsole24ore.com/art/SoleOnLine4/Mondo/2008/03/libano-regole-ingaggio.shtml?uuid

la Repubblica (2007a) 'Afghanistan, Fini attacca D'Alema "Irrituale la tua risposta, non la lettera"', 6 February, http://www.repubblica.it/2007/01/sezioni/esteri/afghanistan-12/fini-ambasciatori/fini-ambasciatori.html

la Repubblica (2007b) 'Medio Oriente, il premier su Hamas "Esiste, aiutiamola ad evolversi"', 12 August, http://www.repubblica.it/2007/07/sezioni/esteri/medio-oriente-35/prodi-hamas-evoluzione /prodi-hamas-evoluzione.html

la Repubblica (2007c) 'D'Alema: "Bravo Bush, è stato coraggioso"', 28 November, http://85.116.228.24/Stampa/Rassegna/rassegna.asp

la Repubblica (2007d) 'Sicurezza, Veltroni contro la Romania. Per le espulsioni varato un decreto legge', 31 October, http://www.repubblica.it/2007/10/sezioni/cronaca/tor-di-quinto/reazioni-uccisa/reazioni-uccisa.html

la Repubblica (2008a) 'Martino: "Se torno alla Difesa via dal Libano e di nuovo in Iraq"', 13 March, http://www.repubblica.it/2008/03/sezioni/politica/verso-elezioni-10/martino-programma /martino-programma.html

la Repubblica (2008b) 'Libano, Berlusconi boccia Martino I soldati italiani devono restare', 16 March, http://ricerca.repubblica.it/repubblica/archivio/repubblica/2008/03/16/libano-berlusconi-boccia-martino-soldati-italiani-devono.html

l'Unità (2007) 'Afghanistan, dall'Italia 10 milioni per la giustizia', 3 July, http://www.unita.it/view.asp?idContent=67163

MAE [Ministero degli Affari Esteri] (2008) 'Rapporto 2020: Le scelte di politica estera', http://www.esteri.it/mae/doc/Rapporto2020_SceltePoliticaEstera_090408.pdf

Romano, S. (2002) *Guida alla politica estera italiana. Da Badoglio a Berlusconi*, Milano: Rizzoli.

Tremonti, G. (2008) *La paura e la speranza: la crisi globale che si avvicina e la via per superarla*, Milano: Mondadori.

Walston, J. (2008) 'La politica estera : il difficile perseguimento di un ruolo influente', pp. 151–171 in M. Donovan and P. Onofri (eds), *Politica in Italia : I fatti dell'anno e le interpretazioni*, 2008 edition, Bologna : il Mulino.

Part II
The Run-Up to the Election

4
The Parties of the Centre Left

Ilaria Favretto

The Prodi government's poor record and the challenge of electoral recovery

Prodi's results during his short second government (2006–2008) were, overall, poor and disappointing. Not surprisingly, his centre-left coalition lost public support at an extraordinarily fast pace, possibly the only record which this government could claim.

A number of factors militated against the Government's success, beginning with its narrow victory (by a mere 24,755 votes). Thanks to the majority premium, Prodi's coalition managed to gain a comfortable majority (60 seats) in the Chamber of Deputies. However, the majority in the Senate amounted to only two seats. This made it impossible for the Government to tackle divisive issues that threatened to tear the coalition apart and were likely to imperil its existence.

Second, a high level of ideological and political divisiveness characterised the coalition. As Alessandro Chiaramonte noted (2008: 216), from 2001 to 2006, during the opposition years, Prodi was extremely successful in coalescing centre-left parties and in putting together an electoral alliance – later to be named l'Unione – which would stand a chance of winning office back from the centre right. Prodi managed to incorporate parties such as Rifondazione Comunista (Communist Refoundation, RC) and Antonio Di Pietro's Italia dei Valori (Italy of Values, IdV), which had not been part of the centre-left alliance in 2001. Moreover, his Unione coalition also took on board small and very small parties such as the Pensioners' Party, Alleanza Lombarda, the Liga Fronte Veneto and Bobo Craxi's Socialists, all of which had either previously stood alone or been part of the centre-right Casa delle Libertà (House of Freedoms, CdL). This turned out to be Prodi's recipe for victory (Cotta and Verzichelli, 2007: 99). However, once the centre-left coalition was elected, its diversity also proved to be its 'Achilles' heel'. As Donatella Campus (2008: 141) put it, in 2006 the Unione made a serious effort to sell the 281-page programme, *Per il bene dell'Italia* ('For the Good of Italy'), as absolute proof that the centre left was not only an electoral cartel, but, more importantly, a solid political coalition capable of forming a stable government. But, as Luca Ricolfi noted (2007: 51), the centre left's programme was merely a 'long and hard-to-digest book of good and vague intents meant to keep together a wide-ranging coalition of parties which, on most issues, aimed at different and conflicting goals'.

Third, unlike Berlusconi's earlier centre-right government, which was, admittedly, also characterised by a high degree of internal fragmentation and division, the centre left suffered from the absence of a party which, on the model of Forza Italia (FI), was strong enough to play a stabilising role within the coalition (Itanes, 2006: 23–24). Although at the 2006 election FI's vote decreased, Berlusconi's party's score (23.7 per cent in the Chamber-of-Deputies and 23.6 per cent in the Senate election) still amounted to almost half of the votes obtained by the CdL (49.7 per cent in the Chamber of Deputies and 49.9 per cent in the Senate). By contrast, the result scored (17.2 per cent) by the Democratici di Sinistra (Left Democrats, DS), the party with the highest vote within the centre-left coalition, was only slightly more than one third of the sum of the votes gained by Prodi's Unione (49.1 per cent).

The great extent of fragmentation which characterised both the centre-right and the centre-left coalitions after 2006 was, though not entirely, the result of the new electoral law passed by the Berlusconi government in December 2005 (Donovan, 2008: 119). With this is mind, it is worth noting – and here we come to another factor that explains the Prodi government's weakness – that the new voting system also increased the weight that far-left parties were able to exert in the centre-left coalition, as they managed to increase the number of seats they had in the Chamber of Deputies (Newell, 2008: 251). This, it goes without saying, further accentuated the Government's inner divisions and tensions, and its ability to deliver.

Throughout 2007, polls reflected the public's disappointment with Prodi and his centre-left coalition (Natale, 2007: 344, 347; Ricolfi, 2007: 143–144, 195–197). Above all, they sent a clear warning that, should the Government fall, as it eventually did in January 2008, the centre left would find it very difficult to regain office. In February 2008, polls placed Berlusconi's centre right at an advantage of almost 10 per cent over the centre-left coalition. However, Berlusconi's extraordinary electoral recovery in 2006, combined with a number of polls which, as the campaign progressed, indicated that the gap between centre right and centre left was shrinking,[1] kept alive hopes that victory might still be possible. As Berlusconi had well shown two years before, a well devised electoral strategy which pushed the right buttons might well do the trick. The paragraphs that follow analyse the strategy, the strengths and the weaknesses of Veltroni's centre-left coalition (which included the newly formed Partito Democratico (Democratic Party, PD) and Di Pietro's IdV).

The PD 'card'

The electoral card which Veltroni's coalition played most insistently during the campaign was the novelty entailed by creation of the PD. This came into being in October 2007 as a result of the merger of the DS – heir of the Partito Democratico della Sinistra (Democratic Party of the Left, PDS) and, before that, of the Partito Comunista Italiano (Italian Communist Party, PCI) – and of Francesco Rutelli's Margherita (the Daisy) – the party which in 2002 brought together the Partito Popolare (the People's Party, the centre-left component of the former Christian Democrats), Lamberto Dini's Rinnovamento Italiano (Italian Renewal) and the Democratici (Democrats). The latter was the party founded by Romano Prodi in 1999. The birth of the PD, that is a single progressive party which gathered together all the moderate reformist parties and put an end to the fragmentation which had long characterised the centre-left area, signalled the culmination of a process that Prodi had promoted ever since his entry into politics in 1995.[2]

Prodi's project had long faced resistance and suspicion both within the PDS-DS and the Margherita. Leading figures within the PDS (renamed DS after 1998), such as Massimo D'Alema, long regarded Prodi's Ulivo (Olive-tree Alliance), the centre-left coalition which successfully won the 1996 election, as a mere electoral alliance that would enable the PDS-DS to regain support while clinging to its social democratic identity. However, the sorry results of the 2001 election (when the DS's vote declined from 21.1 to 16.6 per cent) and the poor electoral recovery at the 2006 election (17.2 per cent) undermined D'Alema's strategy and strengthened, within the DS, advocates of the Ulivo unitary project such as Walter Veltroni (Mulé, 2007: 46, 49). Similarly, the Margherita's support of Prodi's goal of a united centre left went through ups and downs which are well reflected in the electoral and political strategy pursued by Rutelli's party after its formation. In the run-up to the European election of 2004, Rutelli adhered to Prodi's proposal to join a single list – 'Uniti nell'Ulivo' – with the DS, Enrico Boselli's Socialisti Democratici Italiani (Italian Democratic Socialists, SDI) and Luciana Sbarbati's Movimento Repubblicani Europei (European Republican Movement). Later, in February 2005, in the wake of the positive result (31 per cent) obtained by the list, Rutelli's party also decided to join the Federazione dell'Ulivo (Federation of the Olive-tree Alliance), a federation through which centre-left parties were meant to define a common political agenda for the future. However, in the May–June 2005 regional elections, it decided to stand alone in five out of the fourteen regions in which the ballot was held. The huge turn out at the October 2005 primary election (when 4,311,149 citizens voted), which crowned Prodi leader of the centre-left electoral coalition, the Unione, with 74.1 per cent of vote, gave a new spurt to the Ulivo project. However, as the 2006 election approached, the Margherita, whilst opting to join a single list with the DS for the Chamber of Deputies election, decided, out of a matter of electoral calculation, to stand alone for the Senate (Vassallo, 2006: 59–63).

Nevertheless, the consequence of the 2006 election was to silence opponents of the Ulivo project in both parties, as the vote obtained by the Ulivo list in the Chamber of Deputies (31.3 per cent) exceeded by more than 3 per cent the sum of the votes the parties gained in the Senate contest standing separately (the DS and the Margherita scoring respectively 17.2 per cent and 10.5 per cent).

In April 2007 both parties held their national congresses and voted in favour of the merger, meant to take place in October 2007. On 14 October 2007 the newly formed party's primary elections were held and Walter Veltroni was elected national secretary with a vote of 75.8 per cent. Dario Franceschini, previously of the Margherita, was elected deputy. A Constituent Assembly (Assemblea Costituente nazionale) was also elected. This was expected to set up three commissions aimed at drawing up the party's Statutes, Manifesto and Ethical Code.

One of the PD's main goals was the strengthening of bi-polarism in Italy. In Veltroni's mind (Veltroni, 2007a: 15) the bi-polar nature of the party system, had indeed contributed to improving stability in Italian politics since the mid-1990s. However, it had hardly had any impact on Italian governments' capacity to deliver. Both centre-right and centre-left coalitions had, in fact, proved unable 'to solve Italy's structural problems'. In the PD leader's words, these coalitions 'lack political cohesion and are torn by deep ideological and political differences and act more as coalitions "against" rather than coalitions "in favour" of something'. As Veltroni continues, coalitions' fragmentation and Italian political parties' small size is one of the major weaknesses of Italian politics. FI and the DS together total approximately 40 per cent of the votes. This, as other senior PD figures have argued, is in stark contrast with the more pronounced bipartisan share of votes that characterises those European countries, such as Spain, Germany or Britain, that, over the last few years, have proved better able than Italy to pursue major structural reforms (Filippeschi, 2007: 27).

In pursuit of the centrist vote

The PD takes inspiration from the several ideological and political traditions which characterised its founding parties (Veltroni, 2007b: 158–160). However, as Veltroni puts it (Veltroni, 2007a: 30), the aim of the PD is to go beyond 'the twentieth century's political cultures and ideologies' and the PD leader's specification is not accidental. The other long-term goal of the PD is, in fact, to create a party, which starting from the name itself, could signal a break with the traditional Left and, by so doing, become more attractive to moderate and centrist voters. The latter have proved crucial in Italian elections over the last 15 years.

As a number of studies have highlighted, voters who move between coalitions in Italy are characterised by a high degree of de-politicisation and lack of information (Itanes, 2006: 63–65). Most importantly, they tend to reject the right-left divide and rather locate themselves in the centre of the political spectrum. Electoral shifts between coalitions are very few and far between in Italy. Voters do change their voting preferences but this happens mainly within and not between the two main coalitions. The percentages of voters who shifted their vote to a different coalition party without moving to the opposite side were in the 2001 and 2006 elections 22.2 and 20.1 per cent respectively. By contrast, only 5.9 and 8.7 per cent of voters in 2001 and 2006 respectively moved between the two main coalitions (Itanes, 2006: 63–65). However, given the two coalitions' similar sizes and the centre left's narrow victory in 2006, this is a percentage which might well prove decisive for electoral victory and is a target worth pursuing.

True, Veltroni's coalition's focus on the centrist voters in 2008 did indeed entail the risk of losing voters to its left. However, the PD's gamble was that, by emphasising the importance of tactical voting, that is a vote cast for those parties or coalitions that had a realistic chance of securing the majority premium, far-left voters would in the end 'hold their nose' and support the centre-left coalition.

The break with the far left

The observations contained in the preceding section help to throw light on the decision of the centre-left coalition, in contrast to the 2006 election, not to establish an electoral alliance with the far left in 2008. Far-left parties stood alone in the election under a joint list named La Sinistra – L'Arcobaleno (the Rainbow Left, SA) led by Fausto Bertinotti, the former leader of RC. The SA operated as an electoral coalition but, as was repeatedly stressed during the campaign, it was also expected to be the first step towards a future unified political entity.

The far-left parties' unification had long been promoted by parties such as Diliberto's Partito dei Comunisti Italiani (Party of Italian Communists, PdCI), though with limited success. However, the split of the DS's left-wing component – later to be named Sinistra Democratica (Democratic Left; SD) – which followed the DS's decision to merge with the Margherita, gave it a new spurt. The DS's left-wing faction, led by figures such as Fabio Mussi and Gavino Angius, had long manifested its opposition to the party's increasingly evident move to the centre and willingness to dilute its socialist legacy. On 5 May 2007, 21 Deputies and 12 Senators left the party and formed a separate parliamentary group. A number of them were soon to join Boselli's SDI and contribute, in 2007, to the rebirth of the Partito Socialista – the Socialist Party (which stood alone at the 2008 election and was to score the catastrophic result of 0.9 per cent). Nevertheless, the larger proportion, led by Fabio Mussi, participated in December 2007 in the creation of the SA, together with RC, the PdCI and the Greens. The rainbow that was its symbol was intended to be a reminder of the SA parties' anti-war stance (because it is also the symbol of Italy's pacifist movement), while its diverse colours stood for the composite political traditions – from post-communism to environmentalism – which the new coalition was meant to represent.

The PD's decision to discontinue the alliance with the far left was central to its electoral strategy. As was often stated during the campaign, the exclusion of parties such as RC from the coalition testified to the centrist and moderate vocation of the centre-left coalition in stark contrast to a centre right which had proved unable to get rid of its 'extreme' components. Not only did Berlusconi's coalition include the Northern League but it had also offered seats to highly controversial candidates, such as Alessandra Mussolini or Giuseppe Ciarrapico, who never missed an opportunity to make clear their fascist leanings. As Dario Franceschini (betraying a heavy dose of wishful thinking) put it, 'moderate public opinion and decent citizens could never accept a centre-right coalition of this kind and what seemed to be its unstoppable and irreversible move to the right' (*la Repubblica*, 2008a). By contrast, it was hoped, centrist, and possibly even centre-right, voters would be tempted to support a new centre-left party, that is the PD, which, on the model of Blair's Labour or Zapatero's Spanish Socialist Worker's Party (Partido Socialista Obrero Español, PSOE), stood as the most credible political force to promote the country's modernisation (Salvati, 2008).

Radicals welcome but, please, be quiet!

The centre left's pursuit of the centrist vote did not target Berlusconi's electorate only but Pierferdinando Casini's voters too. This was well reflected in the PD's extreme caution when dealing with the issue of alliance with the Radicals.

By December 2007 the experience of the Rosa nel Pugno (Rose in the Fist), that is the political and electoral alliance created in November 2005 between Boselli's SDI and the Radicals, came to an end. There were a number of reasons for this: to start with, the poor result scored by the coalition at the 2006 election (2.6 and 2.4 per cent in the Chamber-of-Deputies and Senate contests respectively). This was far below the sum of the percentages gained by the two parties individually at the previous election (e.g., in 2001 the Radicals scored 2.2 per cent of the proportional vote). Second, one should remember Boselli's interest, in the wake of the PD's formation and the split of the DS's left-wing faction, in acting as a pivotal force around which a large Socialist Party could be recreated.

In the wake of the dissolution of the Rosa nel Pugno, the only way for the Radicals to be able to secure some parliamentary seats, given the electoral system's 4 per cent threshold, was to enter a new alliance, and negotiations started with the newly formed PD. The Radicals' estimated vote was 1.2 per cent. This was a tiny percentage which, however, might, according to some polls, prove crucial to the centre left's victory in regions such as Piedmont (*la Repubblica*, 2008b).

Radicals wished to establish an electoral alliance with the PD similar to the one which the latter established with Di Pietro's IdV, that is, an alliance which would enable the party to preserve its own symbol and identity. Nevertheless, the PD's leadership ruled this option out very soon after the beginning of negotiations and instead offered to allocate a number of the PD's parliamentary seats to Radical candidates in exchange for their party's support. This was so due to the fear of the Radicals' effect on the moderate Catholic vote.

According to a number of studies which were produced on the 2006 election (Donovan, 2008: 131), the inclusion of the Rosa nel Pugno in the Unione coalition had, in fact, had a negative effect on Catholic voters. The Radicals' visibility within, and support for, the centre left had to be as low-key as possible. Former members of the Margherita in particular strongly opposed any arrangement which might again prevent Catholic or moderate voters from supporting the centre-left coalition. A poll conducted in February 2008, the month during which the alliance between the PD and the Radicals was being discussed, seemed to back their fears: whilst 63 per cent of the PD's electorate favoured the move, only 36 per cent of its 'potential' voters did.[3]

A less fragmented coalition

Veltroni's decision to keep the far-left parties out of the centre-left coalition and to rule out an alliance with the Radicals on the model of the agreement with Di Pietro's IdV was fully consistent with the centrist electoral strategy pursued by the PD. However, the reluctance to take on board extra allies also resulted from the fear of giving life to too fragmented a coalition which would inevitably recall the 2006 Unione. The only way for the centre left to signal a break with the Prodi experience was to promise a less divided and less litigious government. The birth of the PD was a start. After that, the creation of a coalition with as few parties as possible was a consistent tactical decision to take. The door was eventually opened to Di Pietro's IdV only. In 2001 Di Pietro's failure to support the centre-left coalition had been one of the key factors contributing to the centre-left's defeat (Newell, 2002: 238). Since then, no centre-left coalition leader has failed to lure the IdV to their side.

The two-party format which eventually characterised the 2008 centre-left coalition was also meant to contrast with Berlusconi's centre-right alignment. As the PD leadership repeatedly argued during the election campaign, the latter still included the Northern League and was, because of it, likely to prove, once again, to be an alliance deeply torn on both domestic and foreign-policy issues (*la Repubblica*, 2008d).

Betting on the 'novelty effect'

In addition to increasing the centre left's appeal to centrist voters, the creation of the PD also put Veltroni's coalition in a position to play the 'novelty card'. This was so not only in respect of the past Prodi government, from whose negative record and experience it had somehow to distance itself, but also vis-à-vis its centre-right opponents. By 2008, after 14 years of political activity, the novelty effect that benefited Berlusconi when he first entered politics in 1994, had faded and the centre left made a serious effort to rob the centre-right leader of the 'novelty flag'. Indeed Berlusconi and his allies did their best throughout the campaign to challenge the purported novelty of Veltroni and his 'new' party. However, the decade Veltroni spent as mayor of Rome in a successful local experience enabled him to step back into national politics with a completely new image. The Veltroni who campaigned for the 2008 election was not the former leader of an electorally declining party (Veltroni was the DS's national secretary from 1998 to 2001) but the successful and competent mayor of the country's capital. In this respect, it is worth remembering that Veltroni, who was first elected Rome's mayor in 2001, was successfully re-elected at the first ballot with 61.4 per cent of the votes in 2006 (http://www.partitodemocratico.it). Veltroni also had the advantage of being much younger (he is 53 years old) than his opponent, Berlusconi (who is 72).

The PD's election campaign did mostly rely on prospective voting, that is a vote cast in favour of a candidate and a coalition for what they promise and not for what they or their opponents have or have not done hitherto. Hardly any reference was made to the past Berlusconi governments or the centre right's weaknesses. Indeed, betting on retrospective voting and focusing the electorate's attention on the past would inevitably have revived memories of the recent Prodi government, which was the last thing Veltroni wanted to do (Sartori, 2008a). During the election campaign it was also suggested that this was a strategy intentionally pursued by the PD to open up room for negotiations with the centre right on a number of institutional and electoral reforms once the election was over. However, the decision not to revamp the anti-Berlusconi rhetoric, which has been central to centre-left political discourse over the last 15 years, also certainly underlay the PD leadership's widespread confidence in the positive electoral effects of their 'novelty' message. Discarding the anti-Berlusconi rhetoric was itself part of a strategy which aimed at conveying the message that this was a 'new' centre left.

Throughout the campaign Veltroni used soft and conciliatory tones towards his opponents. Berlusconi was never even named. He was rather addressed as 'the leader of the Opposition'. Di Pietro and IdV's other figures ran a far less consensual campaign, reviving, for instance, traditional anti-Berlusconi themes such as the conflict of interests. However, they were

regularly rebuked and disavowed by their PD allies. This contrasted significantly with the electoral campaigns run by Rutelli and Prodi in 2001 and
2006 respectively. Both campaigns were characterised by the centre-right
and the centre-left coalitions' reciprocal delegitimation and demonisa-
tion (Newell, 2002: 127ff; and Campus, 2008: 139, 144). One will certainly
remember Berlusconi's description in 2006 of potential centre-left voters
as 'coglioni' (assholes) and his apocalyptic messages of what might happen
should the Left come back to office. These were aimed at polarising the
electoral competition so that disillusioned centre-right voters would not be
tempted to abstain (Cacciotto, 2007: 41–57) and triggered a harsh response
from the centre left. In fact, Prodi centred his campaign on similarly del-
egitimising messages depicting Berlusconi as the embodiment of incompe-
tence and anti-politics (Itanes, 2006: 36, 43).

During the 2008 campaign not only did the centre left and the centre right
discard anti-Berlusconi and anti-communist rhetoric respectively but they
also put forward electoral programmes which were characterised by much
similarity. No obvious differences existed on key issues such as labour and
welfare reforms, law and order and foreign policy. At the same time, both
coalitions carefully avoided ethics-related issues. Berlusconi did not include
Giuliano Ferrara's 'pro-life' list (Lista per la vita) in his coalition and, as we
saw earlier, Veltroni, whilst agreeing to take on board the Radicals, tried at
the same time to limit their visibility and negotiating power as much as possible. Not surprisingly the cover of the edition of the US weekly, *Newsweek*,
that was dedicated to the 2008 Italian elections (7 April 2008) carried a
mixed image of Berlusconi and Veltroni under the title of 'Veltrusconi'.
Furthermore, on a number of occasions the centre right accused Veltroni's
coalition of stealing their ideas and programmes.[4]

The 'Northern question'

The centre left's 'novelty' message was also expected to be reinforced by
Veltroni's decision to carry out a thorough overhaul of the coalition's list of
candidates. 'First Republic' candidates such as Ciriaco De Mita were gently
asked to back down; the number of female and young candidates was increased
and several 'civil-society' candidates, such as Massimo Calearo – the former
President of Federmeccanica, Italy's engineering industry federation – were
picked up.

Calearo was, without doubt, a highly controversial candidate within the
centre left. During the election campaign he did not hide his support for
abolition of 'article 18', that is, the so-called workers' statute article which
safeguards workers from unfair dismissal. Since the trade union-led mass
protest in 2001 that caused the Berlusconi government to retreat from its
planned labour legislation reforms, the centre right had ruled out its abolition. Calearo also proudly declared that he had never voted for the centre

left before (Stella, 2008). His inclusion in the PD's lists as a front-runner for the Veneto region was aimed at projecting the image of a pro-business and cross-class party.[5] Nevertheless, it was also meant to help the centre left reverse the electoral decline that it had been suffering in the northern regions since 1994, a decline which has played a major role in its election difficulties over the last 15 years.[6]

Since the end of the First Republic and the rise of new 'regional' parties such as the Northern League, the centre left has been able to keep control of several important northern cities in the lower part of Lombardy and other northern regions such as Piedmont and Friuli-Venezia Giulia. However, as Marco Alfieri noted in his book *Nord terra ostile* (2008: 12), in several north-eastern areas (e.g., cities such as Varese, Vicenza or Treviso), the centre right has led by 'Bulgarian' percentages. The centre left's electoral decline in the North is well reflected in the loss of membership suffered by the PDS-DS in the northern regions. Party membership declined by 30 per cent, passing, in the years from 1995 to 2003, from 148,114 to 103,183 (Mulé, 2007: 66).

The areas in which the centre left's vote has been most badly hit are characterised by the significant presence of small- and medium-sized export-oriented enterprises. The latter experienced a boom in the 1980s and 1990s and, since then, have been making a crucial contribution to Italy's exports (Alfieri, 2008: 21). As Michele Salvati, one of the PD's founders and leading intellectuals, lamented (Alfieri, 2008: 17) the centre left has proved unjustifiably impervious to these new economic actors' concerns, for instance fiscal pressure, immigration, law and order. Moreover, it has done very little to reverse the deeply rooted identification within the northern electorate between the Left, and State bureaucracy and inefficiency. Neither has it been successful in undermining an image of the Left as hopelessly hostile to private enterprise.

Several scholars have challenged the argument according to which the centre left's electoral decline in the North would reflect a new political and electoral divide between pro-modernisation and anti-modernisation parties. As Luca Ricolfi and Paola Ferragutti have noted (Ricolfi and Ferragutti, 2007: 218), the 'red' regions (Emilia, Toscana, Umbria, and Marche), traditionally a centre-left stronghold, are highly industrialised and far from being economically depressed. At the same time, the modernity/anti-modernity divide doesn't fit with centre-right parties' strength in southern regions such as Sicily (Ferragutti, 2007: 215). It has also been suggested that the centre-right's electoral success in the North relies more on its ability to engage with small and medium enterprises' demands not so much for greater 'modernity' as for less 'modernity' (for instance, greater protection from global competition and developing countries' cheap exports). Such an argument fits well with the popularity within the centre-right electorate of protectionist policies such as those endorsed by Giulio Tremonti's (2008) controversial but also highly acclaimed *La Paura e la speranza: la crisi globale che si avvicina e la via per superarla* (The fear and the hope: the global crisis and the means to overcome it) published in the middle of the election campaign.

This is a huge debate to which it would be impossible to do justice in this chapter. Whatever the reasons underlying northern voters' electoral preferences for the centre right, it is a matter of fact that in 2006 the centre right's vote among self-employed workers, shopkeepers and the owners of small- and medium-sized enterprises was double the vote gained among these categories by the centre left (Itanes, 2006: 97). This was so in spite of the centre right's failure to fulfil election promises, such as tax cuts for those on higher incomes, which had played such a crucial role in its success at the 2001 election (Ricolfi, 2006: 15). In 2006, centre right voters punished FI by casting their ballots for Casini's UDC and Fini's Alleanza Nazionale (National Alliance, AN) while remaining faithful to the CdL. The status quo in the fiscal system left by the centre-right was regarded as a lesser evil compared to what a centre-left coalition, including RC, might have brought about; and very few shifted their votes to the centre left. This reflected a lack of trust in the centre left that Veltroni's party hoped to reverse at the 2008 election (Alfieri, 2008).

The 'Veltronification' of the centre left's image and message

The centre left's strategy for electoral recovery also relied significantly on its leader, Veltroni. As polls indicated (Diamanti, 2008a) from the very beginning of the election campaign, although the centre-left coalition was estimated to be 6–8 points behind the PdL, Veltroni was doing much better and his popularity ratings remained very high throughout the campaign, almost exceeding those of Berlusconi.

Unlike his predecessor, Prodi, Veltroni proved to have extremely good communication and media skills. Furthermore, he was a far stronger candidate than earlier centre-left leaders. In 2001 Berlusconi made considerable use of the instrument of delegitimation of Rutelli, a choice which, admittedly, was driven more by Rutelli's centrist image and media skills than by his leadership and power within the coalition. His party, the Democrats, was far smaller than its DS ally and he was portrayed, by Berlusconi, as the fig leaf for a *de facto* DS-dominated coalition (Newell, 2002: 80). The October 2005 primary elections shielded Prodi from similar accusations. The extraordinary turnout and the huge proportion of the vote in Prodi's favour (74.1 per cent) gave him full legitimacy, so that there was no risk that he could be portrayed as the 'puppet' of any of the coalition parties (Ricolfi, 2007: 23). Like Prodi, Veltroni was elected through well-organised and supported primary elections, but he also benefited from being the leader of the largest party in the coalition.

In light of Veltroni's popularity, the centre left ran a campaign which largely focused on its leader. This further accentuated the trend towards

the increasing personalisation of electoral competition that has characterised Italian politics over the last two decades.[7] The hope was that voters
would in the end choose between the two candidates and not the two
coalitions. Veltroni's face dominated the centre-left coalition's posters, and
several efforts were made to arrange a TV debate between the two candidates (although Berlusconi, not surprisingly, refused to take part in such an
encounter).

The ballot's verdict

In spite of Veltroni's hopes and wishful expectations that the centre-left
strategy described so far would work the miracle of an electoral recovery,
the 2008 results provided the centre right with a resounding victory and a
solid majority both in the Chamber of Deputies and in the Senate. The vote
for Berlusconi's centre-right alliance exceeded that for Veltroni's coalition
by almost 10 per cent.

The only winner within the left-wing camp was the IdV. Its score in the
Chamber of Deputies contest, a spectacular 4.3 per cent, was almost twice
the vote it obtained at the 2006 election (2.3 per cent). By contrast the big
looser was, indisputably, the SA which scored 3.1 and 3.2 per cent in the
Chamber and Senate contests respectively, almost 7 per cent less than the
sum of the votes gained in 2006 by RC, the PdCI and the Greens (which
amounted to 9.2 and 11.3 per cent in the Chamber and Senate contests
respectively). This was a major defeat for the far left which failed to win a
single parliamentary seat (as the SA failed to pass the 4 per cent threshold)
and lost more than 2.5 million votes. It has been estimated that almost one
third of the 2006 far-left electorate voted for the PD (D'Alimonte, 2008);
one quarter approximately abstained; and one quarter voted either for other
parties on the extreme Left or, in larger part, for the centre right (mainly the
Northern League). With this in mind, it is worth noting that Bossi's party
obtained almost 7 per cent in the 'red' region of Emilia Romagna (doub-
ling its vote in cities such as Bologna) and scored extremely good results
in working-class areas such as Milan's deprived neighbourhoods of Quarto
Oggiaro and Gratosoglio.[8] The 2008 election further illustrated the extent
to which parties such as RC have lost touch with their traditional working-
class grass roots.

The *débacle* suffered by the SA provoked a fierce debate within each of its
constituent parties. This focussed on two issues: first, future unification,
which, in light of the sorry election result, parties such as RC were very
happy to shelve; second, the reasons for the defeat. A number of factors
were cited, first, the far left's support for Prodi's government in spite of the
latter's U-turn on the agreed electoral programme. Bertinotti's acceptance
of the post of President of the Chamber of Deputies created a further obstacle in the way of parties such as RC acting as more critical voices within

the coalition. Second, the SA coalition's failure to project a clear image and identity should be mentioned. Traditional symbols such as the hammer and sickle were put aside but no attempt was made to formulate a thoroughly revised political agenda that went beyond past themes and the Left's traditional concerns. Furthermore, as argued by Valentino Parlato, one of the founders and leading commentators of the communist newspaper *Il Manifesto*, the creation of the SA was too last-minute and, most significantly, the result of a decision taken at the top with hardly any connection with the grass roots and civil society (*Corriere della Sera*, 2008a). Lastly, the SA suffered from an ill-chosen and weak leadership. The high-level institutional position held by Bertinotti made the former RC leader an unsuitable candidate to launch the fierce attack on Prodi's record and mistakes which, according to many, the SA parties should have undertaken in order to regain their electorates' confidence (Agnoletto, 2008). Moreover, Bertinotti's age (68 years) conflicted with the image of a new modern radical Left that the SA aimed to associate itself with.

The ballot's verdict (2): Veltroni's 'good result' or 'heavy defeat'?

IdV's and the SA's votes have been easily pigeonholed by political analysts within the 'memorable results' and the 'sorry defeats' boxes respectively. However, when it comes to analysis of the PD's score (33.1 per cent), commentators' opinions have varied enormously. In fact, not much agreement exists on whether Veltroni's vote should be regarded as a minor or a heavy defeat. As Roberto D'Alimonte (2008) has noted, the PD's was a 'good result'. For all the campaign boasts, no one could really expect the centre-left coalition to win. Given the Prodi government's poor record, the outcome might have been much worse. True, compared to the vote gained in 2006 by Prodi's list, Uniti nell'Ulivo (31.3 per cent) – which included the DS and the Margherita – the PD's vote increased by very little. Assuming that the Radicals' contribution amounted to 1 per cent, Veltroni's party grew by less than 1 per cent. However, Veltroni managed to achieve some of the PD's purported objectives: to start with, the creation of a centre-left party the size of other large European social-democratic parties. Second, the strengthening of bipolarism was also secured. As a matter of fact, this was mainly thanks to the SA parties' electoral decline. However, one suspects that the SA parties' exclusion from Parliament, far from bothering the PD's more moderate components, was, in fact, regarded as an achievement. As D'Alimonte argued, an alliance between the PD and the far left, such as the one established in 2006, was unlikely to have resulted in the centre left's victory. Even so, it would have produced a fragmented and unstable government, and, following Prodi's experience, this could no longer be considered a viable option. According to this argument, the PD is only at the beginning of a process of attempted growth likely to require considerable time before it bears fruit. By sticking to its centrist and moderate vocation, the party should aim to increase its appeal among centrist and moderate voters and so to reverse the centre left's decline in the North. As far as far-left voters are concerned, appeals to vote tactically will continue do the trick. Should an alliance be formed, this should be with centrist parties such as Casini's UDC and not with the far left.

The problem is – and here we come to those commentators, such as Ilvo Diamanti or Giovanni Sartori (Diamanti, 2008b; Sartori, 2008b), who looked at Veltroni's result more pessimistically and described it as a 'heavy defeat' – that the PD's project seemed to have very little appeal for centrist voters. The PD's vote, which approximately equalled the vote gained by the Ulivo list in 2006, included almost one third of former far-left voters. This means that, far from making any inroads into the centrist vote, the PD lost several moderate voters to the centre right (or, possibly, to abstention). The PD failed to reverse the decline in the northern regions, as the centre-right's vote in the North and in the North East exceeded that of the centre left by 17 and 19 per cent respectively. It also suffered huge losses in southern regions such as Sicily (Diamanti, 2008b). Furthermore, the 2008 ballot confirmed the centre-left coalition's weakness among professional categories such as self-employed workers and shopkeepers. Unlike the centre-right coalition, whose electorate seems to be evenly spread both from a national and social point of view, the centre left has once again proved unable to rebalance the geographical and social disequilibria which have long characterised its vote (Diamanti, 2008c).

As far as the reasons for the centre left's poor electoral score are concerned, a number of factors should be considered, first, the Prodi government's sorry experience. Veltroni's strategy of attempting to convey an image of novelty – presenting the PD as the *'deus ex machina'* the electorate had been waiting for to tackle economic decline and major structural problems – did not seem to persuade the Italian electorate. The resentment against the centre left was such that Berlusconi was this time able to score a solid victory without making any particularly extravagant promises (as had been the case in 2001). Second, one should mention Berlusconi's ability to react promptly to the birth of the PD and create in February 2008 (two months before the election) the Popolo della Libertà (The People of Freedom, PdL) through the merger of FI and AN and smaller centre-right parties. The PdL's formation prevented the PD from becoming the largest party in Italy's party system. Furthermore, it also enabled Berlusconi to promise the electorate a less fragmented and quarrelsome centre-right coalition – the more so for the fact that, although the Northern League stayed on board, a number of coalition partners both on the right (Daniela Santanchè's La Destra – the Right) and in the centre (Casini's UDC) were left out. One last factor that has been raised by the PD leadership is the small amount of time the party had to convey its message that a new political entity had come to the fore, with a thoroughly revised political agenda and style of policy-making (Vitali, 2008). The PD, it has been argued, is a long-term project and its vote will grow as the years go by. This might be true. However, the PD's inner tensions and divisions following defeat do not seem to promise a rosy future. Neither are they likely to convince the electorate that the old fragmented and litigious centre-left is a thing of the past.

Notes

1. One week before the election, polls issued by market and opinion research institutes such as Demos and Swg put the gap between the two coalitions at 6.6 and 5.0 per cent respectively. See on this, *la Rpubblica* (2008c).
2. On the birth of the Partito Democratico and on the Ulivo project see Salvati, 2003, 2007; Santagata, 2006; Meacci, 2007; Fassina and Visco, 2008. For more on centre-left parties in the years between 2001 and 2006, see Hopkin, 2006; Rose, 2008; and Donovan, 2008.
3. The poll was issued by the market and opinion research institute Ipr. See on this Berizzi (2008).
4. As Paolo Bonaiuti, from the PdL, lamented, the PD plagiarised ideas from the centre right 'as the Chinese did with designer products'. See *la Repubblica* (2008e).
5. On the PD's attempt to defuse the image of a party as one solely concerned with the lower strata, see Veltroni (2007a: 75–76).
6. For instance, according to Caciagli and Corbetta (2002: 51) the centre left's defeat in the North was crucial to Berlusconi's victory in 2001.
7. On the issue of the growing personalisation of Italian politics and the impact of the 'leadership factor' on the electoral result, see Sani, 2002; Newell, 2002: 78, 127ff; Calise, 2006, 2007; Novelli, 2006: 148–150, 183; Barisione, 2007.
8. In the aftermath of the April electoral result, the press placed much emphasis on the Northern League's success in working class areas. On this, see, for instance, *Corriere della Sera* (2008b) and Tondelli and Trocino (2008).

References

Agnoletto, V. (2008) 'Gli errori degli ultimi mesi. Ma la sconfitta della sinistra è strategica', *Agnoletto's Newsletter*, 17 April.

Alfieri, M. (2008) *Nord terra ostile. Perchè la sinistra non vince*, Venice: Marsilio.

Barisione, M. (2007) 'L'orientamento al leader. Forme, effetti e dinamiche', pp. 157–186 in P. Feltrin, L. Natale and L. Ricolfi (eds), *Nel segreto dell'urna. Un'analisi delle elezioni politiche del 2006*, Turin: Utet.

Berizzi, P. (2008) 'La Bonino vale 400 mila voti ma l'intesa può confondere', *la Repubblica*, 21 February.

Cacciotto, M. (2007) 'La strategia del *framing*', pp. 41–57 in P. Feltrin, P. Natale and L. Ricolfi (eds), *Nel segreto dell'urna. Un'analisi delle elezioni politiche del 2006*, Turin: Utet.

Caciagli, M. and Corbetta, P. (eds) (2002) *Le ragioni dell'elettore. Perchè ha vinto il centro-destra nelle elezioni italiane del 2001*, Bologna: Il Mulino.

Calise, M. (2006) *La terza Repubblica. Partiti contro Presidenti*, Rome and Bari: Laterza.

Calise, M. (2007) *Il Partito personale*, Rome and Bari: Laterza.

Campus, D. (2008) 'Campaign issues and themes', pp. 139–155 in J.L. Newell (ed.), *The Italian General Election of 2006: Romano Prodi's Victory*, Manchester and New York: Manchester University Press.

Chiaramonte, A. (2008) 'How Prodi's Unione won by a handful of votes', pp. 203–222 in J.L. Newell (ed.), *The Italian General Election of 2006: Romano Prodi's Victory*, Manchester and New York: Manchester University Press.

Corriere della Sera (2008a) 'Parlato: Fausto? Appartiene al passato. Tante stravaganze, sembravamo la Trinità', *Corriere della Sera*, 15 April.

Corriere della Sera (2008b) 'La notte terribile della *gauche* italiana. E gli operai fanno festa con la Lega', *Corriere della Sera*, 15 April.

Cotta, M. and Verzichelli, L. (2007) *Political Institutions in Italy*, Oxford: Oxford University Press.

D'Alimonte, R. (2008) 'Il 33 per cento? Un inizio, ma il partito non lo vede', *Sole 24 Ore*, 22 June 2008.

Diamanti, I. (2008a) 'Presidenzialismo all'italiana', *la Repubblica*, 17 February.

Diamanti, I. (2008b) 'Quei 7 punti persi dal centrosinistra', *la Repubblica*, 16 April.

Diamanti, I. (2008c) 'La geografia politica di Berlusconi', *la Repubblica*, 19 May.

Donovan, M. (2008) 'The processes of alliance formation', pp. 115–135 in J.L. Newell (ed.), *The Italian General Election of 2006: Romano Prodi's Victory*, Manchester and New York: Manchester University Press.

Fassina, S. and Visco, V. (eds) (2008) *Governare il mercato. Le culture economiche del Partito democratico*, Rome: Donzelli.

Ferragutti, P. (2007) 'Analisi territoriale del voto', pp. 201–216 in P. Feltrin, P. Natale and L. Ricolfi (eds), *Nel segreto dell'urna. Un'analisi delle elezioni politiche del 2006*, Turin: Utet.

Filippeschi, M. (2007) 'Bipolarismo', pp. 18–30 in M. Meacci (ed.), *Partito Democratico. Le Parole Chiavi*, Rome: Editori Riuniti.

Hopkin, J. (2006) 'From federation to union, from parties to primaries: the search for unity in the center-left', pp. 67–84 in G. Amyot and L. Verzichelli (eds), *Italian Politics. The End of the Berlusconi Era?* New York and Oxford: Berghahn Books.

Itanes (2006) *Dov'è la vittoria?. Il voto del 2006 raccontato dagli italiani*, Bologna: Il Mulino.

la Repubblica (2008a) 'Pdl, scoppia il caso Ciarrapico', *la Repubblica*, 10 March.

la Repubblica (2008b) 'PD ai Radicali: "Bonino Ministro". Ma le condizioni non convincono', *la Repubblica*, 20 February.

la Repubblica (2008c) 'Distacco ridotto, Senato in bilico. Rimonta Pd negli ultimi sondaggi', *la Repubblica*, 28 March.

la Repubblica (2008d) 'D'Alema: "il Kosovo divide il centrodestra, non il Pd"', *la Repubblica*, 20 February.

la Repubblica (2008e) 'La sfida di Veltroni: "Già in rimonta". FI: "Il Pd copia i nostri programmi"', *la Repubblica*, 17 February.

Meacci, M. (ed.) (2007) *Partito Democratico. Le Parole Chiavi*, Rome: Editori Riuniti.

Mulé, R. (2007) *Dentro i DS*, Bologna: Il Mulino.

Natale, P. (2007) 'Il primo anno del governo Prodi: segnali contrastanti', pp. 339–349 in P. Feltrin, P. Natale and L. Ricolfi (eds), *Nel segreto dell'urna. Un'analisi delle elezioni politiche del 2006*, Turin: Utet.

Newell, J.L. (ed.) (2002) *The Italian General Election of 2001: Berlusconi's Victory*, Manchester and New York: Manchester University Press.

Newell, J.L. (ed.) (2008) *The Italian General Election of 2006: Romano Prodi's Victory*, Manchester and New York: Manchester University Press.

Novelli, E. (2006) *La Turbopolitica. Sessant'anni di comunicazione politica e di scena pubblica in Italia. 1945–2005*, Milan: Bur.

Ricolfi, L. (2006) *Tempo scaduto: il 'contratto con gli italiani' alla prova dei fatti*, Bologna: Il Mulino.

Ricolfi, L. (2007) *L'arte del non governo. Da Prodi a Berlusconi e ritorno*, Milan: Longanesi.

Ricolfi, L. and Ferragutti, P. (2007) 'Modernizzazione della politica e "questione settentrionale"', pp. 217–237 in P. Feltrin, P. Natale and L. Ricolfi (eds), *Nel segreto dell'urna. Un'analisi delle elezioni politiche del 2006*, Turin: Utet.

Rose, S. (2008) 'The parties of the centre left', pp. 79–95 in J.L. Newell (ed.), *The Italian General Election of 2006: Romano Prodi's Victory*, Manchester and New York: Manchester University Press.

Salvati, M. (2003) *Il Partito Democratico. Alle origini di un'idea politica*, Bologna: Il Mulino.

Salvati, M. (2007) *Il Partito Democratico per la Rivoluzione Liberale*, Milan: Feltrinelli.

Salvati, M. (2008) 'La battaglia del centro', *Corriere della Sera*, 26 March.

Sani, G. (2002) 'La personalizzazione delle campagne', pp. 275–299 in M. Caciagli and P. Corbetta (eds), *Le ragioni dell'elettore. Perchè ha vinto il centro-destra nelle elezioni italiane del 2001*, Bologna: Il Mulino.

Santagata, G. (2006) *La Fabbrica del programma. Dieci anni di Ulivo verso il Partito Democratico*, Rome: Donzelli.

Sartori, G. (2008a) 'Strane elezioni senza battaglia', *Corriere della Sera*, 2 April.

Sartori, G. (2008b) 'Le elezioni dirompenti', *Corriere della Sera*, 24 April.

Stella, G.A. (2008) 'Lo strappo di Calearo', *la Repubblica*, 7 March.

Tondelli, J. and Trocino, A. (2008) 'La nuova Lega: operai e impiegati', *Corriere della Sera*, 16 April.

Tremonti, G. (2008) *La Paura e la speranza: la crisi globale che si avvicina e la via per superarla*, Milan: Mondadori.

Vassallo, S. (2006) 'The regional elections: winning too convincingly?', pp. 47–66 in G. Amyot and L. Verzichelli (eds), *Italian Politics. The End of the Berlusconi Era?* New York and Oxford: Berghahn Books.

Veltroni, W. (2007a) *La nuova stagione. Contro tutti i conservatorismi*, Milan: Rizzoli.

Veltroni, W. (2007b) 'Sintesi', pp. 158–160 in Meacci, M. (ed.), *Partito Democratico. Le Parole Chiavi*, Rome: Editori Riuniti.

Vitali, A. (2008) 'Veltroni, al via la nuova fase', *la Repubblica*, 15 April.

5
The Parties of the Centre Right: Many Oppositions, One Leader

Daniele Albertazzi and Duncan McDonnell

There are few political leaders in Europe who could afford to lose a second general election to the same opponent and still survive to lead their party into another contest. But, then, there are few contemporary leaders comparable to Silvio Berlusconi. Not only does he wield financial and media power which would be unimaginable (and perhaps unconstitutional) for a political leader in any other European democracy, but he has used this power to create a party, Forza Italia (FI), that has been constantly the most-voted in Italy since the collapse of the First Republic. Moreover, around this fulcrum, he has been able to construct a centre-right coalition that has successfully filled the huge political vacuum left by the demise of the old governing parties at the beginning of the 1990s.

Having claimed to be entering politics 'temporarily' in 1994 in order to 'save Italy' from communist rule, Berlusconi has since become one of the longest-serving major political leaders on the continent. Indeed, in the 14 years he has led FI and the centre right, he has seen the leadership of the rival centre left change at least five times.[1] Nonetheless, as his struggling Casa delle Libertà (House of Freedoms, CdL) government entered the 2006 general-election campaign, it looked as though Italy might be finally moving towards a 'post-Berlusconi' era. Nothing could have been further from the truth. Despite losing that election, Berlusconi has not only remained at the forefront of Italian politics, but in 2008 he became Prime Minister once again. Moreover, he did so at the head of a coalition of which he appears more in control than ever, having again created, 'overnight', a new party, the Popolo della Libertà (People of Freedom, PdL).

How and why the period from 2006 to early 2008 paved the way for this turn of events is the subject of this chapter. Taking as our starting point the extremely (and unexpectedly) close results of the April 2006 election, we look at how Berlusconi doggedly sought to topple the Prodi government in what became known as the tactic of the *spallata* ('shoulder charge'). This strategy was not fully supported by his allies and, as we will see, in the period between April 2006 and December 2007, Italy often appeared to have multiple oppositions, with the junior parties of the CdL located in concentric circles around Berlusconi and FI. To use an astronomical metaphor, we might say that at the centre of the CdL universe the Berlusconi sun stood out in its glaring refusal to recognise the legitimacy of the Prodi government, and FI alone remained constant in its call for fresh elections as the only possible solution to Italy's problems. Around this sun, at varying degrees of orbit, we find first the Lega Nord (Northern League, NL) followed by Alleanza Nazionale (the National Alliance, AN), and finally the Unione dei Democratici Cristiani e dei Democratici di Centro (Union of Christian Democrats and Centre Democrats, UDC) as a sort of far-off Pluto, with doubts about whether it could even still be considered a planet in the Berlusconi solar system at all. This universe of multiple, concentric oppositions survived until mid-November 2007 when – after the budget vote in the Senate saw the government survive yet another *spallata* – it was called into question not only by the UDC, but also by AN. Just, however, when it appeared that his position as the fixed, essential point around which the centre right revolved was most under threat, Berlusconi founded a new party which would incorporate FI and anyone else who was willing. In other words, to continue the metaphor, the Berlusconi sun moved to a new system and let the CdL parties figure out whether they could live without its energy or not. While this was to some extent a gamble, it was one which paid off when the Prodi government then indeed fell in January 2008 and Berlusconi returned to power three months later.

The two-year *spallata* and the death of the CdL

To a large degree, the roots of Berlusconi's 2008 victory can be traced back to the start of the 2006 campaign. Then, the CdL government had failed to achieve most of the key pledges of Berlusconi's 'Contract with the Italian People' on which it had been elected in 2001 (Ricolfi, 2006) and the public mood was one of pessimism regarding the state of the economy and standards of living (Guarnieri and Newell, 2005). Moreover, the coalition had appeared divided with FI and the NL on one side and the more traditional politicians of AN and the UDC on the other (Albertazzi and McDonnell, 2005). After five years of declining ratings in the polls and centre left victories in sub-national and European elections from 2002 onwards, the image thus presented by the centre right in 2006 was of a tired, failed and bickering alliance – quite in contrast to the dynamic centre left, which had welcomed back as leader Romano Prodi, the man who had defeated Berlusconi in 1996 and now seemed set to carry his coalition to victory. As the campaign approached, and the centre right saw important pillars of Italian society (the employers' Confindustria and the *Corriere della Sera* newspaper) either line up against it or keep a distance (the Church), many members of the CdL had resigned themselves to an apparently inevitable defeat (Briquet and Mastropaolo, 2007). This was clearly shown by the centre right's electoral law, introduced at the end of 2005, the main purpose of which seemed to be to make it difficult for whichever side won to govern – hardly the move of a government that believed it had a reasonable chance of being re-elected.

As it turned out, the centre left won by the narrowest margin in Italian history. In the Chamber of Deputies election, it secured the majority premium by just 24,755 votes. In the Senate, the CdL in fact received 270,001 votes more than the Unione within Italy – although, due to the regional basis on which the Senate's majority premium is awarded, and the CdL's mistakes in the overseas constituency (Chiaramonte, 2008), the centre left still finished up with a two-seat majority. It may well be, as James Newell (2006) has argued, that the predicted centre-left triumph in 2006 was a mirage constructed by the media and the political world itself. Nonetheless, the sensation on the morning after the election was that the centre left's victory in fact amounted to a partial defeat, given the expectations that had been generated. By extension, the centre right appeared to have made a remarkable 'comeback', considering the situation in which it had found itself at the beginning of the campaign.

In the election's aftermath, Berlusconi refused to recognise the centre-left victory for a series of reasons, ranging from allegations of electoral fraud to the fact that the more productive northern regions of the country had tended to support the CdL. While the latter is, of course, a rather difficult argument to sustain in a democracy, Berlusconi perhaps had a point in arguing, as he did in a letter to *Corriere della Sera*, that 'there are neither losers nor winners' and that 'we should not dismiss the possibility of a partial and temporary agreement to work together in order to tackle the pressing institutional, economic and international commitments of the country' (Berlusconi, 2006a). Certainly, given the centre left's wafer-thin advantage in the Senate and the fact that it only enjoyed this majority due to the perverse effects of the electoral law, a 'national unity' government would not have appeared unjustifiable. Likewise, the announcement of a new general election within months, perhaps under a new electoral law, would also have seemed reasonable, especially since Prodi himself had said on 28 February 2006 that, in the event of a 'draw' (which is essentially what then transpired), a new general election would have to be held.

In any case, the Manichaean nature of Italian political competition meant that there was no chance of Berlusconi recognising the Unione's win graciously, or of Prodi considering any compromise gesture – such as offering the opposition the presidency of one of the chambers of Parliament, as had been the practice between 1976 and 1992 when the Italian Communist Party held the presidency of the Chamber. While Berlusconi and the NL refused to recognise the legitimacy of the centre left's incumbency, on the centre left there were renewed expressions of the view that Berlusconi's own democratic credentials were in doubt. Indeed, the refusal by each side to accord full democratic legitimacy to the other has rendered inter-coalition dialogue extremely difficult throughout the short history of the Second Republic – a problem exacerbated in April 2006 given the nature of the centre left's victory and the highly acrimonious election campaign that had preceded it.

It was in this climate that the new government faced its first test with the May 2006 local elections. Consistent with his *spallata* approach, Berlusconi urged voters to hand 'a first eviction notice to the Left', which he accused of having fraudulently occupied the institutions of the state (McDonnell, 2007). Rather than providing a *spallata*, however, the elections were the second (after the general election) of a hat-trick of CdL defeats in 2006, with the third coming in the constitutional referendum on 26 June. This latter result had been widely expected as, although the reform had been officially presented as a CdL bill, its focus on 'devolution' was seen and presented as the price of the NL's participation in government. Considering the opposition to this aspect voiced not only by AN and the UDC, but also by some southern figures within FI, it was not surprising that the reform was defeated in the referendum by a 61 per cent 'no' vote.

At a meeting of the AN leadership following the referendum, Gianfranco Fini announced that 'the CdL as we knew it is over' (*Corriere della Sera*, 2006) and it became increasingly clear that he had a firm eye on the future. Fini, of course, was well aware that, were the centre left to remain in power for the full five years, it was highly unlikely that the next election in 2011 would see another face-off between Prodi and Berlusconi (who turned 70 in 2006) and that his own ambitions as a potential future leader of the centre right would be better served by a longer period in opposition. For this reason, despite the centre left's weakness both in Parliament and, increasingly, in the polls, he was unlikely to welcome a fall of the Prodi government and new elections. Rather, like the many actors in the wide and variegated world of the centre left whose main point of unity was their opposition to Berlusconi, Fini, along with UDC leader, Pierferdinando Casini, appeared to hope that, the more time went on, the greater the chances that Berlusconi's grip on the leadership of the centre right would weaken.

Nonetheless, as has often been the case over the last 15 years, Fini's rebellious stance proved to be more rhetorical than real – perhaps understandably given the fear of AN being re-marginalised on the Right and of Fini's own prime-ministerial aspirations thus vanishing forever. The case of the UDC, however, was quite different. It quickly disassociated itself in June 2006 from the tactic of the '*spallata* at all costs', refusing, for example, to vote against the Government over continued funding for the Italian mission in Afghanistan. Its position became more explicit when, on 16 September 2006, Casini told a UDC meeting that, now it was not in government, the party was no longer obliged to follow the CdL line. The most visible example of the extent to which the UDC had moved came just over two months later on 2 December 2006 when it decided that, rather than participate in an anti-Government protest alongside the other parties of the CdL, in Rome, it would hold its own rally in Palermo. As if to reinforce the point, Casini then declared: 'the CdL no longer makes sense: Berlusconi, Fini and Bossi can hold leadership meetings on their own' (Luzi, 2006). This sense of division was reinforced by repeated UDC references to the existence of 'two oppositions', and to the possibility of centrist alliances with moderate members of the Unione who had opted not to join the Partito Democratico (Democratic Party, PD). Regular centre-right splits in parliamentary votes also continued to occur. For example, the UDC again pursued its own course regarding financing for the mission in Afghanistan when, on 27 March 2007, FI, AN and NL senators abstained.

Given the rhetoric of the 'two oppositions', however, it is interesting that little mention was made of the fact that the UDC then ran with the other parties of the centre right in 27 out of the 29 largest city councils and in all eight provinces in which elections were held in May 2007. These elections saw the centre right finally break its six-year losing streak (since the 2001 general election) and fed the on-going media speculation about the Prodi government's imminent collapse. While these contests highlighted the continuing *electoral* unity of the centre right, however, there still remained strong differences in terms of the behaviour of the CdL parties as 'oppositions' to the centre left. As promised in the run-up to the vote (and consistent with the *spallata* campaign), Berlusconi subsequently called for a general election and, for several weeks, there was a public debate within the centre right about whether its leaders should officially request that the President, Giorgio Napolitano, dissolve Parliament. Having initially been against the idea, AN leader Gianfranco Fini changed his mind and on 13 June joined with Berlusconi and NL leader, Umberto Bossi, in asking for a meeting with Napolitano – a move dismissed by Casini as a futile propaganda stunt (Bei, 2007).

If the UDC thus continued to pursue a different orbit on the margins of the Berlusconi solar system, where it did find itself in agreement with the rest of the CdL was on the question of ethical issues – one of the main cards played by the centre-right opposition over the course of 2006–2008. Aware of the divisions within the centre left – particularly between the former Christian Democrats and former Communists who were now merging to form the PD – the centre right sought to exploit these by focusing attention on questions such as civil unions and gay marriage. This reached its height with the holding of the 'Family Day' rally in Rome on 12 May which, according to the organisers, saw over a million people in attendance, including not only various CdL members, but also the centre-left Justice Minister and former Christian Democrat, Clemente Mastella.

While the junior partners of the centre-right opposition can be viewed as moving around the central sun at different distances and varying orbits, there also appeared in the Berlusconi solar system during this period what could perhaps be termed an unidentified object in the shape of media-savvy and telegenic industrialist, Michela Brambilla. She led the Circoli della Libertà (Freedom Clubs), in whose creation, from the end of 2006, Berlusconi had been instrumental. The activities of these clubs appeared to be driven by two fundamental aims: (a) to increase the appeal of the centre right among professionals and middle-class voters – resentful at what was perceived as the centre left's hostility towards them; (b) to underline the lack of popularity of the Prodi government by organising meetings with 'ordinary citizens' (to be broadcast on the movement's own television channel, set up by Mediaset professionals). This was all presented as giving the common people an opportunity to vent their frustration. Brambilla's creation of course bore a strong resemblance to FI's own 'clubs' of 'ordinary citizens' (as opposed to the 'branches' run by traditional parties); and the 'manifesto' of values the Circoli published in November 2006 mirrored Berlusconi's leading ideas.[2] In it, the clubs were presented as an opportunity for citizens to fight the 'Nanny state', to combat those who 'preach class warfare' and to oppose excessive taxation (Circoli della Libertà, 2008).

Over the course of 2007, Brambilla was extremely active in organising town meetings with disgruntled voters and was able to attract much media attention through her stinging attacks on the Government and the political class as a whole. Although the figure of 5,000 active clubs by the summer of 2007 was certainly much inflated, Brambilla did manage to secure large quantities of airtime and column inches. In this sense, she can be viewed as an excellent example of Berlusconi's power to make or break political careers at the drop of a hat. Having stated on several occasions that he saw Brambilla as his likely successor as FI leader (e.g., Romano, 2007a and 2007b), and with prominent FI politicians such as Marcello dell'Utri taking the very unusual step of complaining in public about the space and role she had been given,[3] Berlusconi was able to use Brambilla to send messages not only to his allies, but also to those within FI itself. One of these messages was undoubtedly delivered on 21 August 2007 (*Corriere della Sera*, 2007a), when it was announced that Brambilla had registered the name and symbol of the Partito della Libertà (Party of Freedom), whose subsequent emergence we will discuss in the next section.

Of course, Berlusconi's resort to Brambilla and the Circoli also highlighted how, in his calls for fresh elections at every turn, he had become isolated from his allies apart from the NL (which, however, occasionally seemed open to an accord with the centre left on federalism). Having conceived of his role, since the day he lost the 2006 election, as requiring him to provoke the Government's fall at any cost, the longer that government clung to power, the more desperate and one-dimensional his strategy seemed. Over the period, he had almost constantly refused to enter into dialogue about institutional and electoral reform, or to support the Government on matters of national interest such as funding for Italy's mission in Afghanistan. By November 2007, when the centre left had been in power for a year and a half, the tactic of the '*spallata* at all costs' appeared to have reached its make-or-break moment, as the budget came up for discussion in the Senate and with Berlusconi confidently predicting that the Government would fail to secure enough votes to get the measure through. As it turned out, on 15 November, it was approved in the Senate, with 161 votes in favour and 157 against. This was widely greeted as a defeat for the '*spallata*'. Indeed, in what seemed an attempt to distance himself from Berlusconi, Fini accused him in a front-page article for the *Corriere* on 16 November, of ignoring the fact that 'the government will fall only once it is certain that a new general election will not take place using the current electoral law' (Fini, 2007). As the weekend of 17–18 November approached, therefore, Berlusconi looked more alone and lacking in ideas than he had for many years. The sun which had dominated not only the centre-right universe, but that of the Second Republic, appeared to be fading. However, Sunday 18 November and its aftermath would show that this was merely an eclipse.

The birth of the Popolo della Libertà and the final *'spallata'*

On that day, in piazza San Babila in Milan, Berlusconi announced the creation of a new party that, he promised, would soon incorporate FI. Its initial name, the Partito del popolo italiano delle libertà ('The Italian People's Freedom Party') would later be shortened to Popolo della Libertà (People of Freedom, PdL). The other parties of the centre right were also invited to merge with the PdL, since this was said to be 'what people wanted' (*la Repubblica*, 2007). Berlusconi's 'invitation', however, sounded very much like a threat. Two weeks later, having announced (somewhat implausibly) that the PdL had already attracted 1.2 million members, Berlusconi insisted: 'I hope that everyone from the centre right joins us. If they do not, it will be their problem as they are destined to be isolated on the margins of petty party politics' (*La Stampa*, 2007b). In short, Berlusconi's allies were, 'at Berlusconi's command' (Donovan, 2008: 87), supposed to surrender their autonomy, dismantle their parties and accept his leadership once and for all.

The populist style of the PdL's launch was not out of character (Tarchi, 2007) and the move attracted a lot of media coverage. A few days after the piazza San Babila announcement, Stefania Prestigiacomo – a well-known FI politician and former minister – admitted on television that neither she nor any of her colleagues had been consulted about whether FI should enter the PdL. Indeed, a number of FI figures expressed sentiments of puzzlement and concern in the aftermath of the announcement.

The leaders of the other CdL parties were also very critical of Berlusconi's initiative. Fini and Casini issued a joint statement dismissing it as 'propagandistic' and another of his 'populist sorties' (*La Stampa*, 2007a; Calabresi, 2007).

Fini later defined the move as a *'coup de théâtre'*, comparing Berlusconi to a comedian (*La Stampa*, 2007c). As for the NL, Bossi had reiterated already in the summer that his party was not interested in merging with anyone (*ANSA*, 28 August 2007). Once the birth of the PdL was announced, Bossi argued that Berlusconi's initiative would cause relationships within the centre right to deteriorate (*la Repubblica*, 2007). The anger and disappointment was such that for a few weeks the media even speculated that AN and the UDC might merge with one another, rather than join the PdL (*La Stampa*, 2007d).

For all the furore that the announcement caused, the merger idea was certainly not new; indeed, many CdL politicians had declared themselves in favour of it in the past. The significance of this move by Berlusconi thus lay not so much in 'what' he was proposing, but rather in the 'how' and the 'when'. The 'how', because unification had previously always been discussed in terms of a progressive rapprochement between allies which, despite their differences, all claimed to draw inspiration from the values of European-style conservatism (Urso, 2005); the 'when', because, as we have seen, the move coincided with the umpteenth instance of the Prodi government not falling as Berlusconi had predicted, with figures such as Fini publicly criticising the CdL leader's strategic abilities.

Berlusconi had in fact started talking about the need for a unitary conservative party as far back as 1994, only a few months after creating FI (Donovan, 2008: 90), and had even gone as far as publishing a collection of speeches entirely dedicated to the idea (Berlusconi, 2006b). Following the very convincing victory of the centre right in 2001, FI parliamentarian Ferdinando Adornato had organised several conferences and meetings aimed at facilitating the process of unification, and launched a 'manifesto of values' in 2005, which was designed to become the founding text of the new party (see appendix to Berlusconi, 2006b). Adornato had also devised a 'road map' to unification, to be achieved through a process involving the grassroots of all the centre-right parties except the NL.[4]

There were two reasons why this plan was destined to fail. First, given the new electoral law introduced by the CdL in 2005, the constituent parts of the CdL had more incentive to stand separately in the 2006 elections. The return to a proportional system meant that Berlusconi's allies could try to negotiate an adjustment to the power relations within the alliance (depending on the votes they were able to gain). This was predicated on the expectation that FI – which had underperformed in local and European elections in 2004 and 2005 – would continue to pay the heaviest price for the Government's lack of popularity at the 2006 election.

Second, a strategy of unification based on constituent assemblies and negotiations between interested parties would inevitably have entailed an open and prolonged challenge to Berlusconi's leadership by the UDC (and possibly also AN). Therefore, once convinced of the necessity to move beyond the CdL four-party coalition, Berlusconi decided to create a new party on his own terms by staging a repeat of 1994 – when he had created FI almost overnight, announced its birth through the television channels that he owned, and presented the nation (and his future allies) with a *fait accompli* that was to revolutionise politics in the country for years to come (Ginsborg, 2004: chapter 6). Similarly, in 2008, Berlusconi's carefully crafted media operation put him again at centre stage, confirmed his ability to set the political agenda on his own terms, and re-established his position as the (only possible) leader of the centre right.

Understanding fully the need for such a dramatic move requires going back in time to consider how relations between the centre-right parties had developed following the creation of the Berlusconi-led alliance in the mid-1990s. After the 1994 general election, Berlusconi had managed to convince the NL to govern alongside the former fascists of the Italian Social Movement (Movimento Sociale Italiano, MSI) (at that time in favour of centralisation and the 'strong state') and former Christian Democrats – very much the symbol of the 'old regime' of Italy's 'First Republic'. The centre right had thus configured itself in terms of multiple, concentric circles of opposition to the centre left, and attachment to Berlusconi, as he was the only one who could keep such a motley crew together (Diamanti and Lello, 2005). Berlusconi had thus emerged as the fulcrum of the alliance. Closest to him in the mid-1990s were the former Christian Democrats, whose leaders had been elected to Parliament on FI's lists. At a greater distance – however, as it later transpired, generally loyal to him – were the former fascists of the MSI – soon to turn into AN; and, finally, furthest away was the NL, which was competing for votes with FI in the industrial heartland of northern Italy (Albertazzi and McDonnell, 2005).

During Berlusconi's second five-year experience in government between 2001 and 2006, the centre right could again be understood in terms of multiple, concentric circles of opposition to the centre left. However, each of Berlusconi's allies had by then re-positioned itself vis-à-vis the Prime Minister and his party. AN had moved towards the centre, having embarked on a process of progressive, but irreversible, transformation into a respectable, conservative party. While this meant it had come closer to FI and Berlusconi in terms of values, it also implied that its language was in fact more moderate and far less populist than that of the FI leader. It is important here to remember that, despite its roots in neo-fascism, AN and its leader have not played the 'anti-communist' card to anything like the same extent as Berlusconi during election campaigns. Moreover, Fini has shied away from denying the legitimacy of the centre left as a governing force in the way that Berlusconi has consistently done. Finally, for its part, the NL, while not giving up its radical identity, had 'reinvented' itself as a faithful ally of Berlusconi, providing staunch support to the Prime Minister (with some exceptions) in exchange for approval of a federal reform of the Constitution (Albertazzi and McDonnell, 2005).

In fact, it was now the UDC that had moved furthest away from the Prime Minister. Having embarked on a campaign to weaken Berlusconi's leadership, the UDC's leaders began attacking his alleged 'Peronism', often refusing to provide support for Government policies dear to the Prime Minister, such as the reform of legislation regulating the amount of exposure parties can receive in the media before elections (the *par condicio* law), or the attempt to introduce legislation specifically aimed at protecting Berlusconi's close associate, Cesare Previti, from prosecution (Amyot and Verzichelli, 2006: 33).

There were several reasons why the UDC decided to position itself as the 'enemy within' the centre-right alliance. After all, this was the party which, being closest to the 'centre' of the political spectrum, needed to keep its distance from the more extreme elements within the CdL in order to maintain its identity. A good example came with the party's insistence that the strict Bossi-Fini immigration law be accompanied by an amnesty for those illegal immigrants already in Italy. Moreover, the UDC's strategy of progressively distancing itself from a government with low approval ratings had been shown to pay off, as the party benefited from moderate voters deserting FI in the second-order elections held in 2004 and 2005 (Albertazzi, 2009). Finally, given the very poor poll ratings for Berlusconi as Prime Minister (Pasquino, 2007), it finally seemed possible, towards the end of his tenure in office, to imagine a centre-right alliance that no longer depended on his leadership and could even be led by a centrist. For all these reasons, the UDC developed a much more autonomous profile throughout 2004 and 2005, and, as explained in the previous section, maintained a distinctive identity, even when the parties of the centre right found themselves in opposition after the 2006 election. Any attempt by Berlusconi to re-establish his hegemony over the centre right would thus have had to start by neutralising the challenge posed by the UDC.

Berlusconi's decision to create the PdL, therefore, must be interpreted as, first and foremost, an offensive move. However, it was also, to some extent, a defensive one. A few months earlier, the young media-savvy mayor of Rome, Walter Veltroni (cfr Chapter 4), had launched the PD, the unified party incorporating the two largest members of the centre-left coalition. This had attracted much media coverage and had been sold to Italian voters as a way of reducing the fragmentation of the Italian political system, by giving the country its first ever large, moderate reformist party of government (Veltroni, 2007). Clearly, unifying the Right would have had the effect of spoiling the PD's efforts to sell itself as *the* novelty of Italian politics.[5] In November 2007, therefore, we could say that Berlusconi presented the UDC and other minor parties of the Right with an unenviable choice: either merge with his new party (and thus accept a subordinate position within yet another of his tightly controlled creations) (Calise, 2000) or risk not being represented in Parliament due to the vote thresholds required for parties running alone.[6]

In the aftermath of the announcement of 18 November 2007, there was a rush by political figures and the leaders of small parties, such as Gianfranco Rotondi and Alessandra Mussolini, to join the new 'creation', alongside Brambilla's Circoli (see previous section). Among Berlusconi's major allies however, the mood was for an all-out rejection (possibly in the hope that the PdL would turn out to be a short-lived stunt and that Berlusconi would be forced to reconsider).[7] In December 2007, the leader of AN, Gianfranco Fini, went as far as declaring that there was 'no chance that AN will dissolve and be incorporated into Berlusconi's new party' (*Corriere della Sera*, 2007b).

This type of response, however, was predicated on the assumption that the Prodi government would survive for at least another year or until a change in the electoral law had been introduced. In fact, the rules of the game were turned upside down just a few weeks later with the Government's fall on 24 January 2008. Faced with an upcoming general election, AN had to perform a humiliating U-turn, choosing to merge with the PdL after all.[8] Having recently suffered a rightward split led by former government minister, Francesco Storace, and with many well-known figures of the radical right (including Storace himself) involved in talks to join Berlusconi's new party, AN (as a much-watered-down, would-be conservative party) would have risked becoming redundant in the eyes of voters. In addition, by leading his party to merge with the PdL, Gianfranco Fini (who has consistently enjoyed high rates of approval among the Italian electorate) presumably believes that he has put himself at the forefront in the race for the leadership of the centre right (whenever Berlusconi relinquishes it).

As we know, the successful '*spallata*' finally came when the Prodi government was brought down by Clemente Mastella and Lamberto Dini (both of whom, it seems fair to say, presumably had some form of contact with Berlusconi before the crucial vote). As new elections were then scheduled for the spring of 2008, and with AN's U-turn in his pocket, Berlusconi sought an electoral alliance with the NL, which was eager to maintain its autonomy (see note 2). As for the UDC, the party was presented with the choice either of merging with the PdL (which, for a party of between 3 and 7 per cent would have meant all but disappearing within it) or of fighting the election on its own – thus facing the possibility of electoral annihilation (cfr. Chapter 11). Reassured by the stability of its vote (Hine and Hanretty, 2006: 115–116), the UDC took a gamble and ran on its own – emerging after the election as the only party outside the two main coalitions that managed to maintain a parliamentary presence (of 35 deputies and 3 senators). Nonetheless, at the end of this process of 'forced' (partial and incomplete) unification of the centre right and following an election in which the PdL with its allies obtained about 47 per cent of the vote, it is clearly Berlusconi who has now emerged, once again, as the winner of yet another round in Italian politics.

From Berlusconi to Berlusconi. And again.

Commenting on the election, the editor of *la Repubblica*, Ezio Mauro, attributed Berlusconi's ability to stage a seemingly 'eternal come back' to the new kind of populism he is able to offer: 'a modern populism, which can overcome his government's poor performance for five years, his age ... the outlandish nature of his promises ... the endless disputes with the judiciary' (Mauro, 2008: 47). Like other contemporary European leaders (Albertazzi and McDonnell, 2007), albeit far more successfully, Berlusconi has expertly exploited the populist box of tricks, tapping into (and fomenting) an anti-political and anti-party mood that was already rife in Italy in the 1990s and, if anything, is even stronger today. At the beginning of his political career, Berlusconi promoted himself as the 'saviour' who could fill the political vacuum left by the demise of the old governing parties in the wake of the 1990s investigations into political corruption, offer a new and dynamic kind of politics, and provide a 'bulwark' against the advance of the communist Left, following the disappearance of Christian Democracy. Besides coming forward with the 'right' political product, Berlusconi was, of course, also able to package it professionally and effectively to communicate it, due to his unique position as media tycoon and financial entrepreneur.

Fifteen years later, not much has changed in this respect, as Berlusconi still possesses his large media empire. According to some observers, the connection between the cultural conditioning that started in the 1980s with Berlusconi's channels promoting a pro-American, individualist, consumerist and escapist culture, and his eventual political triumph 'is a fundamental one' (Ginsborg, 2004: 51; also Sartori, 2000). As he became Prime Minister for a second time in 2001, Berlusconi provoked various controversies on the national and international stages, due to his continuing key position in the Italian media system, his attempts to silence opposition and his unwillingness to resolve his clear conflict of interests (Hibberd, 2007: 882). For this and other reasons (especially his recurrent troubles with the justice system) he has been declared 'unfit' to lead Italy by international newspapers and magazines of both the Left *and* Right (McDonnell and Albertazzi, 2005) – condemnations that clearly cut no ice with the majority of the Italian electorate which keeps returning him to office.

At the time of writing, Berlusconi's continuing and unresolved conflict of interests appears to be one of the few certainties of a centre right still very much in flux. AN and FI, despite the rhetoric, still survive as separate entities;[9] meanwhile, the Government now relies on the support of the NL, following that party's impressive electoral performance (cfr Chapter 10). This situation, as Berlusconi knows, is not without risks: while the NL has been very loyal to him since it re-joined the centre right alliance in 2000, and was amenable to compromises in exchange for federal reform between 2001 and 2006, it is now in a much stronger position than it was then (when its support was not essential to the survival of the governing majority). This being the case, it is impossible to predict what the NL will seek to gain in exchange for another five years of loyal support (and how well its requests will go down with the PdL's southern constituencies). As for the UDC, its decision to remain outside the PdL and join the opposition may have weakened it in the immediate term – as the party cannot play any role in the allocation of public funds to those southern constituencies that have provided faithful backing. However, having preserved its autonomy, the UDC may find itself once more in a strong bargaining position should its support become essential in the future to the electoral success of one of the two main blocks – especially if Berlusconi starts encountering troubled electoral waters, as he did not long after his 2001 victory. These uncertainties aside, what we can conclude about the centre right at the end of its two-year period in opposition is that, while the solar system may have changed considerably, its sun not only remains the same, but appears to be more powerful than ever.

Notes

This chapter reflects the ideas of both authors and is the product of their joint collaboration. In terms of its writing-up, Duncan McDonnell took responsibility for the first two sections and Daniele Albertazzi for the latter two.

1. At times, it has even been unclear whether the centre left has had a single, easily identifiable leader at all (Pasquino, 2005).
2. For an analysis of Berlusconi's speeches, see Benedetti (2004). See also Bolasco, Giuliano, and Galli de' Paratesi (2006).
3. In recent months, dell'Utri has referred to Brambilla as a figure of 'no importance' (*Corriere della Sera*, 8 April 2008).
4. The NL is a regionalist populist party (Biorcio, 1991; McDonnell, 2006) which has posited itself as the representative of the interests 'of the north' against the alleged voracity of 'Rome', and has been able to create a very distinctive sub-culture in parts of northern Italy (Cento Bull and Gilbert, 2001). If it were to lose its radical, territorially based identity by merging with its allies, many of its supporters would not be willing to follow. The NL thus expressed no interest in Adornato's project in 2005.
5. The supposed 'novelty' of the PD has been one of its major selling points since its creation. As Veltroni said in his first speech as leader 'what Italy needs is a party for the new millennium: a force for change…a party which does not appear out of thin air, but yet is completely new' (Veltroni, 2007).
6. For details of these thresholds see the introductory chapter by Newell, p. 4–5.
7. It is important to keep in mind that at the time of Berlusconi's announcement no-one knew that elections would be held only a few months later.
8. It must be stressed, however, that at the time of writing this has still not happened, although FI and AN have kept their promise to create a single parliamentary group. As could be seen by the 'sharing out' of ministerial positions and governmental jobs after the election, AN and FI still very much survived as separate entities.
9. The merger had initially been planned for the autumn 2008; however it was later postponed to February 2009 (La Stampa, 2008).

References

Albertazzi, D. (2009) 'In bed with the enemy – infighting among governing parties and the return of the centre', in D. Albertazzi, C. Brook, C. Ross and N. Rothenberg (eds), *Resisting the Tide – Cultures of Opposition in the Berlusconi Years*, London: Continuum.

Albertazzi, D. and McDonnell, D. (2005) 'The Lega Nord in the second Berlusconi government: in a league of its own', *West European Politics* 28(5): 952–972.

Albertazzi, D. and McDonnell, D. (2007) 'Introduction: the sceptre and the spectre', in D. Albertazzi and D. McDonnell (eds), *Twenty-First Century Populism: The Spectre of Western European Democracy*, London: Palgrave.

Amyot, G. and Verzichelli, L. (2006) 'Introduction: end-of-term anxieties and improvisation', pp. 29–46 in G. Amyot and L. Verzichelli (eds), *Italian Politcs – The End of the Berlusconi Era?* New York and Oxford: Berghahn Books.

ANSA (2007) 'Lega Nord: Bossi, no al partito unico', 28 August.

Bei, F. (2007) 'La Cdl divisa al Colle: crisi insostenibile', *la Repubblica*, 14 June.

Berlusconi, S. (2006a) 'Dalle urne né vincitori né vinti', *Corriere della Sera*, 15 April.

Berlusconi, S. (2006b) *Verso il partito della libertá*, Milano: Mondadori.

Benedetti, A. (2004) *Il linguaggio e la retorica della nuova politica italiana: Silvio Berlusconi e Forza Italia*, Genoa: Erga edizioni.

Biorcio, R. (1991) 'La Lega Come Attore Politico: Dal Federalismo al Populismo Regionalista', pp. 34–82 in Mannheimer, R. (ed.), *La Lega Lombarda*. Milan: Feltrinelli.

Bolasco, S., Giuliano, L. and Galli de' Paratesi, N. (2006) *Parole in libertà. Un'analisi statistica e linguistica*, Rome: Manifestolibri.

Briquet, J-L. and Mastropaolo, A. (2007) 'Introduction', pp. 37–58 in J-L. Briquet and A. Mastropaolo (eds), *Italian Politics: The Center-Left's Poisoned Victory*, New York and Oxford: Berghahn.

Calabresi, M. (2007) 'Casini: "Non serve il populismo: Silvio, non puoi cancellare Fini"', *la Repubblica*, 22 November.

Calise, M. (2000) *Il Partito Personale*, Rome: Laterza.

Cento Bull, A. and Gilbert, M. (2001) *The Lega Nord and the Northern Question in Italian Politics*, London: Palgrave.

Chiaramonte, A. (2008) 'How Prodi's Unione won by a handful of votes', pp. 203–222 in J.L. Newell (ed.), *The Italian General Election of 2006: Romano Prodi's Victory*, Manchester and New York: Manchester University Press.

Circoli della Libertà (2008) 'Perché i circoli', http://www.circolodellaliberta.it/chi_siamo.php.

Corriere della Sera (2006) 'La Cdl un'esperienza conclusa', http://www.corriere.it/Primo_Piano/Politica/2006/06_Giugno/30/galluzzo.shtml, 30 June.

Corriere della Sera (2007a) 'Brambilla registra PdL. Berlusconi titolare', http://www.corriere.it/Primo_Piano/Politica/2007/08_Agosto/21/brambilla_pdl_logo.shtml.

Corriere della Sera (2007b) 'L'intervento del leader di An all'assemblea del partito all'ergife: Legge elettorale, lo stop di Fini', http://www.corriere.it/politica/07_dicembre_09/fini_ostruzionismo_vassallum_e9d35680-a646-11dc-b0eb-0003ba99c53b. shtml.

Corriere della Sera (2008) 'Dell'Utri: se vinceremo le elezioni, i libri di storia saranno revisionati', http://www.corriere.it/politica/08_aprile_08/dellutri_storia_resistenza_959d1b0a-0578-11dd-8738-00144f486ba6.shtml.

Diamanti, I. and Lello, E. (2005) 'The Casa delle Libertà: a house of cards?', *Modern Italy* 10(1): 9–35.

Donovan, M. (2008) 'Il centro-destra: conflitti, unità e mobilitazione permanente', pp. 87–108 in M. Donovan and S. Onofri (eds), *Politica in Italia. I fatti dell'anno e le interpretazioni*, Mulino: Bologna.

Fini, G. (2007) 'Caro Silvio, adesso voltiamo pagina', *Corriere della Sera*, 16 November.

Ginsborg, S. (2004) *Silvio Berlusconi*, London: Verso.

Guarnieri, C. and Newell, J.L. (2005) 'Introduction: 2004 – a year "on hold"', pp. 29–46 in C. Guarnieri and J.L. Newell (eds), *Italian Politics: Quo Vadis?*, New York and Oxford: Berghahn Books.

Hibberd, M. (2007) 'Conflicts of interest and media pluralism in Italian broadcasting', *West European Politics* 30(4): 881–902.

Hine, D. and Hanretty, C. (2006) 'Games advanced democracies play: the coalition crisis of April 2005', pp. 105–122 in G. Amyot and L. Verzichelli (eds), *Italian Politics – The End of the Berlusconi Era?* New York and Oxford: Berghahn Books.

la Repubblica (2007) 'Il Cavaliere a Milano: "Forza Italia si scioglierà nella nuova formazione"', 18 November.

La Stampa (2007a) 'Lo scontro CDL in ordine sparso. Fini e Casini Nasce l'asse anti-Cavaliere', 24 November.

La Stampa (2007b) 'Centrodestra dialogo a singhiozzo. Nuovo partito Berlusconi sceglie il popolo "Il 53 per cento lo vuole nel nostro simbolo"', 3 December.

La Stampa (2007c) 'Centrodestra l'ultimo affondo. Fini: Silvio comico. E' rissa nell'ex Cdl', 10 December.

La Stampa (2007d) 'Centro destra senza Silvio. Lite Fini-Pdl. An e Udc pensano a costruire la "cosa bianco-azzurra"', 17 December.

La Stampa (2008) 'An: via libera al Pdl. Dubbi, ma si' unanime alla fusione con Fi', 27 July.

Luzi, G. (2006) 'La Cdl è finita, basta vertici', *la Repubblica*, 5 December.

Mauro, E. (2008) 'L'eterno ritorno del Cavaliere', *la Repubblica*, 16 April.

McDonnell, D. (2006) 'A weekend in Padania: regionalist populism and the Lega Nord', *Politics* 26(2): 126–132.

McDonnell, D. (2007) 'Eviction cancelled: The 2006 local elections', pp. 81–98 in J-L. Briquet and A. Mastropaolo (eds), *Italian Politics: The Center-Left's Poisoned Victory*, New York and Oxford: Berghahn

McDonnell, D. and Albertazzi, D. (2005) 'Enough vaccine? The Berlusconi years', *Modern Italy* 10(1): 3–8.

Newell, J.L. (2006) 'The Italian election of 2006: myths and realities', *West European Politics* 29(4): 802–813.

Pasquino, G. (2005) 'Too many chiefs and not enough Indians: the leadership of the centre left', *Modern Italy* 10(1): 95–108.

Pasquino, G. (2007) 'The five faces of Silvio Berlusconi: the knight of anti-politics', *Modern Italy* (12)1: 39–54.

Ricolfi, L. (2006) *Tempo scaduto. Il contratto con gli italiani alla prova dei fatti*, Bologna: Il Mulino.

Romano, A. (2007a) 'Berlusconi sta bene, il polo no', *La Stampa*, 6 May.

Romano, A. (2007b) 'La leadership che manca', *La Stampa*, 28 May.

Sartori, G. (2000) *Homo Videns*, Bari: Laterza.

Tarchi, M. (2007) 'Italy: a country of many populisms', pp. 84–99 in D. Albertazzi and D. McDonnell (eds), *Twenty-First Century Populism: The Spectre of Western European Democracy*, London: Palgrave.

Urso, A. (2005) 'Il partito unico c'è già: basta farlo', *Liberal*, 32, October/November 2005.
Veltroni, W. (2007) 'Un'Italia unita, moderna e giusta', speech delivered in Turin on 27 June 2007, http://www.repubblica.it/2007/06/sezioni/politica/partito-democratico5/discorso-integrale-veltroni/discorso-integrale-veltroni.html.

6
The Processes of Alliance Formation

Mark Donovan

This chapter comprises four parts. First, it suggests that alliance developments were among precisely the most significant features of the election. From this perspective, the major outcomes were:

1. the electoral baptism of the new Partito Democratico (Democratic Party, PD), resulting from the unification of the two largest forces on the centre left, the Democratici di Sinistra (Left Democrats, DS) and the Margherita – democrazia è libertà (Margherita – Democracy is Liberty);

2. the electoral baptism of the new *'rassemblement'* party, the Popolo dell Libertà (People of Freedom, PdL) led by Silvio Berlusconi, unifying Forza Italia (FI), the National Alliance (Alleanza Nazionale, AN) and a number of much smaller formations;

3. the failure of the new alliance of left-wing parties in La Sinistra-L'Arcobaleno (The Rainbow Left, SA) to gain parliamentary representation;

4. the success of the centrist alliance, the Unione di Centro (Union of the Centre, UDC);

5. the failure of the far-right list, La Destra–Fiamma Tricolore (The Right–the Tricoloured Flame, D–FT), to gain any parliamentary representation.[1]

6. the radical 'defragmentation' of the party system at the parliamentary and consequently governmental levels: a major development for a party system usually defined as one of 'fragmented bipolarism'.

Not all these outcomes may be permanent. A degree of fluidity of party organisation and party-system structure has existed since the collapse of the so-called First Republic, in 1992–1993, and continues. In fact, as examined in part two, a sequence of confusing alignments of parties, quasi-parties, alliances and sub-alliances developed after 1994 in which alliances were both about unity to defeat a common enemy and competition within alliances to gain strategic advantage or simply to survive. Central to this multi-directional competition were institutional distinctions between extra-parliamentary organisations and the formation of parliamentary groups. In examining this complexity, this part of the chapter also considers the issue of the term 'poles' which defines the principal framework used by political scientists, at least, for understanding the fundamental difference between the so-called First Republic, and the Second, that is, the shift from a tripolar to a bipolar party system.

Third, in the penultimate section the chapter considers the specificities of the alliance-building processes that took place in the years 2006–2008, including those processes that ended in non-alliance. The most remarkable examples of the former were, as indicated, the formation of the PD and PdL. Both processes, however, involved parties' breaking with forces with which they had previously been allied. Finally, the chapter draws some conclusions about party alliance developments in Italy and the nature of the current party system.

Alliances and the 2008 elections: what happened?

From the perspective of alliance-building, the story of the 2008 election is dramatic. The result even led it to be argued that 'possibly a second phase of the Italian transition' had begun (D'Alimonte, 2008). It is this structural, systemic development that is considered here, and not other arguments as to the election's significance, such as the possible consolidation of an illiberal democracy (Ignazi, 2008).

What happened at the systemic level that was so important? The nature of the party system changed. The dominant analytical description of the party system that has been under construction since 1993–1994 has been that of 'fragmented bipolarism'. Thus, whilst the Cold-War party system that collapsed in 1992–1993 was tripolar, without government alternation, the new party system is bipolar, with government alternation. Indeed, by 2006 it was argued that alternation was too frequent. Since 1992, no government had been re-elected. One major reason for this is the infighting within governments, based as they were on large, heterogeneous, even 'negative' coalitions – that is, ones formed not primarily to govern, but to prevent the other side from governing. Consequently, although the bipolar configuration was fairly well consolidated by 2001, calls for a return to 'neo-centrism' remained strong, particularly from within the business world. And many believed this remained possible because the bipolar structure was dependent on the survival of Berlusconi and his party, Forza Italia (FI) – which many doubted.

Party-system fragmentation was rooted largely in the disintegration of the traditional parties when the Cold-War party system collapsed. This fragmentation was then consolidated by the interaction of alliance processes and new institutional rules, notably the new (1993) electoral system but also the very generous public financing of even the smallest parties with parliamentary representation. The further electoral reform of 2005, moreover, encouraged fragmentation – at least in the 2006 election, by abolishing single-member constituencies and reintroducing proportional representation, albeit preserving the majoritarian logic by introducing a seat bonus for the plurality party, or coalition of parties, at the national level (in the Chamber, at least). The 2005 rules led to the two main alliances each comprising some 12–13 lists for the Chamber of Deputies, and 16–17 for the Senate in 2006 (Donovan, 2008a: 117–118). In all, there were some 30 lists, several of which were themselves composite! The victory of the Unione, as the pan-left alliance was known, led to a government coalition comprising eight parties, a record which few welcomed, for it implied incoherence and instability. And, indeed, the government lasted only two years.

In 2008, things went very differently. The centre left alliance comprised just two lists, that of the centre right three. The new government comprised only two parties, the PdL and the Northern League (NL). The third, and very small, Movement for Autonomy (MPA) did not enter the Cabinet. And whilst this time 'third forces' took a large share of the vote – nearly 16 per cent in the Chamber of Deputies – only one 'third party' entered Parliament – the Union of the Centre. As a consequence, the new parliament had only six groups in each chamber (see Table 6.1), including the Mixed Group, compared to 10 and 13 (in the Senate and Chamber respectively) at the outset of the previous parliament (Papavero and Verzichelli, 2008). The two largest groups, furthermore, now took 490 of the 630 Chamber seats (78 per cent) compared to 354 (56 per cent), in 2006, and 265 Senate seats (82 per cent) compared to 157 (49 per cent). In sum, at the parliamentary level, and

Table 6.1   Number and size of groups in Parliament, 2008

Group	Chamber	Senate
Northern League Padania	60	26
People of Freedom	273	146
Union of the Centre	35	11[1]
Democratic Party	217	119
Italy of Values	29	14
Mixed of which:	16	6
Linguistic minorities	3	–
Movement for Autonomy	8	2
Independents	5	4
Total	630	322[2]

Notes:
1 Actually Union of the Centre, plus the South Tyrol People's Party, plus the Autonomies.
2 The figure includes seven Life Senators.

Sources: http://www.camera.it/organiparlamentarism/239/260/documentoxml.asp and http://www.senato.it/leg/16/BGT/Schede/Gruppi/Grp.html – accessed 10 July 2008

consequently the governmental level, the system was no longer one of *fragmented* bipolarism.

The PdL dominated the Government. The Prime Minister (PM) and 10 ministers came from its ranks, compared to the League's two ministers. And though the League had another two ministers without portfolio, the PdL had seven. In other words, including the PM, the PdL occupied 85 per cent of Cabinet offices and 80 per cent of all ministerial offices.

The simplification of representation at the parliamentary level was remarkable, even brutal. On both left and right a single large party dominated, flanked by a much smaller, more radical one. On the left, the radical party, IdV, was not from the traditional, socialist left, but was a product of the 1990s crisis and subsequent transition, being led by the former public prosecutor, Antonio Di Pietro, who had come to symbolise the judicial scourging of political crimes and misdemeanours during the crisis. Indeed, the traditional, radical left failed to gain representation – perhaps the single most shocking outcome of the election, given that the four forces that

Table 6.2 'Third' forces, Chamber of Deputies (PR vote), millions; and share of the vote

'Third' force votes	1994		1996		2001		2006		2008	
	No.	%	No.	%	No.	%	No.	%	No.	%
The Right-FT	xx	xx	xx	xx	xx	xx	xx	xx	0.89	2.4
MS-FT	a		0.34	0.9	0.14	0.4	a		d	
Northern League	a		3.78	10.1	A		a		a	
Pannella/PR	a		0.70	1.9	0.83	2.2	b		b	
Union of the Centre	a		a		A		a		2.05	5.6
Segni Pact	1.81	4.7	b		A		xx	xx	xx	xx
PPI	4.29	11.1	b		B		b		b	
European Democracy	xx	xx	xx	xx	0.89	2.4	b		xx	xx
Italia dei Valori	xx	xx	xx	xx	1.44	3.9	b		b	
Socialist Party	b		b		B		b		0.36	1.0
Communist Refoundation c	b		3.21	8.6	1.87	5.0	b		1.12	3.1
Workers' Communist Party	xx	xx	xx	xx	xx	xx	xx	xx	0.21	0.6
Critical left	xx	xx	xx	xx	xx	xx	xx	xx	0.17	0.5
Other	1.36	3.3	0.63	1.6	0.38	1.0	0.17	0.5	0.89	2.48
Total excluding RC/SA	7.46	19.1	5.45	14.5	3.68	9.9	0.17	0.5	4.57	12.58
Total including RC/SA	7.46	19.1	8.66	23.1	5.55	14.9	0.17	0.5	5.69	15.68

Notes:
a = formed part of the centre-right alliance
b = formed part of the centre-left alliance
c = in 2008: The Rainbow Left (SA)
d = allied with The Right in 2008

Source: Ministry of the Interior, http://elezioni.interno.it/ind_elez.htm

comprised it had obtained over ten per cent of the (Chamber) vote in 2006. Thus, Communist Refoundation, the Partito dei Comunisti Italiani (Party of Italian Communists, PdCI) and the Greens had obtained 5.8 per cent, 2.3 per cent and 2.1 per cent respectively, and they had been joined, in forming the Rainbow Left, by the Sinistra Democratica (Democratic Left, SD). This new formation had split from the DS in protest at the formation of the PD. Now, jointly, the Rainbow Left gained only 3.1 per cent of the vote – see Table 6.2. Many of their former voters switched their support to the PD; others abstained (Marcotti and Vanelli, 2008). Another one per cent of the vote was split between the Worker's Communist Party and the Critical Left.

In total, 'third forces' (those outside the two main alliances) received 15.7 per cent of the vote (see Table 6.2), and whilst the two million voters who supported the Union of the Centre (essentially the UDC), gained representation in Parliament, over three-and-a-half million, some ten per cent of the electorate, did not. At the same time, turnout declined, from 83.6 per cent in 2006 to 80.5 (for mainland Italy), a decrease of over a million voters. These unrepresented voters create a degree of uncertainty about future vote outcomes and the structure of the party system since the re-emergence of an electorally viable, traditional, left is not inconceivable.

The radical right also failed to get elected as an independent force, the D–FT alliance getting 2.4 per cent of the votes and no seats. Some heirs to the Fascist-nostalgia radical right were nevertheless elected thanks to their inclusion in the PdL.

Analysing alliance processes and party-system restructuring

Since 1994, parties have ceased to be the only, or even the main actors in the party system. Rather, alliances have dominated elections and been central to parliamentary, and hence governmental, organisation. These have been, on the left: the Progressisti in 1994, the Ulivo in 1996 and 2001, the Unione in 2006; on the right: the Alliance for Good Government and the Freedom Alliance in 1994, the (differently constituted) Freedom Alliance in 1996, the Casa delle Libertà (House of Freedoms, CdL) in 2001 and 2006. In 2008 there was a return to the significance of parties, above all, the PD and the PdL. Alliances still mattered, but were dominated by two organisations intended to be more or less single, integrated structures – that is, disciplined parties. In fact, the reality deviated from this somewhat. The PD tended to divisions over prominent ethical issues between its Catholic and lay-socialist components, whilst the PdL was an agglomeration, or *rassemblement*, of parties and party fragments – dominated, nevertheless, by Berlusconi. Still, both the PdL and the PD formed single groups in Parliament, where party discipline generally has tended to be fairly strong, albeit not sufficiently strong to have prevented the fall of several governments, most notably Prodi's in 1998 and 2008, Berlusconi's in 1994 and 2005 (although in the latter case, the entrepreneur formed another, almost identical coalition straight away). All these incidents reflected conflict *within* the parliamentary majority such that, in essence, the broad-based alliances of 1994–2006 synthesised unity, in opposing the rival alliance, with the *internal* struggle to survive or gain advantage. The construction of the PD and PdL were major steps not only towards party-system simplification, but also towards creating disciplined, hierarchical structures within the two poles, able to support stronger, perhaps 'prime-ministerial' government. This possibility was more evident on the right than the left.

This dual trend, towards simplification and hierarchy, may mean that the distinctions between the various levels of alliance-formation are declining in importance. Thus, at the time of the election, the PdL was still an agglomeration of different organisations. Above all, the National Alliance (AN) 'party on the ground' (in villages, towns, cities, provinces and regions around the country) remained organisationally independent and determined not to dissolve itself without its various middle elites, that is local and regional party secretaries and so on, becoming formally recognised as leaders at these different levels in the new party. By the end of July 2008, however, Forza Italia and the AN had agreed a programme of organisational integration, including the smaller parties, that assigned 70 per cent of posts to FI, and 30 per cent to AN with the smaller parties' representation probably to count as part of FI's 70 per cent. The process was intended to be completed by February 2009 to enable the new party to enter the European People's Party via the 2009 European Parliament elections. The analytical point is that the party system outside of Parliament was being simplified to become congruent with the one in Parliament.

Of course, a degree of territorial complexity remained central to the party system's structure. The NL and MPA are not nation-wide parties. The NL gained 18 of its 25 senators and 41 of its 60 deputies in Lombardy and the Veneto, and none south of Piedmont and the Marches whilst the MPA essentially originates in a split from the Sicilian UDC, with both its senators and four of its eight deputies elected on the island (plus two in Campania, and one each in Calabria and Apulia). But the simplification process remains clear, and is one driven by logics integral to the practice of effective parliamentary government. This logic was not easy to put into practice. Until 2008, extra-parliamentary party logics dominated. Parliamentary rules state that a parliamentary group may not be formed unless it comprises a minimum of 20 elected MPs in the Chamber, and 10 in the Senate – unless derogations are made. Such derogations were made extensively in the 2006–2008 parliament, assisting an increase in the number of groups in the Chamber from eight to fourteen.[2] This, however, was still less than the number of extra-parliamentary parties represented in Parliament since groups were often composite. The formation of the PdL and PD implies that most of the minor parties represented in Parliament are in the process of becoming tendencies and/or factions within parties, rather than remaining parties themselves. This process is not entirely clear-cut. For example, in 2008 the PD 'hosted' a small number (nine – six deputies, three senators) of Radicals, a party with a highly distinctive tradition which has struggled to survive independently. Its inclusion within the PD is 'uncomfortable' for itself and the PD, exacerbating as it does the lay-religious tension within the new party. It is unlikely, though, that the number of parliamentary groups will bloom, contrary to the trend of the past 15 years. This is despite the fact that the importance of political visibility and the ability to influence the agenda if constituted as an autonomous group did see Di Pietro's IdV establish its own groups, in 2008, notwithstanding the undertaking it had given to the PD not to do so. In fact, by mid-July the leader of the PD, Walter Veltroni, was publicly disassociating himself from the radicalism of IdV and its leader.

The process of simplification that the organisation of party and parliamentary government is undergoing appears to reflect the strikingly simple depiction of party-system development over this past 15 years: the shift from tripolarism to bipolarism, and consequently from permanent government by the Christian Democrats and their allies before 1992–1994, to repeated alternation since then. There is no doubt as to the importance of this change. Alliance structures have evolved largely as a means of strategic coordination focusing on competition for government. Yet there has been more to political competition than that. As indicated above, alliances have also been about competition *within* left and right, within the nascent 'poles', and the fragility of government majorities has reflected this. Competition within poles has implications, moreover, for the evolution of the party-system structure. Parties can hope to participate in a majority in four different ways, each with different consequences for party-system structuration: (1) as part of a large, single alliance, such as the pan-left and pan-right alliances of 2006; (2) as an independent centre party (or alliance) embracing the median member of Parliament and able to furnish a majority to left or the right, as sought, most notably, by the Pact for Italy in 1994, NL in 1996, and the UDC in 2008; (3) as an independent force on the left or the right flank, as sought by the D-FT and the SA in 2008; or (4) as a single party, or at least dominant party, within a coalition. These different strategies are all ones by which parties seek both to contribute to being part of a parliamentary majority, and to win votes against their *allies*. Indeed, such competition is strategic, involving the attempt to shape the very structure of the party system. Let us consider this further.

If there are more than two (relevant) parties, then, in numerical terms, there is either limited, or extreme (six or more parties) pluralism (Sartori, 1976). We know further, from Sartori, that what additionally matters for understanding party-system dynamics is the degree of ideological stretching present. Systems can be ideologically polarised, and thus tend to tripolarism, or not, and so tend to bipolarism. Today, few party systems are polarised. Most parties are coalitionable, that is, they are not excluded from government on principle. In Sartori's model, the unit of analysis is essentially the 'pole', rather than parties. But in the absence of polarisation, the logic and language of poles is less over-riding. The logic of competition for government still exists, but where the nature of the political regime is not at stake, plain inter-party competition is more salient. More complex patterns of interaction can be identified than either 'bipolar' or 'tripolar'. In fact, they already have been. For example, when the German liberal party, the FDP, was the 'coalition king-maker', deciding between the SPD and the CDU-CSU, the German party system was envisaged as 'triangular' (Pappi, 1984), whilst the French party system, between 1974–1981, comprised a 'bipolar quadrille' (Knapp and Wright, 2006: 255–256). And so on.

If one maintains the core insight of the significance of competition for government, perhaps redefining it in terms of competition between alternative *'blocs'*, then one can envisage competition between more than two parties as itself potentially *multipolar*. The question that arises is what distinguishes poles from parties. Perhaps a 'cluster' of parties such as the radical left in Italy (Wolinetz, 2004), constitutes a pole? The answer must lie in whether third, fourth and fifth, and so on parties, or clusters, are institutionalised within the *structure* of the party system. But what is structural institutionalisation? Party institutionalisation itself, that is financial viability and electoral and membership strengths, and so on (Maor, 1997: 66–76), is essential, since a large, but weakly institutionalised party can destabilise the system if it disintegrates (Mainwaring and Torcal, 2006) – which is why the robustness, or otherwise, of FI was so important. Many posited its collapse as the premise for restoring tripolarism. But systemic institutionalisation clearly must also have a systemic dimension as such, and this must regard logics of government formation and support.

One can thus hypothesise that the Union of the Centre will be institutionalised as a centre party/alliance, and constitute a specific 'pole', to the extent that it has the requisites to survive as a party, *and*, systemically is either relevant for government formation and survival or, is seen to be able significantly to influence public policy (by offering or denying support). This is, in effect, to re-state Sartori's criteria for the 'relevance' of parties. But perhaps that is the point. Parties matter to party-system structure if they establish themselves as part of the structure as such – a 'pole'; not merely as parties within the system as, for example, the Radicals or the South Tyrol People's Party. Equally, had the D-FT or SA gained parliamentary representation, they would have had a chance of institutionalising themselves as 'wing' poles. In sum, one is hypothesising a potential five-pole party system rather as von Beyme (1985) identified a potential 'natural' five-fold structure to party systems. But 'poles' may also be rooted in additional cleavages, perhaps like the NL, which has consistently challenged the predominance of the left-right principle. Certainly competition between the League and other (centre-)right-wing parties has mattered to election outcomes and executive formation at multiple levels of government.

Such multipolar competition may challenge, or work alongside left-right competition-for-government. It depends on the circumstances. Centre and 'wing' poles can co-exist with a two-bloc alternating system. Nevertheless, successful large parties might seek to reduce multipolarity (and 'multipartyness'), institutionalising 'their' conflict as not merely dominant, but as entirely exclusive (Mair, 1997). The creation of the PD and PdL constituted powerful moves in this direction. The construction of the PD was aimed at establishing the hegemony of the centre left, within the left, as much as at defeating the right. And the PdL's construction, first by Berlusconi, then by Berlusconi and Fini, was an electoral and organisational challenge to their allies. Intra-bloc competition is thus not only significant, but potentially dramatic, since through it parties may seek *permanently* to defeat their 'natural' allies – whereas their principal foes will endure, by the nature of the system constructed.

We can sum this up by saying that the evolution of the Italian party system since 1994 has taken place via competition *within* left and right, as well as between them (see also Donovan, 2008b). In 2007–2008, the process of competition *within* left and right took an apparently decisive turn – *via* alliance-building which appears to be consolidating as party-building – as happened with the Margherita–DL between 2000–2002. It is time to see just how alliance-building between 2006–2008 led to the six major outcomes identified in the introduction.

Alliance restructuring, 2006–2008

Whilst the 2006 election saw the formation of two 'catch-all' alliances, the 2008 election saw a far more exclusive process of alliance-building. The question is, how and why? A prior question, though, is: 'why now?' Giovanni Sartori, had urged such action for a decade, claiming that it was in the national interest as well as the self-interest of the larger parties. These latter would gain in terms of parliamentary seats, in the number of portfolios acquired if and when they won elections, and in their greater influence over policy. The country would gain by having more cohesive and hence more stable governments, better public policy and clear accountability to the electorate. The larger parties, however, could run independently of their smaller allies only if they could be guaranteed that their principal rivals on the other side would reciprocate. If they did not, then, given the predominance of MPs elected in Single Member Constituencies (SMCs) using the plurality formula, between 1993 and 2005, a one-sided electoral massacre would result. And the smaller parties could veto electoral reform discriminating against them by threatening to bring the Government down. This would block the passage of the proposed legislation, yet those parties would remain indispensable to their government ally in the subsequent election.

The 2005 electoral reform alone did not lead to the self-assertion of the larger parties, as the 2006 election demonstrates. Still, the replacement of SMCs by multiple member constituencies did mean that the absence of alliances on one side would *not* bring that side's near annihilation – as it had done for the Partito Popolare Italiano (Italian People's Party, PPI) in 1994. Defeat would be defeat, but not calamitous defeat. In fact, the bonus mechanism guaranteed the winner a majority of 55 per cent of (Chamber) seats, and no more. The institutional opportunity therefore existed for strategic innovation by the major parties. Context, however, was also vitally important in two regards. First, the expectation that the Left would lose the election. Unlike in 2006, there was no close battle to be fought in order to win the bonus. Second, the perception that Italy was facing a growing political crisis which the party system, as currently configured, was contributing to, rather than helping to solve. In fact, anti-party sentiment, always a significant feature in Italian politics (Morlino and Tarchi, 2006), was growing, encouraged by Berlusconi's semi-permanent mobilisation, from the 2006 election onwards, against the Government (Donovan and Onofri, 2008), with the entrepreneur still managing to present himself as a political outsider.

These contextual considerations had informed the launch of the PD in 2007. Whilst its origins to some extent lie in the formation of the Ulivo in 1996, an extraordinary strategic development that had brought reformist ex-communists and Catholics together, the following decade had left unresolved the key issues of how strongly integrated these very different forces should become, and of how wide the alliance should extend, particularly leftwards. The attempt to create a degree of centralised decision-making power within the strongly centre-tending Ulivo, in 2004–2006 had failed, as initially had the quite different strategy of allying the entire left. This latter then came to fruition as a result of the 2005 electoral reform and the subsequent competition for government in 2006. After the narrow victory of the pan-left Unione in 2006, however, the different identities comprising it had reasserted themselves, creating an image of litigious fragmentation.

After the 2006 election, Berlusconi set about unifying the right from the bottom up, attempts to unify it from the top-down in 2005 having failed due to the resistance of his principal allies, Gianfranco Fini of the National Alliance (AN), and Pierferdinando Casini, the *de facto* leader of the UDC (Donovan, 2008c). Mobilisation for the election thus gave way to mobilisation against the new government, whose majority was allegedly fraudulent, and then to mobilisation against the Government's unpopular economic policies. This street-level mobilisation outflanked Fini and Casini. It also put the government under pressure so that every mistake, real or apparent, that it made became magnified. The Government's popularity slumped, whilst anti-party sentiment grew, thanks also to the fact that Berlusconi was campaigning not only against the Government, but also against his allies, the UDC above all, but also AN, both of which were accused of having prevented him from carrying out his political revolution whilst in government, placing party interests before the country's.

The process of unifying the moderate left, the DS and the Margherita, developed under this pressure. The PD's manifesto, published on 12 February 2007, declared its aim to be to provide a solution to the threat of decline facing Italy as a result of both external challenges (globalisation) and domestic weaknesses, not least political. The two parties' overlapping congresses, 19–21 and 20–22 April 2007, brought forward the date for their unification, though in a still unspecified form, to late 2007 – early 2008. In the wake of the poor May-June local elections, it was then decided to mobilise voters directly to elect the leader of the new party and to do so already that October. Opinion polls had long shown that the prospect of unifying the major parties on left and right was very popular, and the left needed to respond to the challenge being mounted by Berlusconi. Over the summer of 2007, the gathering momentum of the centre left's unification process then reinforced Berlusconi's campaign to create a single party of the centre right.

In fact, in December 2006 a highly successful national rally of Berlusconi's supporters in Rome (spurned by the UDC) had already capped months of local rallies, and this had been preceded, in November, by a national convention of the new Freedom Clubs (Circoli della Libertà). These had been created that autumn, at Berlusconi's suggestion, by Michela Brambilla, the dynamic and telegenic former President of the Young Entrepreneurs of Confcommercio (a business association), to be open to all supporters of the right, independent of party affiliation. At the December demonstration, Berlusconi declared: 'We here are the people of freedom…We here today are already the unitary party of the centre right, we are already the party of liberty.'[3] Over the winter of 2006–2007, Berlusconi provoked turmoil within FI, urging local leaders to merge their supporters' clubs with Brambilla's and other, cultural, associations. The UDC in particular, however, continued to assert its independence of Berlusconi, whilst Fini, though keen to consolidate the alliance with FI, also feared annexation so long as Berlusconi still dominated. In the May-June elections, nevertheless, constrained by the electoral system, the centre right remained united. In August, amidst immense speculation about Berlusconi's plans, it was revealed that Brambilla had registered the name 'Partito della Libertà' for the 2009 European elections – on Berlusconi's behalf. Increasingly, the mobilisation of the electorate and party rank-and-file, plus the agglomeration of party fragments, especially Christian Democratic and nationalist-fascist, around FI was pressuring AN and the UDC not merely to continue to acknowledge Berlusconi's leadership, but to accept a much stronger version of it.

On 14 October, 2007, the popular election of the PD leader took place. It was an immense success for the centre left. An unexpectedly large number of people (3,536,317) voted, and the leading candidate, Veltroni, gained a convincing 76 per cent of the vote. The strong public appeal of this operation appears to have convinced Berlusconi to bring matters to a head on the right. On Sunday 18 November, when non-left voters were again being mobilised *en masse*, this time to demand early elections, and even whilst the evening media were announcing that Berlusconi's allies had just publicly declared him guilty of 18 months of failed leadership, the entrepreneur made his so-called *discorso del predellino* ('running-board speech') in Piazza san Babila, at the heart of Milan's fashion district (the video-clip link shows Berlusconi talking to the media whilst standing on the sill of his car door).[4] In this seminal speech, Berlusconi announced the formation of the People's Freedom Party, into which FI would dissolve itself. Other parties could join him – or not. He hoped so, but it was their choice. This was an ultimatum. And one made from a long-prepared position of strength. Just the previous week-end, the founding convention of a new party, The Right, had taken place, the result of another rightward split in AN, and one warmly supported by Berlusconi. Now, a series of minor and micro-parties, such as the Christian Democrats for Regional Autonomy (CDA) and The Right, rushed to declare their intention of joining this great new project. The only parties angrily to reject this quasi-diktat were the largest ones: the League, the AN and the UDC.

Several weeks of confusion followed Berlusconi's audacious bid to impose his authority. All sorts of developments seemed possible, including the collapse of the centre-right alliance entirely, electoral reform to avoid the impending referendum, and even an 'institutional' government led by the President of the Senate to implement such reform. Clarity was brought about as a consequence of early elections being called on 6 February 2008 following the Government's defeat – essentially in line with Berlusconi's intentions and long-declared expectation – in a Senate vote on 24 January. Impending elections forced leaders to make alliance decisions. Yet perhaps critical to the lost vote was Veltroni's decision, announced on 19 January, to run alone at the next election, whenever it was held, and whatever the electoral system, challenging FI to do the same (Ostellino, 2008). With the PD's door shut to them, the tiny centrist UDEUR (Unione Democratici per l'Europa, Democratic Union for Europe) had to find a new ally to survive, and the most obvious one was Berlusconi.[5] The even smaller, recently formed, Liberal Democrats, led by Lamberto Dini, and already semi-detached from the Unione, made the same calculation.

Veltroni's move, was as audacious and imperious as Berlusconi's had been two months previously. It restated the identity of the PD as a party seeking to provide a solution to Italy's problems not just via its programme, but also via its nature, that is its restructuring of the party system around two key actors, itself and Berlusconi. It was a strong move in the direction not so much of bipartism as of the creation of two 'people's parties', that is, two electorally strong, government-minded, centripetally orientated parties, able to dominate coalition formation and provide stable, cohesive government (Smith, 1989).

The four left parties, which had sought unsuccessfully to overcome their rivalry and formalise their *de facto* cooperation (in Parliament, at least) ever since the formation of the Democratic Party, were now obliged to reach agreement. Only Communist Refoundation could expect to overcome the four per cent threshold in the Chamber of Deputies, so the PdCI, the Greens and SD had to ally with it if they – and a decent-sized left, were to survive. The Rainbow Left thus came into being.

The tiny Socialists ended up running alone. Ever since the disintegration of the Italian Socialist Party in the maelstrom of judicial investigation in the early 1990s many of its successor fragments had steadfastly refused to join the DS, the Italian Communist Party's (PCI's) reformist heir, given both their long history of conflict and the belief that the PCI was indirectly responsible for the judicial cyclone. By contrast, the Radicals, who had been in an uncomfortable alliance (known as the Rose in the Fist) with the Socialists since the 2006 election, now accepted being 'hosted' by the PD – that is, they had candidates in safe seats, but were not allowed to display their symbol on the ballot papers, consistent, to that extent, with Veltroni's decision that the PD should run alone.

The visible exception to this rule regarded Di Pietro's IdV which was believed to have the electoral weight needed to win some regions for the left in the Senate. This mattered because whilst Veltroni was convinced Berlusconi would win a majority in the Chamber, the outcome in the Senate was uncertain. Allied to the IdV, the PD could realistically hope that Berlusconi would end up with only a narrow majority there, considerably weakening him. For this reason, and given that a fundamental break had been made, not least with the traditional left and the by now heavily compromised UDEUR,[6] the PD made this one formal alliance.

Despite the PD making only two deals, both were controversial. The arrangement with the Radicals upset the Catholic Church and many from the former Margherita, whilst that with Di Pietro upset many because the IdV was, in its own way, very radical. And in a way that challenged the prospect of 'normalising' Italian politics, since the party continued to regard judicial action against Berlusconi and several of his business-cum-political allies as central to re-establishing the rule of law.

With the election called, Fini made a sharp U-turn, agreeing now to co-found the/a new PdL with Berlusconi. Indeed, the two leaders went further: the new PdL would put forward a single list, with its name and symbol only. If the several minor parties that had rushed to join the party still wanted to, well and good, but their names and symbols would not appear. There was to be no repetition of 2006. This was another major strategic development. The UDC did not participate in this decision and suffered splits in opposite directions: the Liberal Popolari in favour of joining the PdL, the White Rose in favour of building, at last, a centre pole.[7] In the end, Casini decided to (re-)ally with the latter, perhaps because Fini's rapprochement with Berlusconi ended Casini's chance of becoming Berlusconi's 'heir', as leader of the centre right. This decision created a delicate situation for Berlusconi in Sicily, since the UDC's votes, and those of the MPA, formed largely of ex-UDC adherents, would be decisive for the important Senate vote. In the end, the PdL was forced to ally also with the MPA, so that the NL and the MPA, two regional parties, each contested half the country's constituencies, on a north-south basis. Casini's decision to run alone also led to another, significant strategic development, for the election result did indeed result in the resurrection of a centre pole.

The PdL's exception to its rule of burying all past party identities was made first with the League. Its leader, Umberto Bossi would not enter the PdL, so an alliance was justified in terms of the League being a regional, not national party. The newly formed Destra fought hard for the same privilege, having only just founded itself as the flag-bearer of the right's historic identity, long abandoned by the AN elite. Refused such a deal by the PdL, the Destra formed an alliance with another Fascist nostalgia party, the MS-FT, and ran independently.

As a result of these several alliance processes, media attention came to focus on seven parties/alliances as most likely to win representation: see Table 6.3, which also identifies their approximate left-right identity, and relationship to government formation. In the event, the system was 'truncated', the two 'extremes' not entering parliament. The system now looks like a 'pentapolar' party system, with two dominant blocs, left and right (Table 6.4).

It should not be assumed that this structure is symmetrical. First, it will be more difficult for the UDC to form a coalition with the parties to its left than to its right, and many expect that it will be drawn back into the right

Table 6.3.   Anticipated main parties/alliances, prior to the April election

Far Left	Radical Left	Centre Left	Centre	Centre Right	Right	Far Right
Rainbow Left	IdV	PD	UDC	PdL	NL	D-FT
		Centre left government core		Centre right government core		

Table 6.4   The parliamentary party system, after the vote

Left bloc		Centre	Right bloc	
IdV	PD	UDC	PdL	NL

bloc. Second, the parties to the left of the UDC are divided not only between IdV and the PD, but also within the PD, not least over the apparent impossibility of the party joining in its entirety any of the European parliamentary groups in 2009. Third, the (far) left may re-establish itself via the 2009 European parliamentary elections, so further fragmenting the left. Indeed, the PD is split between those seeking to woo the UDC, and those seeking to restore relations with the (far) left.

Conclusions

The left (generically) suffered a major defeat in the 2008 election even whilst championing structural change that may be the most important development of recent Italian political history. The PD's strategic innovation, the decision to run alone, reversing 15 years in which building alliances had dominated, had three principal outcomes. First, it encouraged Berlusconi to do the same, leading to the substantial defragmentation of the party system. Second, these developments did not lead to the PD achieving the electoral breakthrough in the centre that it sought. Veltroni had hoped that his decision to run alone would allow the PD to establish itself as the dominant party of the left, but with a clearly moderate identity. The failure to break through in the centre was a strategic defeat for the new party. The reason for it may be the UDC's decision also to run alone. This resurrected a centre 'pole' for which voters unsympathetic both to Berlusconi's right and to the left, even in its new, moderate garb, could vote. Where the PD did gain votes, though not that many, was from the (far) left. This so-called useful vote resulted from the fact that in the Chamber election, and in many places in the Senate election, a vote for the SA was a wasted vote, in terms of the contribution it could make to efforts to defeat Berlusconi. The third principal outcome of the PD's radical alliance strategy, then, was to weaken the left overall, at least in the short-term, by prompting the disappearance, albeit perhaps only temporarily, of the (far) left in Parliament.

Whilst the bipolar structure of the party system has been substantially confirmed, its precise nature is not entirely clear. It seems likely that the right will dominate in the short- to medium-term at least so that the crucial question is whether the left will be able to win another election in the medium-term. If not, Italy will again find itself with a predominant party system.

Notes

1. The spatial terms 'left', 'right' etc. are controversial (Donovan, 2008c). Here, 'left' and 'right' are used, as value-free, systemic terms: Italy has a fundamentally 'bipolar' party system comprising, essentially, a 'left' and a 'right'. However, to indicate the presence of gradations within left and right, the terms centre left and centre right, far left and far right are also used. The terms 'far left', 'far right'

apply primarily, but not exclusively, to the Rainbow Alliance and the Destra. Many would argue that the terms 'centre left' and 'centre right' are inappropriate for, respectively, the IdV and both the Northern League and the PdL, particularly given the defection from Berlusconi's alliance of the more clearly centrist UDC in 2008 (Ignazi, 2008).

2. See http://legxv.camera.it/organiparlamentarism/239/260/documentoxml.asp
3. See the reproduction of Berlusconi's speech on the Forza Italia website: http://www.forzaitalia.it/silvioberlusconi/pdf/ilPopolodellaLiberta.pdf
4. E. Sogilo, *Corriere della Sera*, 19 November 2007. See: http://www.youtube.com/watch?v=mtW3wV08xao
5. The party's leader, Clemente Mastella, had also stated that he would bring the Government down to try to delay a referendum package on electoral reform likely to make very difficult the survival of small parties. On 16 January, the Constitutional Court gave the go ahead for the referendum to take place that spring.
6. Its leader was a seasoned Christian Democratic *notable* who had refused to join the Margherita, when it was formed in 2002, in order to maintain his party's centre identity and coalition-bargaining power. Since the party's electoral strength was rooted in clientelism, this position smacked strongly of self-interest first and foremost, and principle nowhere. This perception was reinforced when Mastella's wife, the Campania regional assembly president, was placed under house arrest, on 16 January 2008, for suspected corruption. The attempt, then, to save his party by switching sides, that is transformism, led the public, as polls revealed, to have a very negative attitude towards him and his party.
7. The White Rose was subsequently renamed, for legal reasons, the Movimento Federativo Civico Popolare (the Popular Federal Civic Movement).

References

D'Alimonte, R. (2008) 'Riforme per consolidare "la svolta"', *Il Sole 24 Ore*, 11 May.

Donovan, M. (2008a) 'The processes of alliance formation', pp. 115–35 in J.L. Newell (ed.), *The Italian General Election of 2006: Romano Prodi's Victory*, Manchester and New York: Manchester University Press.

Donovan, M. (2008b) 'The "centre" between structure and agency: the Italian case', in M. Donovan and J.L. Newell (eds), The Centre in Italian Politics, special issue of *Modern Italy* 13(4): 415–428.

Donovan, M. (2008c) 'The centre right: conflict, unity and permanent mobilization', forthcoming, in M. Donovan and P. Onofri (eds), *Italian Politics. The Frustrated Aspiration for Change*: New York and Oxford, Berghahn.

Donovan, M. and Onofri, P. (2008) 'Instability, antipolitics and the frustrated aspiration for change', forthcoming in M. Donovan and P. Onofri (eds), *Italian Politics. The Frustrated Aspiration for Change*: New York and Oxford, Berghahn.

Ignazi, P. (2008) 'La destra trionfante', *Il Mulino* 57(3): 432–440.

Knapp, A. and Wright, V. (2006) *The Government and Politics of France*, London: Routledge.

Mainwaring, S. and Torcal, M. (2006) 'Party system institutionalization and party system theory after the third wave of democratization', pp. 205–227 in R.S. Katz and W. Crotty (eds), *Handbook of Party Politics*, London: Sage.

Mair, P. (1997) 'E.E. Schattschneider's *The Semisovereign People*', *Political Studies* 45(5): 947–954.

Maor, M. (1997) *Political Parties and Party Systems*, London: Routledge.

Marcotti, P. and V. Vanelli. (2008) 'Ricerche, sondaggi, studi di caso. Dalla Sinistra arcobaleno alla Lega? I flussi elettorali raccontano un'altra storia", *Il Mulino* 57(3): 529–533.

Morlino, L. and Tarchi, M. (2006) 'La società insoddisfatta e i suoi nemici. I partiti nella crisi italiana', pp. 207–244 in L. Morlino and M. Tarchi (eds), *Partiti e caso italiano*, Bologna: Il Mulino.

Ostellino, L. (2008) 'Veltroni: "Correremo da soli" ', *Il Sole 24 Ore*, 20 January.

Pappi, F.-U. (1984) 'The West German party system', *West European Politics* 7(4): 7–26.

Sartori, G. (1976) *Parties and Party Systems*, Cambridge: Cambridge University Press.

Smith, G. (1989) 'Core persistence: change and the "people's party"', *West European Politics* 12(4): 157–168.

von Beyme, K. (1985) *Political Parties in Western Democracies*, Aldershot: Gower.

Wolinetz, S.B. (2004) 'Classifying party systems. where have all the typologies gone?', Winnipeg: Canadian Political Science Association, http://www.cpsa-acsp.ca/papers-2004/Wolinetz.pdf

Part III
The Campaign

7
Campaign Issues and Themes

Donatella Campus

An unusual campaign

The most important Italian political scientist, Giovanni Sartori (2008), wrote in the influential newspaper, *Corriere della Sera*, recently that the 2008 campaign had been 'a strange election without a real fight' (*strane elezioni senza battaglia*). The core of Sartori's argument is that the leader of the Partito Democratico (Democratic Party, PD), Walter Veltroni, adopted a style of campaigning expressive of a commitment to fair play – leading him to avoid directly attacking his adversary, Silvio Berlusconi,[1] or replying aggressively to the centre right's attacks. Rather, by emphasising the novelty of the PD and its programmatic platform, he chose to focus on and encourage 'prospective voting'. This, Sartori objects, is a curious strategy to adopt 'when one is trailing in the polls by seven percentage points'.

As a matter of fact, the 2008 election campaign was the least negative and/or animated of those of the Second Republic and the first one in which Berlusconi's character and conflict of interests were not really at the centre of the political debate. At the previous elections the centre left's preferred strategy had been one of attempting to demonise Berlusconi and transform the contest into a referendum on him as a person. On the actual efficacy of such a strategy, there is an open and on-going debate. While it is commonly believed that negative campaigns contribute to the degeneration of politics and discourage voters from participating, it is argued that in some elections such a 'dramatising mobilisation' (*mobilitazione drammatizzante*) has been profitable for the centre left since it has prevented abstentions by leftist voters from being more numerous than they would otherwise have been (Mannheimer, 2002). In any case, the 2008 election took place after several appeals to the contestants to show mutual respect and after a number of meetings had taken place between Berlusconi and Veltroni in an attempt to reach agreement on a reform of the electoral law. Thus, it would have been difficult for Veltroni suddenly to change his attitude and to return to the old electoral strategies. By emphasising his own personal characteristics of flexibility and temperance, from the very beginning of the campaign the leader of the PD stressed his desire to focus on the electoral platforms rather than on personalities. In this respect, he seemed to be quite in line with Italian voters who appeared somewhat tired of the excessive personalisation of politics that had characterised political life in the Second Republic. In fact, according to a poll carried out between 18 and 20 February 2008, almost 60 per cent of voters claimed that that they would base their electoral choices on the platforms while only 24 per cent said that the identity of the candidate Prime Ministers would be the determining factor.[2]

In such an unprecedented context, Berlusconi too was less motivated to fight with his usual passionate and aggressive style. He was leading in the polls by a margin of around 7 per cent.[3] This was a gap that would not, perhaps, have been impossible for the centre left to close, but it was large enough to give Berlusconi confidence that he would win the election. After AN and the Union of Christian Democrats and Centre Democrats (Unione dei Democratici e dei Democratici di Centro, UDC) had challenged him by demanding a change of leadership at the end of his last government, subsequent events – Berlusconi's extraordinary recovery in the 2006 election, the foundation of the Popolo dell Libertà (People of Freedom, PdL) and so on – had succeeded in restoring his image and his primacy within the centre right. Moreover, the often conflictual relationship with his two potential successors and rivals, Gianfranco Fini and Pierferdinando Casini, was rendered much less intractable by Casini's and the UDC's refusal to join the newly created PdL. Casini's withdrawal made it easier to guarantee second place in the hierarchy of the new party to Gianfranco Fini. To sum up, in the 2008 election campaign, not having to demonstrate anything to his political allies or having to answer particularly vicious personal attacks from his adversaries meant that Berlusconi could opt for a much more relaxed style of campaigning. In addition, Italy's economic conditions, with GDP falling and the public finances not in a healthy condition, suggested keeping flamboyant electoral promises to a minimum. For the first time, 'the man of the Italian dream' (Campus, 2002) seemed to have understood the gravity of the country's economic difficulties and adopted a cautious and moderate approach to solving problems. In contrast to the enthusiastic tones of the 2001 'Contract with the Italian people', the 2008 electoral programme of the PdL stated clearly, 'We will neither perform, nor promise, miracles'. Thus, in a climate of general preoccupation with Italy's prospects and of widespread disillusionment among citizens, the 2008 election campaign passed off as one of the least memorable (or entertaining) of the Second Republic. Only in the last few days before the vote, when he mounted a heavy attack on the judiciary (by saying that its members should be subject to regular mental-health checks) did Berlusconi elicit a strong reaction from the centre left. However, by that time it was too late to attempt to change the course of events by again questioning the suitability as Prime Minister of a man entangled in a web of judicial proceedings.

Electoral platforms and the 'Veltrusconi' hypothesis

The return, in 2005, of an electoral law embodying a significant element of proportional representation combined with the end, in 2008, of large coalitions, had produced a multiplication of independent party lists and electoral programmes. However, it should be stressed that the 2008 election was in reality a 'two-party' contest between the PdL allied with the Northern League, on the one side, and the PD allied with Italia dei Valori (Italy of Values, IdV), on the other. This competitive dynamic was clearly confirmed by the election outcome, which heavily penalised all the other minor parties, including the Rosa Bianca-UDC and the radical left. For this reason, what is really interesting from the point of view of the role of issues in the campaign is a comparison of the PdL's and the PD's electoral manifestoes.

First of all, it was noticeable that there had been a general simplification, and an increasing centralisation, of the platform-drafting process, especially in the case of the centre left. Both programmes were short and concise: about ten pages for the PdL, whose programme was structured in terms of seven main points ('the seven missions for the country's future'); about 35 pages for the PD, whose programme was structured in terms of 12 areas of government intervention. This confirmed, in the case of the PdL, an already consolidated tendency; for, past centre-right coalition programmes had also been short. But it marked a difference for the centre left whose manifestoes had previously been quite detailed and of conspicuous length (indeed in 2006 the Unione presented a text that was 281 pages long). However, the real difference as far as the centre left was concerned, lay in the drafting process. While in the centre right camp the processes whereby programmes have been worked out and drafted have never been highlighted or publicised, in 2006 the centre left had based its drafting on a well-publicised participatory and bottom-up process through the so called 'Factory for the drafting of the programme' (*Fabbrica del programma*). The *Fabbrica* was intended to gather suggestions and information through hearings and regular seminars. Later on, the leaders of the parties forming the Unione met to discuss and approve the final version of the manifesto. This last step created tensions and conflict among the coalition partners (Campus, 2008), but at least the whole drafting process had appeared to be a commendable effort to bring together and reconcile different viewpoints. Nothing of the sort was replicated in 2008. Partly due to time constraints that prevented an excessively protracted process of soundings of the party base and of civil society, and partly because of the leader's intention to keep the process of drafting the programme under his direction and control in his headquarters, named 'the loft', the manifesto was written by means of procedures that were highly centralised in the PD as well.

The second interesting feature of the two programmes is the similarity in the issues on which they focus. If one compares the headings used in the two manifestos, the parallels between them emerge with remarkable clarity (see Table 7.1). Both parties stressed as their priorities: the importance of helping business and firms through appropriate fiscal policies (in the PdL programme this aspect is included in the illustration of the first mission); reform of the system of public finance; protecting citizens from crime. Both emphasised the family as the fundamental unit of social life and the community, focusing on it as the main recipient of social services. The two main parties competed on the same sets of issues without attempting to establish any specific 'issue ownership'; that is, they did not try to focus public attention on any special theme not mentioned by their adversaries.[4] Of course, in several cases, the two platforms proposed different measures to deal with the same problems, as – significantly – in the case of immigration and crime, for example; however, the general perception was that not only did the PdL and the PD identify the same priorities, but also that they were closer than before on the measures of reform to be promoted. Almost 75 per cent of respondents to a poll carried out at the end of February 2008 declared themselves in agreement with the statement that all parties say the same things.[5] This impression was reinforced by Berlusconi's ironic claim that Veltroni had stolen his platform (*Corriere della Sera*, 16 March) and Veltroni's reply that it was Berlusconi who had moved toward the centre left's position, especially on taxes (*Corriere della Sera*, 17 March).

The third point worth highlighting is that, in both electoral platforms, economic issues were central. This seems to match quite closely the list of

Table 7.1   Headings used in the PdL's and PD's programmes

PdL's seven missions	PD's areas of government action
Encouraging economic development	Public finance
Supporting families	A fiscal policy to encourage economic development
Law and order	Law and order for citizens and firms
Social Services (health/education/ universities, etc.)	The right to fair judicial decisions within reasonable time periods
Sustaining southern Italy	Action-oriented policies for the environment
Promoting federalism	Welfare state: more equality and support for families, to achieve better growth
Reforming the public finance system	Culture, education, research: more autonomy in pursuit of fairness and excellence
	Stronger firms, better able to compete
	Competition as the condition for growth
	Governing democracy
	Beyond duopoly, in the age of digital television

Table 7.2   Italian citizens' priorities

What is the most important issue that the new government will have to deal with?	**%**
Labour and unemployment	20.4
Wage increases	16.0
Inflation / control of prices	10.6
Tax cuts	9.6
Criminality	8.0
Reform of the social security system	7.2
Economic development	5.4
The processing of refuse	5.0
Social services (education/health/welfare)	4.2
The costs of politics	2.6
Improvements to the system of justice	2.6
Illegal Immigration	2.6
The environment	1.8
Electoral reform	1.4

Source: ISPO poll published in *Corriere della Sera*, 23 March and available at www.sondaggipoliticoelettorali.it

citizens' priorities as illustrated by the poll results shown in Table 7.2. Clearly, Italian voters were worried about the state of the economy. They appeared shocked by the rise in the prices of oil and food; they were concerned by low salaries, trailing behind most other European countries. Italian entrepreneurs worried about losing market shares under the threat of fierce competition from the countries of the Far East. This feeling of uncertainty and fear may well explain why six of the first seven items listed in Table 7.2 concern the state of the economy. Never could the famous slogan coined by the Clinton campaign in 1992, 'It is the economy, stupid', have been more appropriately employed in an Italian campaign.

As is well known, Italy's severe economic problems have a number of deep-rooted causes that include: an inefficient public administration, infrastructural insufficiencies, excessively high fiscal pressure. Although in the past the centre right was often tempted to cast blame for these problems on the EU and, in particular, on the introduction of the Euro, what emerges from the 2008 electoral platforms is that both parties were well aware of the necessity for structural reform and willing to intervene in the areas of public administration, labour and welfare. Good intentions, however, are not enough: all of the required reforms will be difficult to achieve given the predictable resistance of the trade unions and other special interests. For this reason, uncertainty about the outcome of the Senate contest and the apparent similarity of the two programmes led mass-media and political observers to advance the idea of a 'grand coalition' or, as *Newsweek* called it, a 'Veltrusconi' government. As the American magazine's correspondents wrote,

> The basic agenda for Italy may be better addressed by keeping that coalition together. Much of what needs to be done is painful. A weak government can't make it work, and the country's two leading politicians could conclude they are better off taking joint responsibility rather than shouldering the blame for the pain alone. (Nadeau, Barigazzi and Dickey, 2008)

This suggestive hypothesis was the object of lively media discussion for several days, but was made irrelevant by the large victory of the centre right. With a comfortable majority in both chambers of Parliament, Berlusconi has gained the opportunity to introduce structural reform without the opposition's support. Now, as the *Economist* wrote, 'he has no more excuses for putting off reforms. This will be his biggest test; hope, for Italy's sake, that he passes it' (*Economist*, 17 April).

The Alitalia story

In the midst of what was quite a boring campaign when even Berlusconi seemed to have lost his talent for *coupes de théâtre*, a sensitive issue suddenly broke to the surface and monopolised media attention: the sale of the state-owned airline Alitalia to Air France-KLM. For a long time Alitalia had faced a serious financial crisis. In 2007 the Government took the decision to sell an Alitalia that already appeared to be in its death throws. An initial attempt at an auction had failed because all the bidders pulled out. Then the sale of the company to Air France-KLM was planned. The deal with Air France was not without cost: above all, it implied a downsizing of Malpensa airport in Milan since it was clear that the French-Dutch company would have abandoned Malpensa, instead re-invigorating Rome's Fiumicino airport as its preferred hub.

In early 2008 the sale of Alitalia became a matter of urgency: its management warned that the company had cash sufficient to keep it in operation for only a few more months after which it would face the risk of liquidation. Air France still wanted to buy Alitalia but it would do so only on the basis of certain conditions including numerous job cuts. Predictably this arrangement encountered the opposition of both the trade unions and the regional council of Lombardy, feeling that the region's interests were placed in jeopardy by the proposal to abandon Malpensa.

The deal with Air France raised two different issues that could be profitably exploited by the centre right: national identity and the North/South divide. First, the sale of Alitalia would have led to the dismemberment of what was (aside from one or two other low-cost airlines) the country's only national air carrier. Thus, opposition to the sale and its disadvantageous terms could be transformed into an appeal to national pride. In fact, Berlusconi promptly intervened not only to denounce the Air France-KLM offer as unacceptable, but also to ask Italian business people to come forward with an alternative deal. To the battle cry, 'I will stop Air France!' (*Corriere della Sera*, 29 March) Berlusconi launched a crusade to rescue a national symbol and declared his intention of putting together a group of Italian investors. He presented Alitalia's disappearance as a matter of national reputation, stressing that even Greece and Portugal, commonly regarded as countries less industrialised than Italy, had their own national airlines.

Strangely enough, even though it was not totally unexpected, Berlusconi found an ally in the radical Left, worried about the job cuts required by the Air France deal and keen to stress the inability of the PD to defend blue-collar workers' interests. While the PD and the UDC dismissed Berlusconi's proclamations as a campaign gesture, the leader of the Sinistra Arcobaleno, Fausto Bertinotti, urged that the proposal of an alternative to the Air France bid be taken seriously (*Corriere della Sera*, 23 March).

The second reason why the Alitalia crusade was advantageous for the centre right concerned the consequences of the restructuring of Malpensa airport, as proposed in the Air France-KLM plan. Cutting down on the number of flights out of Malpensa was a thorn in the flesh for Lombardy and, in general, for all the Northern regions since it would mean large job cuts and economic losses for the whole Milan area. The choice of Air France to give preference to Rome's Fiumicino airport as the third hub rekindled the rivalry between the political and historical capital, on the one side, and the city that is regarded as Italy's economic and business capital, on the other. The argument in defence of Milan airport became pivotal in giving new force to the Northern League's long-standing claim that the north of Italy has never been adequately supported by the central government and, in particular, by centre left governments. The stress put on the antagonism between Rome and Milan was also designed to embarrass Walter Veltroni who, as outgoing Mayor of Rome would, in the circumstances, be damaged regardless of whether he asserted or denied that he had the interests of that city especially close to his heart.

In short, if the Alitalia issue was a very profitable one for the centre right, it posed a difficult problem for Veltroni and the PD. The deal with Air France had been sought by Prodi's government, worried as it was about the financial crisis at Alitalia and not wanting to protract the bidding process with the risk of losing the only potential investor. However, given the widespread sense of outrage that Berlusconi had been able to arouse at the prospect that the Air France offer would go ahead, Veltroni found himself in a sort of double bind: he could either loyally support the centre-left government and risk losing ground in the north of Italy (Verderami, 2008) where the PD's appeal was already running out of steam; or he could join his ally, Antonio di Pietro and his IdV (which had already chosen to defend Malpensa), and leave Prodi to face the liquidation of Alitalia on his own.

As had already happened on previous occasions, for instance in the 2006 campaign with the inheritance-tax issue (Campus, 2006), the centre right had finally discovered a winning campaign issue, and it stuck to it as long as possible. Berlusconi's declarations about possible rescue plans to save Alitalia fuelled the trade unions' opposition to the Air France plan to cut the Alitalia workforce by several thousand people. At the beginning of April the planned sale fell through after unions rejected the proposed job cuts. Time was running out before the mid-April poll; so it was clear that the Alitalia problem could not be solved immediately and would end up as an item high on the agenda of the next government. No other outcome could have been more positive for Berlusconi. He had managed to scupper the deal with Air France without being obliged to put an alternative offer on the table.[6] In sum, it was a very effective move in the electoral game.

Still in the background, but potentially disruptive: the ethical issues

If Alitalia was a sensitive issue with a big impact on the campaign, then ethical matters – the other potentially sensitive issue, as always in recent Italian campaigns – was effectively kept off the agenda and had little impact.

Italy has one of the most restrictive legal and regulatory systems in Europe with respect to issues such as human reproductive technologies, gay rights and stem-cell research. Notwithstanding the pressure exerted by civil-rights movements and by several sectors of Italian society, until now governments have always been resistant to liberalising measures in these areas. Indeed, in 2004, under the second Berlusconi government, a law that actually restricted access to assisted reproductive services was introduced. The sponsors of a 2005 referendum attempting to strike from the legislation some of the new limitations were defeated because of widespread abstentions and the failure of turnout to reach the required 50 per cent in order for the result to have legal validity. In early 2007, under the second Prodi government, the question of the legal rights of gay couples provoked a heated discussion not only between the centre left majority and the conservative opposition, but also within the centre-left among whose ranks there are several Catholic politicians and a small but vocal group of *'teo-dems'* (leftist politicians who identify with the Church's thinking on ethical issues). Eventually, a cross-cutting alliance between conservatives and Catholics was able to stop the introduction of new, more liberal legislation.

As is well known, both the centre left and the centre right have roots in the Catholic tradition insofar as they include parties which themselves include remnants of the old Christian Democratic Party. Moreover, both sides need to be able to appeal to Church-goers. While it has been shown that, in the transition from the First to the Second Republic, Catholic voters have aligned themselves with secular parties (Diamanti, 1997) and are attending church in ever declining numbers (Pisati, 2000), it remains the case that this large group of voters is not indifferent to the Church's social doctrine and ethical teachings.

From this point of view, the centre right has always been the more homogeneous of the two coalitions. Politicians who have secular views on ethical issues consist of a small minority, the majority being quite deferential in the way it relates to the Vatican, and therefore not inclined to question the existing legislation. By contrast, the centre left and, in particular the PD, faces a sharp internal cleavage between liberals and *teo-dems*. As happened in the 2006 election campaign (Campus, 2008), so too in 2008 the centre left tried to avoid a potentially disruptive discussion about moral issues and bioethics. In fact, in its electoral programme, the PD hardly mentioned such issues at all aside from a generic commitment to making provision for living wills and to the introduction of legislation extending the rights of married individuals to non-married couples (but without explicitly mentioning gay rights). However, the latent conflict between the secular and the Catholic components of the new party exploded as part of the process of alliance-building. Veltroni's decision that his party would run alone, avoiding any re-edition of ideologically heterogeneous electoral cartels like the Ulivo, did not prevent the PD from attempting to include representatives of some of its former allies in its own lists. A merger with Di Pietro's IdV proved not to be a viable option, so it was eventually decided to establish an electoral alliance between the two parties. But such an arrangement was rejected in the case of the Radicals. Although interested in reaching an agreement with Marco Pannella's party, the PD leadership was adamant in its refusal to allow the Radicals to run in tandem with the party and thus to have their own symbol on the ballot paper, forcing them to accept instead the alternative offer of having a limited number of candidates hosted by the PD's own lists. The Radicals were not really satisfied with this arrangement, but the only alternative open to them was to contest the election independently – in the knowledge that in that case they were virtually certain not to surmount the four per cent vote threshold that they would have had to surmount if they were to obtain any Chamber-of-Deputies representatives whatsoever. Inclusion of the Radicals was, however, strongly opposed by others in the PD. Worried about the Radicals' very liberal views on ethical issues, the *teo-dem* group demanded additional candidacies for its own spokespersons in the highest positions on the lists in order to be able to counter the potential for Radical activism in the new Parliament. In the meantime, a well-respected Catholic magazine, *Famiglia Cristiana*, called the electoral agreement between the PD and the Radicals a 'Veltroni-style stew in a Pannella-style sauce' (*un pasticcio veltroniano in salsa pannelliana*).

The attack by *Famiglia Cristiana* was just one of the indirect messages sent to the PD by the Church hierarchy and by influential Catholic circles during the election campaign. Through the declaration of the secretary of the Italian Bishops Conference (Conferenza Episcopale Italiana, CEI), bishop Giuseppe Betori, the Church instructed Catholic voters to make their choices on the basis of such incontestable values as the right to life, the traditional family, and promotion of the common good (*Corriere della Sera*, 19 March). Moreover, the CEI demanded a reform of the electoral system, in particular a modification of the closed-list system to allow the casting of preference votes. Asserting voters' rights to choose among the individual candidates presented by their chosen parties was clearly functional to the principle the Catholic church has been advancing for a long time: the duty of the Catholic voter to support those politicians, whether of the centre right or of the centre left, who are willing to defend and to advance the Church's moral and social doctrines. This attitude exemplifies quite well the political strategy of the Church in the Second Republic. No longer tied to just one party, as it had been in the case of the Christian Democrats, the Church has consistently pursued the objective of conducting its crusade in defence of 'the sanctity of life' across the whole party spectrum (Hanafin, 2007: 10).

In light of this, it is quite clear why the PD preferred to avoid openly addressing any controversial issues of a moral or bioethical nature in what was already a difficult campaign. Yet the PdL was not particularly keen to do so either. Apart from an explicit mention of the family as an entity formed by the union of a man and a woman, and the commitment to preventing any legislation that would allow or encourage the practice of euthanasia, none of the 'Seven missions' listed in the PdL's programme dealt with moral or bioethical issues. Apparently satisfied with the existing legislation on abortion, artificial insemination, and stem-cell research, the leadership of the PdL chose not to follow conservative intellectuals and opinion leaders, such as Giuliano Ferrara, down the path of calling for more restrictive pro-life legislation. Well aware that voters had other priorities, as Table 7.1 shows, Berlusconi avoided campaigning on such issues, preferring to concentrate attention on economic policies and law and order. For this reason, he also refused to make an electoral alliance with Giuliano Ferrara's pro-life movement.

In conclusion, in 2008, as had already been the case in 2006, ethical issues were not really central to the political debate, notwithstanding the efforts of certain vocal minority groups. It should not be assumed that they will not return to the glare of the political and media spotlight in the coming months and years. In fact, on the one hand, movements for liberal reform are likely to continue to press for change; on the other hand, the Catholic Church and its supporters are still deeply engaged in a crusade to defend the sanctity of life. However, while it can be predicted that ethical issues will be the subject of continuing debate and controversy, it is also likely that the governing majority will not push for them to be placed on the legislative agenda and will prefer to leave the current state of affairs unchanged.

Conclusion

The 2008 campaign reflected voters' fears about the state of the economy in general, and their own households' economic circumstances in particular. Both Berlusconi and Veltroni campaigned on the issue of how to save Italy from economic recession and to reform the public administration. From the point of view of understanding the actual outcome of the vote, crucial questions are the extent to which the electoral programmes had an impact on voting choices and whether the PdL's proposals appeared more convincing. It is well known that only a minority of voters read and understand election manifestos in any detail. Even more difficult is it for voters to discriminate between programmes when they are as similar as those of the PD and the PdL were in 2008. Therefore, the hypothesis that can be advanced is that voting choices will have been subject to a strong incumbency effect, with voters being by-and-large convinced that the centre right was likely to do better than the direct heirs of Prodi's government. Indeed, Prodi's government had deeply disappointed voters as the constant decline in its popularity had shown.[7]

During his campaign to win the leadership of the PD, Veltroni had already articulated issues, policy positions and proposals that were quite different from those of the Prodi government. In the 2008 general election he tried to distance himself even more decisively from the Prodi experience. In fact, the PD could reasonably claim to be a new political subject and Veltroni's decision to stand alone without forming an electoral alliance with the radical Left encouraged the view that he was ready to bring significant change to the centre left. However, he did not have enough time to establish his credentials. Therefore, the PD was held at least partially responsible for the centre left government's failures and setbacks.

If Veltroni was inevitably destined to pay a price for the Prodi government's mistakes and liabilities, then the incumbency effect may well not exhaust the list of factors responsible for the PdL's victory. For instance, perhaps for lack of time, but also for the lack of novel ideas, Veltroni was unable to establish a political agenda different from the one on which Berlusconi was easily thriving. In some ways, the impression given by the electoral programme, and even more by Veltroni's speeches around Italy, was that the PD did not campaign on 'position issues', that is 'those that involve advocacy of government action from a set of alternatives over which a distribution of voter preferences is defined' (Stokes, 1966: 170). However, given the characteristics of the electoral context, one may presume that only by being able to differentiate itself from its adversaries, did the PD have any real chance of closing the gap in the polls.

In this regard, time was certainly a crucial factor: it should be remembered that the 2008 election was held much earlier than would have been the case had the 2006 legislature run for its full term. It is true that the fundamental weakness of the Prodi government – its extremely small majority in the Senate – made it seem likely that it would be unseated quite quickly and that elections would take place sooner rather than later. However, nobody could really predict exactly when the Government would collapse or when elections would be called. Both of the party system's two most important entities, the PD and the PdL, were actually formed in the space of a few months. This meant that the possibilities for putting in place elaborate processes of platform-drafting – such as those that had been employed by the Unione in 2006 with its *Fabbrica del Programma* – were limited. From many points of view, such circumstances represented a step backwards; for, involving party members, sympathisers, and civil-society groupings in the drafting of electoral platforms is not only an ideal opportunity to gather information and useful suggestions, but also an opportunity to reinforce the links between politicians and citizens. As was shown quite well in the 2007 French presidential elections, when voters are asked to express their opinions they appear willing to do so, and are even enthusiastic about participating. Although their methodologies and styles were different, both Nicolas Sarkozy and Ségolène Royal invested time and energy in a process of soundings that not only elicited more participation, but also helped to put a number of issues more clearly at the centre of the political debate.[8] Until Italian politicians are able to sponsor more effective mechanisms of participation, it is unlikely that substantive policy issues will play any really significant role in the determination of election outcomes.

Notes

1. Never referring to him by name, but calling him, bizarrely, the 'principal representative of the camp opposed to us.'
2. Demos Eurisko poll published in *la Repubblica*, 25 February, and available at www. sondaggipoliticoelettorali.it
3. I am here taking an average value. Of course, the margin between the two coalitions varied during the course of the campaign depending on when the polls were carried out. In addition, different research institutes came up with varied figures, but these were always within the range of a few percentage points of each other.
4. According to one line of research (Budge and Farlie, 1983; Budge et al., 1987), the analysis of electoral programmes can shed light on whether electoral competition amounts to a debate over common sets of issues (confrontation theory) or whether parties emphasise different issues (issue ownership) and acquire full control of some of them.
5. See the results of the Eurisko poll published in *la Repubblica*, 25 February 25.
6. At the time of writing (July 2008) Alitalia was being kept alive by a huge emergency loan by the Italian Government, much to the preoccupation of the European Commission. There were still rumors circulating about rescue plans by a group of Italian investors, but no concrete offer had formally been made.
7. After just a few months, trust in Prodi's government was reduced to 45 per cent and reached a low of 35 per cent in the summer of 2007. All of the polls were

originally published in *la Repubblica* and are now available at www.sondaggipo
liticoelettorali.it

8. Sarkozy chose a platform-drafting process that was internal to his own party, but given detailed publicity through the mass media. From March 2005 to October 2006 (the election was held in April 2007), the Gaullist party organised 18 conventions, each devoted to a specific theme. Then members of the party's rank and file were asked to express their opinions through a consultation process (Ventura, 2007). Royal adopted a model of participative democracy by exploiting new technologies. Through her website, she organised a huge number of hearings and meetings geared to development and drafting of the programme (Vaccari, 2008).

References

Budge, I. and Farlie, D. (1983) *Explaining and Predicting Elections: Issue Effects and Party strategies in Twenty-Three Democracies*, London: Allen and Unwin.

Budge, I., Robertson, D. and Hearl, D. (1987) (eds) *Ideology, Strategy and Party Change: Spatial Analysis of Post War Election Programmes in 19 Democracies*, Cambridge: Cambridge University Press.

Campus, D. (2002) 'Two coalitions in search of an issue: the role of policy stands in the campaign', pp. 183–197 in J.L. Newell (ed.), *The Italian General Election of 2001. Berlusconi's Victory*, Manchester and New York: Manchester University Press.

Campus, D. (2006) 'The 2006 election: more than ever a Berlusconi-centred campaign', *Journal of Modern Italian Studies* 11(4): 516–531.

Campus, D. (2008) 'Campaign issues and themes', pp. 139–155 in J.L. Newell (ed.), *The Italian General Election of 2006: Romano Prodi's Victory*, Manchester and New York: Manchester University Press.

Diamanti, I. (1997) 'Identità cattolica e comportamento di voto', pp. 317–360 in P. Corbetta and A. Parisi (eds), *A Domanda Risponde*, Bologna: Il Mulino.

Hanafin, P. (2007) *Conceiving Life. Reproductive Politics and the Law in Contemporary Italy*, Aldershot: Ashgate.

Mannheimer, R. (2002) 'Le elezioni del 2001 e la mobilitazione drammatizzante', pp. 179–197 in G. Pasquino (ed.), *Dall'Ulivo al governo Berlusconi. Le elezioni del 13 maggio 2001 e il sistema politico italiano*, Bologna: Il Mulino.

Nadeau, B., Barigazzi, J. and Dickey, C. (2008) 'Taking out the trash', *Newsweek*, 29 March.

Pisati, M. (2000) 'La domenica andando alla messa', *Polis* 14(1): 113–136.

Sartori, G. (2008) 'Strane elezioni senza battaglia', *Corriere della Sera*, 2 April.

Stokes, D. (1966) 'Spatial models of party competition', pp. 161–179 in A. Campbell, P. Converse, W. Miller and D. Stokes (eds), *Elections and the Political Order*, New York: Wiley.

Vaccari, C. (2008) 'Surfing to the Élysée: the internet in the 2007 French elections', *French Politics* 6(1): 1–22.

Ventura, S. (2007) 'L'irresistibile ascesa dell'uomo indispensabile', *Ideazione* 14(2): 123–124.

Verderami, F. (2008) 'Così addio Nord', *Corriere della Sera*, 18 March.

8
The Low-Intensity Media Campaign and a Vote That Comes from Far Back

Franca Roncarolo

In the light of two passionate and high-intensity media competitions such as the ones that took place in 2001 and 2006, the 2008 campaign seemed much less lively and engaging. Though several observers (Diamanti, 2008; Feltrin and Natale, 2008; Ignazi, 2008; Mannheimer and Natale, 2008) have suggested that the 2008 election will turn out to have been a genuinely critical one, there was no hard media campaigning in the immediate run up to it. As we shall see in the following paragraphs, this was true both from the standpoint of journalistic coverage (which was, on the whole, minimal and lacked prominence) and with regard to politicians' use of the media (which was limited and less exciting than in other cases). The result was that, after a notably lacklustre campaign, nobody expected that the country that just two years before had – at least apparently – been equally split, would give an advantage of more than 12 points to the centre-right coalition, even though the victory of PdL was widely regarded as a foregone conclusion (Sani, 2008).

Several factors conspired to produce this result, starting from the fact that the campaign had only a limited appeal for the media. This was due, first, to the lack of any of the atmosphere of expectation that is usually created by the long cycle linking successive general elections (Marletti, 2006) through a continuous series of intermediate ones, and to the lack of the suspense produced by unexpected recovery of the candidate who is trailing in the polls. A further reason for the lack of interest was that political actors seldom produced those appealing events that grab journalists' attention, but need large resources in terms of time and organisation. That is to say, such events were exactly what was in very short supply during the 'concentrated' 2008 campaign, which was not prepared by anything like the two-year run-ups that had preceded the campaigns of 2001 and 2006.

The low-intensity media campaign did not imply, however, that the political communication system played no relevant role. It did, but in an indirect way, helping, through its framing activity and its coverage of issues such as security, to set the agenda according to which voters would make their choices.

In order to develop this analysis, the remainder of the chapter focuses on three main aspects. First we will consider the limited visibility of the campaign in the media and the climate of opinion that prevailed during the competition. Second we will further describe the main political actors' communication strategies and their effects on media coverage. Finally, we will consider the electoral agenda and the way in which issues were framed.

The poor visibility of the election campaign in the media and the negative climate of opinion

The limited amount, and the lack of vibrancy, of media coverage of the 2008 campaign broke decisively with a long-standing tradition that had seen considerable attention devoted to politics in general and to national elections in particular. Actually, the break was not completely new, having already been apparent during the 2006 campaign (Roncarolo, 2008b), but this time it was even clearer and more accentuated.

Only at the beginning, during the week following the announcement of the date of the election, and in the final days of the campaign, did as many as three of the seven principal television channels start their evening news bulletins with an item about the election or about an issue relevant to it. For the remainder of the time the average was lower and sometimes – as, for example, during the last two weeks of March – so low that for several days not a single television station decided to open its prime-time news edition with a reference to the contest (see Figure 8.1).

It is interesting to note that the visibility of the campaign was particularly limited on 'Studio Aperto', the news bulletin broadcast by Italia1 which, of the Berlusconi-owned TV stations, is the one that is most oriented towards young people (who are supposed to be less interested in politics than their elders): on that channel, indeed, only five opening news items out of one hundred had a political theme. Even more interestingly, it was neither the public television channels nor Silvio Berlusconi's, but the third major network, owned by the media branch of a telephone company (Telecom Italia Media), that gave the greatest visibility to election news. Its small but influential channel, La7, has a tradition of attempting to use political news as a means by which to distinguish itself and thus to attract at least some parts of the audiences that are otherwise drawn to its two larger competitor networks (see Table 8.1).

The picture is not very different if we turn from broadcasting to the print media: although the press paid slightly more attention, not even the dailies focused most of their front pages on the election campaign. This was to the extent that, if we consider the 11 most important national newspapers

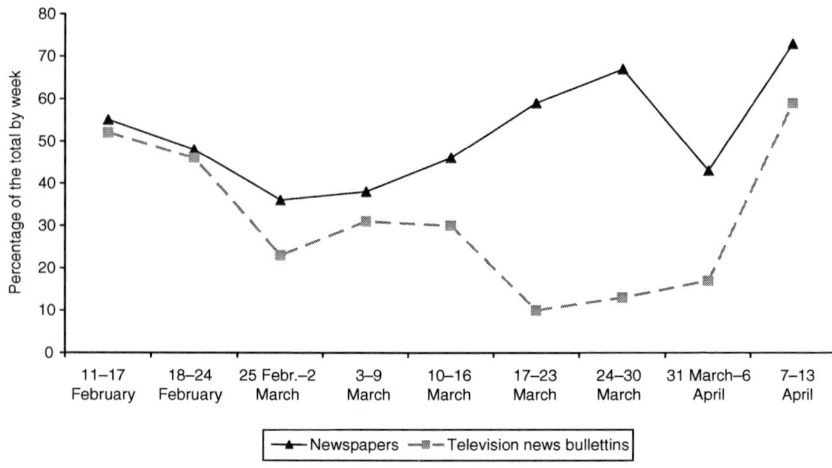

Figure 8.1   Proportions of opening news itmes focused on the election campaign in seven television news bulletins and eleven newspapers

Source: Observatory of Political Communication

Table 8.1   Percentage of news bulletins' opening items that focused on the campaign, by TV channel

Tg1	31%
Tg2	31%
Tg3	38%
Average Rai	33%
Tg5	38%
Tg4	30%
Studio aperto	5%
Average Mediaset	24%
La7	47%

Source: Observatory of Political Communication

during the period from 11 February to the Sunday of the vote (14 April) we discover that only during four of the nine weeks involved did the opening news item concern the competition on at least one day out of two. This figure becomes even more telling if we consider which dailies did make room for politics on their front pages (Table 8.2).

The only newspapers that were almost always interested in the election campaign were partisan dailies: *il Giornale*, owned by Berlusconi's family, and *Libero*, a more independent – but not less conservative – newspaper.

Table 8.2   Proportions of opening news focused on the election campaign by newspaper

Corriere della Sera	31%
La Stampa	55%
Il Messaggero	37%
Average in information dailies	41%
la Repubblica	59%
L'Unità	69%
Il Giornale	94%
Libero	96%
Il Manifesto	29%
Liberazione	42%
Average in openly partisan dailies	72%
Il Sole 24 Ore*	13%
Avvenire**	4%
Average in the dailies sponsored by interest groups	9%

Notes:
* *Il Sole 24 Ore* is the daily of the National Industrial Association (Confindustria)
** *Avvenire* is the daily of the Conferenza Episcopale Italiana (Italian Bishops' Conference, Cei)

Source: Our elaboration of Observatory of Political Communication data

Some distance behind these two, we find two more politically aligned newspapers: *L'Unità*, (the former Communist Party's newspaper) and *la Repubblica*, a centre-left daily that has always been so politically committed as to deserve the label of quasi-party paper.[1] On the other hand, the so called 'information press' – that is to say, those dailies that are less politically committed – and even some that side with the left, like *Liberazione* and *il Manifesto*, gave very limited coverage of the election campaign on their front pages. The same was true of *il Sole 24 Ore*, the main financial newspaper, and the Italian Bishops' Conference's daily, *Avvenire*.

This lack of attention is to be explained, in part, by the process whereby, even though it has hitherto taken place to a more limited degree than elsewhere (Hallin and Mancini, 2004; Roncarolo, 2002), the Italian media have acquired a growing autonomy from the main political actors, turning to the market and giving their news by a rationale whereby the values of political partisanship are no longer the most significant ones. The first, obvious, consequence is that, even in the country that was once the homeland of 'parallelism' between information and political systems, coverage of party politics, as in all mediated democracies, has decreased. However, this is less evidence of a genuine lack of interest in the campaign than of a different style of coverage, one that is to be explained in terms of the function of the media in supplying cognitive maps to voters (Belluati, 2008a). On the one hand, indeed, as is usual in the third generation of political communication, there were many different channels – from the Internet to the free press – through which a rich information flow continuously ran, offering people news that could be picked out and easily and quickly consumed.[2] On the other hand, especially in the newspapers, despite the campaigns' limited visibility, those voters who were interested could find in-depth analysis of it. Indeed, while the opening news items often focused on events that did not concern the election campaign, in almost every daily paper, on almost each day, there was at least one leading article offering analysis and comment on the key themes in the political debate (see Figure 8.2).

The gap between the limited visibility of election coverage and the relative abundance of editorials can be explained by the scarcity of newsworthy events, a feature of the 2008 campaign that was due both to the fact that political actors did not have time to organise them,[3] and because of the electoral strategies adopted by the two main leaders. Actually, Walter Veltroni's decision to 'run alone' was a very effective move both from the standpoint of political communication and from that of media logic. However, its effect failed to last; for it lacked further events capable of retaining journalists' attention to it (not least because the campaign tour, which took Veltroni around the country in a campaign bus, was neither completely new[4] nor especially interesting to the media). It had, consequently, only a short-term appeal, and one that was quickly annulled by the many disputes that arose from the process of candidate selection. So, though the decision not to form an instrumental electoral alliance created the impression that there was real political innovation here, and though it attracted positive comment on

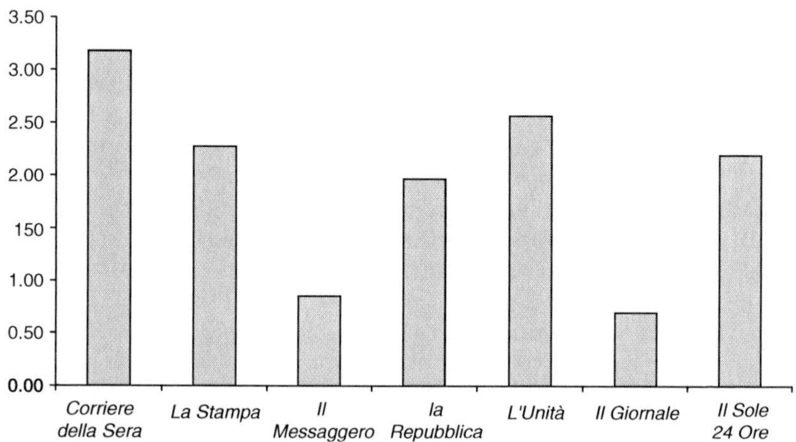

Figure 8.2   Daily average of editorials and comments on 2008 election campaign
Source: Observatory of Political Communication

the part of political observers and journalists, subsequent decisions about which candidates to place at the head of electoral lists largely disappointed expectations of change. They seemed to be driven more by considerations of an opportunist kind than by a genuine political project, thus feeding editorials with the suspicion that an old political style continued to operate beneath the appearance of novelty. On the other hand, as we will see below, Berlusconi's coalition had too large an advantage to force him to engage in a truly demanding campaign.

It was precisely this advantage that was the most important aspect of the campaign and in all probability the main reason for its limited visibility in the media. The point is that the climate of opinion in 2008 was driven by two main factors, both of which helped to create a negative framework and make the campaign less interesting. First, as a consequence of various political problems, there was very widespread disapproval of Prodi's government, and during its time in office, the consequences of this disapproval were reinforced by what at the very least was an ineffective communications strategy (Roncarolo and Belluati, 2008). At the same time, the opposition's ratings were almost equally poor (see Figure 8.3).

According to the polls, even though the majority of Italians felt more positively towards the opposition than towards the Government, when Parliament was dissolved public opinion was very unfavourable towards both. This was not really surprising given the 'anti-political' mood the media had amplified for many months. There were two dimensions to this. On the one hand, extensive (although often very critical and negative) coverage was given to the resurgence of Italy's recurring anti-political movement. During the months spanning 2007 and 2008 this movement was led by Beppe Grillo, a comedian and an explosive speaker who crystallised the widespread disenchantment with the political elite and made it visible, by creating arenas (like his blog, which attracts 160,000 hits daily) and opportunities for protest against politicians' failure to tackle the country's problems.[5] On the other hand, newspapers and television channels fed these negative attitudes, by acting as an echo chamber for popular outrage at politicians' perks. Such attitudes were in their turn fuelled by the publication, in May 2007, of *La Casta*, a best-selling book by two journalists, Sergio Rizzo and Gian Antonio Stella, who described the wide-ranging privileges of a deeply entrenched political class. And they were also expressed with great emphasis, in, for example, *la Repubblica* through coverage which, even at its less intense moments, amounted to an average of almost one article a day (Figure 8.4).

Stressing the 'decay of a nation [...] that is quickly losing speed [...] while the political strata are the most static and immobile,'[6] Italian journalism ended up masking the widespread demands for political solutions. And day by day it persuaded itself that there was no room for change. This belief was then strengthened by the polling figures, which remained basically stable. Although such figures are obviously a very imperfect indicator of the state

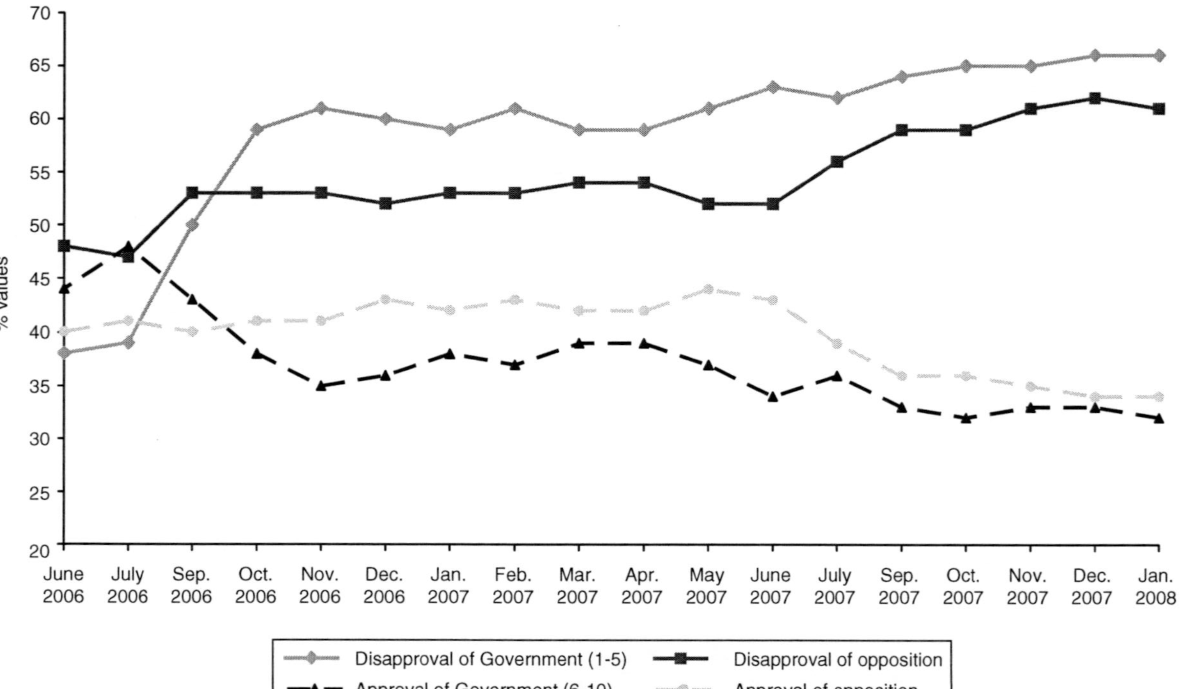

Figure 8.3 Approval ratings of Government and opposition

Source: Ipsos

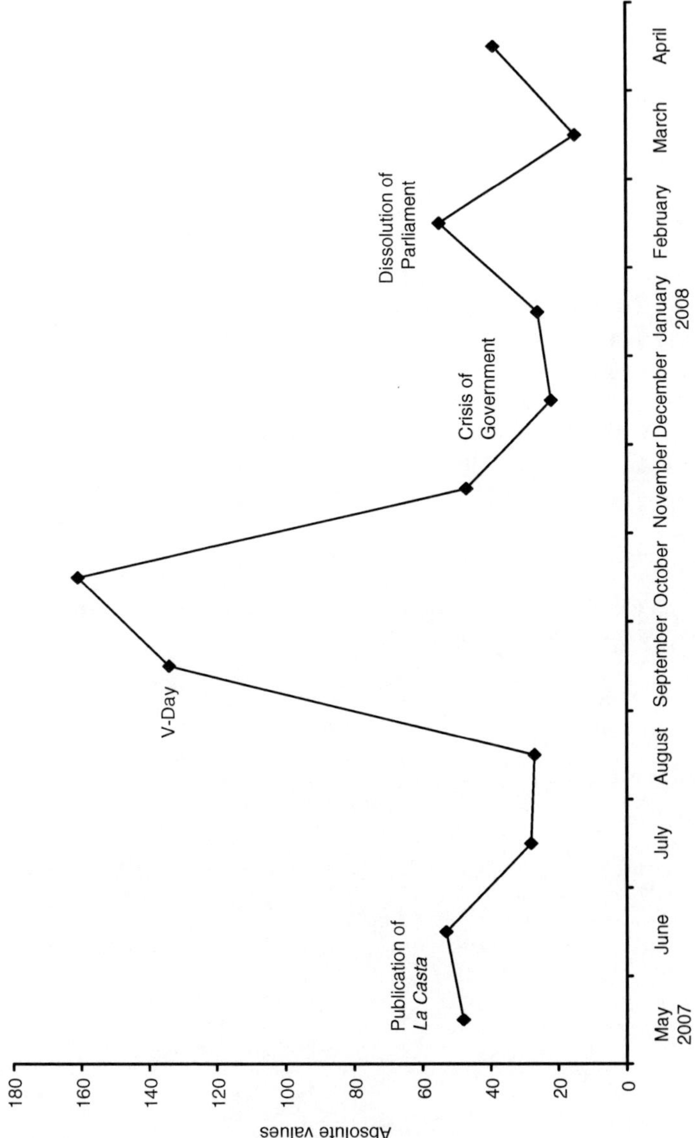

Figure 8.4   la Repubblica articles containing the word 'anti-politics'

of public opinion, they are influential because of the use the media make of them – and their stability makes it easy to appreciate why they were so scarcely reported by the media or debated in the public arena (see Table 8.3). As Table 8.4 clearly shows, the climate of opinion was also very stable, but people had a very clear perception of how the campaign was going (see Table 8.4).

Leaving aside the problem of the usual under-representation in the Italian polls of those who vote for the centre right,[7] what is interesting here is the appearance of immobility that this picture of Italian society gives. Portraying Italy as a country where the majority was frozen in terms of its preferences (or hostilities) while others were increasingly disenchanted with politics, the press contributed to producing a distorted image of reality, where nothing was happening and the most important issues concerned the chances of negotiating a wide agreement among all political actors.

To what extent did the two main leaders contribute to the creation of this mood? And even more importantly, to what extent did the media focus on the campaign with which they tried to win votes, thus developing the well-known process that, from the early 1990s, began the presidentialisation of Italian politics?

Table 8.3   Electoral estimate of voting in the 2008 general election (%)

'If the general election were held today which party would you vote for in the Chamber of Deputies ballot?'

	18–20 February	5–10 March	25–26 March
Centre-left coalition (PD+IdV)	39.0	38.5	39.1
Centre-right coalition (PdL+LN)	45.4	45.2	45.7

Source: Atlante politico, Dernos & Pi. poll for *la Repubblica*, www.sondaggipoliticoelettorali.it

Table 8.4   Public perceptions of the likely winner (%)

'In your opinion, which of the following will win the 2008 general election?'

	February	March	March
Democratic Party	21.6	21.7	22.1
The Centre	0.6	0.8	0.6
People of Freedom	56.7	57.2	55.6
I don't know	20.9	20.3	21.7
No	3,500	6,401	6,303

Source: Ipsos cit. in Vaccari (2008: 180)

The electoral face of Italian presidentialisation and the leaders' media campaigns

As Calise (2005: 88) has noted, 'Italy represents, in most respects, an ideal-type for the presidentialisation of the political system'; and, since the early 1990s, the country has seen a very high degree of personalisation in election campaigns. In many respects, the 2008 campaign marked a continuation of this process, one that was greatly enhanced by the nomination of Veltroni as leader of the main centre-left party. If in the early 1990s Berlusconi had transformed the personalisation of local elections 'into a massive nation-wide undertaking', setting 'a standard for personal campaigning with no comparable precedents in modern mass democracies' (Calise, 2005: 99), then the leader of the new Democratic Party broke with the traditional diffidence of the Italian left towards the media. Unlike Prodi, the former Mayor of Rome is naturally skilled in communication strategies. And he is as used as Berlusconi to communicating with citizens both directly and through the media (Roncarolo, 2008c). Not surprisingly, in 2006, after a first term as Mayor of Rome, he was re-elected on the first ballot with 62 per cent of the vote, while – less than two years later – he began his general election campaign by choosing to identify himself with the successful American Democratic leader, Barack Obama.

Veltroni's style of campaigning and leading the Democratic Party (Partito Democratico, PD) reinforced at least two of the three developments that are considered to be meaningful indicators of the 'electoral face' of presidentialisation:[8] 'the growing emphasis on leadership appeals in election campaigning' and the tendency of media coverage of politics to be focused more on leaders (Poguntke and Webb, 2005: 10). But, despite a range of circumstances that might have been expected to result in an even greater degree of presidentialisation, this much debated process[9] was subject to various limits in the 2008 campaign.

The first of these had to do precisely with the consequences of the changed electoral offer due to Veltroni's decision to break with the old practice of forming very inclusive coalitions. This choice – and the consequent acceleration given to construction of a new and larger party of the centre right, bringing together Forza Italia and Alleanza Nazionale and eschewing any electoral alliance other than with the Lega Nord (Northern League, NL) – helped immediately to simplify the party system. But in the context of the 2008 campaign they also had the consequence of increasing the number of candidates for the position of Prime Minister. Legally, these candidates had to be given a minimum amount of space and visibility by the media. Indeed, while in the 2006 election there were only two competing leaders – although the number of parties in the two coalitions was so high that, after the election, there were 30 parliamentary groups – in the 2008 campaign there were about 20 candidates competing, at least formally speaking, to become the future head of government. The consequence can be seen if we look at the presence of the main party leaders on television: those watching political television programmes had a greater chance of encountering a 'minor-party' candidate than one of the two main leaders (see Figure 8.5).

Besides the disproportionate level of activism of these minor-party candidates, two further elements favoured this over-representation: media attention to the leading characters in 'David-and-Goliath' type stories, and the obligations created by the so-called *par condicio* law.

As Figure 8.5 clearly shows, the greatest visibility was given to politicians leading parties that might have held the balance of power in the event of a political tie – an outcome that many observers considered highly probable in the case of the Senate contest – or that might have anyway played a more relevant role; and this favoured greater pluralism.[10] Needless to say, politicians like Bertinotti and Casini – who out of choice or necessity, were competing against the two 'giants' of the electoral competition – or like Daniela Santanchè – who, from the standpoint of media logic, had the additional advantage of being a woman – were very appealing to journalists. Moreover, being the leaders of small political formations, they did not have to share their air-time with other politicians to the extent that Berlusconi had to – with, for example, Maurizio Gasparri and Gianfranco Fini – or Veltroni had to, with Dario Franceschini, Piero Fassino and Emma Bonino.[11]

By contrast, the print media were much more strongly focused on the two main candidates, and – at least on their front pages – showed greater interest in those with a realistic chance of winning leadership of the country. Relatively speaking, therefore, they ignored the other contenders.

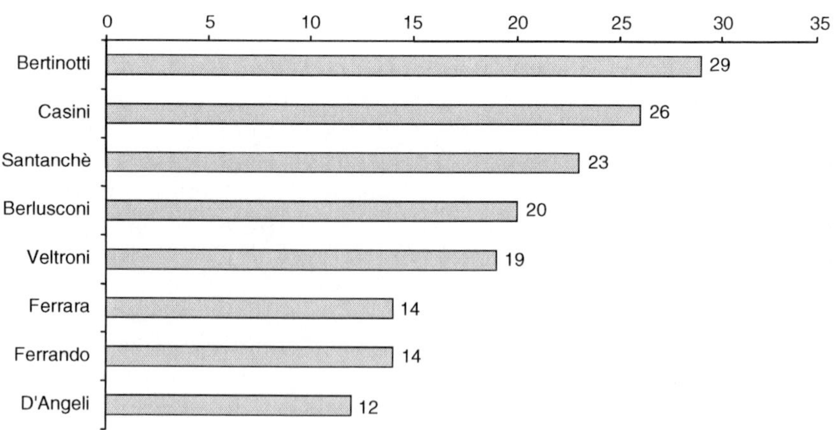

Figure 8.5   Prime-ministerial candidates participating in TV current affairs programmes: Number of appearances, 7 February – 10 April 2008

As we can see in Figure 8.6, only Berlusconi and Veltroni had a relatively high index of visibility,[12] maintaining weekly averages of 17.6 and 14.6 points. And Berlusconi – the expected winner – continuously held the top position from the beginning of March onwards, while the leader of the PD had maximum visibility only during the second half of February. This was the time when he was at the heart of political debate – but also of several controversies – because of his decisions to replace Ciriaco De Mita (former general secretary of the DC and a parliamentarian of more than 40 years standing) with a younger candidate, to include members of Radical Party in the Democratic Party's lists, and to place a famous secularist scientist, Umberto Veronesi, at the head of the party's list in Lombardy. These were decisions that caused a furore such as to induce both the main Catholic daily (*Avvenire*) and the Catholic weekly magazine (*Famiglia Cristiana*) to publish very critical articles.[13]

Generally speaking, though, neither Berlusconi nor Veltroni on the whole enjoyed the degree of attention that might have been expected in a critical election (Norris et al., 1999). Not only did they fail to reach the maximum index of visibility, but they always remained well below the ceiling of 28 points. Besides the effect of the other factors already mentioned, the style of campaigning adopted by Berlusconi and Veltroni may have helped limit their visibility. First, their contrasting needs meant that neither of them appeared very much on television. On the one hand, Berlusconi was in the comfortable position of leading the polls. On the other hand, Veltroni was engaged in the difficult task of unifying a still 'hypothetical' party (Berselli, 2008) with two souls (one comprising the former Christian Democrats and the other the former Communists) which were still far from being integrated. Second, the early general election did not leave them enough time to organise the broadcast campaign or to take full advantage of the absence of the limits which the *par condicio* law imposes on the last 30 days of the campaign.

As always, the most visible candidate in the electronic media was Berlusconi. Even though he did not this time conduct the kind of inflammatory campaign that he had in the past, the leader of the PdL was interviewed for several news bulletins and participated in various talk-shows. He appeared on RAI's most popular political programme, 'Porta a porta', where he blamed all of Italy's problems on the Prodi government, but – unlike 2001 – he took good care not to sign any 'Contract with the Italian people'. And a few days before the vote, participating in a Mediaset talk-show, 'Matrix', he again showed his well-known impatience with rules: after his interview had finished, he walked back onto the set and took the place of the anchorman, Enrico Mentana, to explain how to vote.[14] Such an unexpected and unscheduled move caused great embarrassment to Mentana, who was forced to end the programme abruptly in order to avoid a breach of the law.

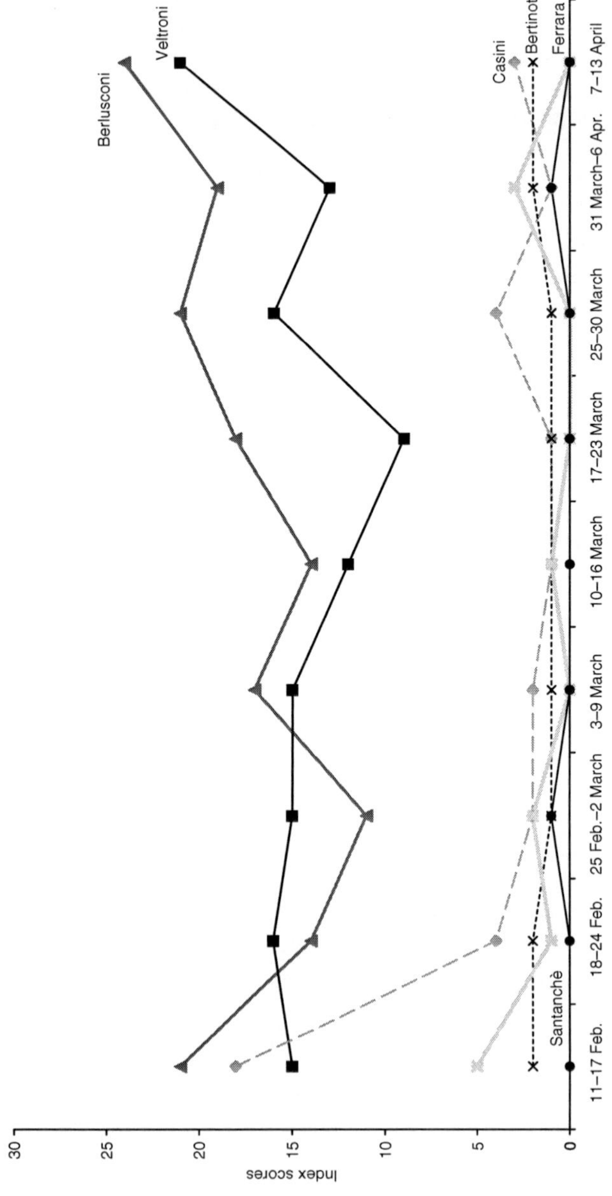

Figure 8.6 The visibility of leaders on the front pages of daily newspapers

Source: Observatory of Political Communication

It is interesting to note that on the last day of the campaign – but only on the last day, not for weeks as had been the case in 2006 (Roncarolo, 2008a) – Berlusconi 'invaded' the television channels. On Friday 12 April, at 7.00 p.m. he was in the studios of the Tg4 news bulletin, of the three news bulletins broadcast by the Mediaset channels the one that was always most favourable to him. At 8.00 p.m. he opened the Tg5 news bulletin with a very long interview, and half an hour later appeared on the successful political programme, 'Otto e mezzo', broadcast daily by La7. Then, at 10.00 pm he took Veltroni's place on 'Matrix', and finally he closed the parade with an appearance on Rai Uno's 'Electoral Tribune' – where all 15 leaders of parties or coalitions had five minutes each – and a last interview on the third channel of public television. The only programme that did not include an appearance by Berlusconi – and consequently neither by Veltroni – is one that did not take place at all, namely, the sought-after face-to-face television debate. Being the frontrunner, and enjoying a large advantage, the leader of the PdL denied Veltroni the chance to challenge him in public, exploiting the ambiguities of a law – the *par condicio* – that was intended to guarantee democratic competition but in some cases, risks paralysing it. So, confirming his decisive style of operating, he ignored all the pressures and protests – including those deriving from the publication of a huge critical advertisement by Sky TV[15] – and continued on his course, sure of his voters' basic indifference to issues of this kind.

For his part, Veltroni adopted a somewhat different communication strategy, one that was aimed at achieving two goals: the already-mentioned integration of the PD's constituent parts, and a reduction of the gap separating him from Berlusconi, anticipating that this would change the climate of opinion by influencing the media and the public's perceptions of the competition. All things considered, this was exactly what Berlusconi had almost successfully done in the 2006 election campaign. But, unfortunately for him, the leader of the centre-left formation was not in a position to exploit in full the power of the media to drive the social construction of reality, because he had neither Berlusconi's resources nor the time that would have been necessary to do it without giving up running the 'real-life' election campaign. In order to overcome these basic obstacles, Veltroni tried to maximise his chances by connecting the two aims, that is to say by trying to use his tour through 110 Italian provinces as an opportunity to attract media coverage. Exploiting the fact that – as has been observed – he 'is possessed of Sarkozy-like energy' (Hooper, 2008), the former Mayor of Rome criss-crossed Italy in a large, green eco-friendly bus, followed by a second green bus for the press, completing a 12,600 km tour from northern to southern Italy. He met large and enthusiastic crowds and – against a background of large banners proclaiming the PD slogan 'A Modern Italy. We can do it' – made stump speeches, delivered without notes, laden with Obama's themes (novelty, hope and rejuvenation). The result was newsworthy enough to gain him the attention of the foreign as well as the Italian press (Dinmore, 2008). But there were many limits. The tactic of never referring to Berlusconi by name – calling him, instead 'the main exponent of the coalition opposed to us' – avoided both demonising his opponent and the risk of placing the spotlight on him; however, it ended up reducing the attention of journalists, who were less strongly attracted by a less personalised competition. And while for some time Veltroni was quite successful in sowing seeds of doubt about who would win, claiming that the gap with PdL was lessening, he never succeeded in being completely convincing. Moreover, as time went on, the series of always-similar images from the always-similar squares and theatres that the television news bulletins continued to broadcast, evening after evening, lost all attraction.

Of course the news bulletins were not the only opportunity the voter had of seeing Veltroni on television. He appeared on almost all of the same programmes as Berlusconi, playing a kind of chess game with him, aimed at avoiding anybody having any advantage, however small.[16] But on the whole the leader of the PD was less visible in the media than his opponent, without obviously being able to rely on an effective and deep-rooted political organisation, with a genuine presence on the ground, like that of the Northern League.

The election agenda in the media

In terms of the electoral agenda too, Veltroni was in quite a weak position. Generally speaking, the agenda was very thin from both the quantitative and the qualitative standpoints. As the data show, coverage of the 2008 campaign included discussion of a very limited number of issues, which in most cases focused on the campaign itself. Once again, it is difficult not to be astonished by the gap between the size of the vote won by the centre right and the poverty of the debate that produced it. Whether one considers newspapers (Cannone, 2008; Mazzoni et al., 2008) or television programmes (Bobba, 2008; Legnante, 2008) the empirical evidence is basically the same. During the 2008 campaign political actors addressed those concerns that lay at the core of citizens' agendas only sporadically (see Figure 8.7). In all other cases their statements focused on arguments about how the campaign should be run, about whether or not certain alliances should be formed, and according to what criteria candidates should be selected (although voters would not be able to express any preference among them, since the lists were 'closed').

If one then considers the election agenda from the standpoint of the potential for 'issue ownership' (Petrocik, 1996) it is easy to see how unfavourable to the centre left it was. The only policy issue among the top five themes was Alitalia. But – as is well known – while it was supposed to be a resource whereby the government and the centre left could gain support, it ended up

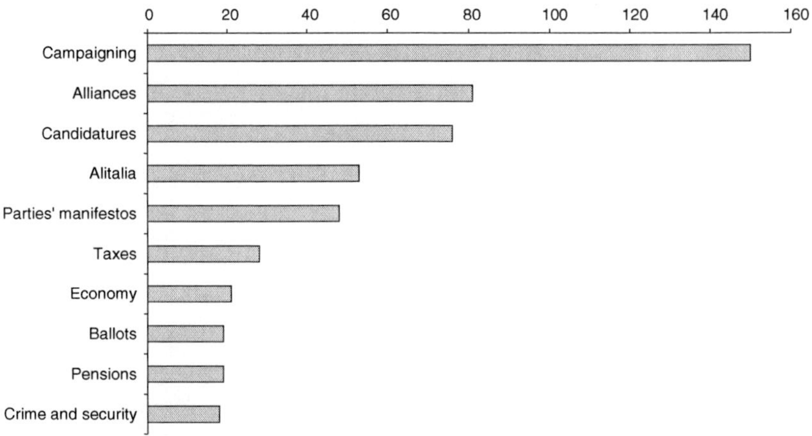

Figure 8.7   The ten most frequent themes of the opening items of television news bulletins

Source: Observatory on Political Communication

being a difficult issue, one on which the leader of the PdL was more success-ful at positioning and presenting himself as the 'presidentiable' candidate. The centre right then had ownership of most of the themes we see in the list and – for this reason too – looked more believable.

Veltroni discussed many issues, however. He presented an electoral pro-gramme with a mixture of various topics, like increased security 'but also' targeted public spending; cutting taxes 'but also' fighting tax evasion.[17] He talked about a Modern Italy, but he never captured the heart of cen-trist voters or the imagination of the media. Moreover, while he engaged strongly with electoral themes, calling for a 'clean slate' of candidates and for less adversarial politics, these issues showed themselves to be secondary for many voters.

Berlusconi was, by contrast, more successful in tuning in to the mood of the majority. Given the context of a severe international economic crisis, he sought to give the impression of a sober, wise, statesman who does not promise too much, but who can cure the ills of his troubled homeland far better than a younger rival who, in the end, was proposing similar solu-tions. He exploited demands for 'strong leadership', which were becoming louder in Italy, as in France (Diamanti, 2007). And without directly talking of insecurity – except in some selected cases – he offered an answer to the demands for 'protection' that television broadcasts had greatly contributed to create, both with their framing processes and as a consequence of their agenda-setting power.

If we look at the content of television news programmes' opening items in the nine weeks before the vote – whether presented as political or not[18] – we see, for example, that there were four main kinds of item, which we can subdivide as follows:

a. news focused on the theme of security/insecurity because of criminality;
b. news focused on the economic crisis (which is another source of insecurity);
c. foreign news;
d. other news (soft news, events that cannot be placed in any thematic frame, etc.).

According to Bobba's (2008) data, during the election campaign, on average, more than 50 per cent of opening items on television news broadcasts fell into one of the first two categories, telling the public stories about various kinds of risk and threat. This evidence is not surprising if we consider that, in recent years, the coverage of events connected with the insecurity issue has become increasingly important in Italian public debate. Although the trends in crime figures fail to justify this rapidly increasing attention, in five years the volume of crime news has more than doubled, driving the issue to the front of the stage in the media arena (see Table 8.5).

Needless to say, if the two variables – the increasingly prominent representation of risk on television and the centre right's large majority in the ballot boxes – are connected, they are not connected in any direct or simple way. But it is difficult to believe that fuelling the widespread perception of living in an unsafe world did not have any effect on the cognitive schemes of voters (Belluati, 2008). Insecurity was, indeed, the general thematic framework within which people took their decisions about voting: whether or not to vote, and if they did, which party to vote for, the one closest to their heart, or the one with the better chance of actually winning. Although most voters simply confirmed their past political preferences (Natale, 2008), the unexpected willingness of Italians to wield the 'useful vote', as a strategic tool to maximise the political efficacy of the government, may also derive from this situation.

Table 8.5   Trends in television coverage of the issue of insecurity

	2003	2004	2005	2006	2007	Percentage increase 2007–2003
RAI	10.7	13	11.5	19.1	22.3	210.7
MEDIASET	11.2	12.5	10.7	18.9	25.6	227.3
LA7	6.9	9.8	8.4	17.7	22.0	320.1

Source: Centro d'Ascolto dell'Informazione Radiotelevisiva

Conclusion

In the end the most salient features of the 2008 election campaign in the print and broadcast media were three in number. First, in comparison with previous competitions the campaign was short, plunged as always in the flow of permanent campaigning and driven by a climate of opinion that was very unfavourable to the centre left because of the legacy of mistrust left by the Prodi government. Second, coming after a period of anti-political protest greatly emphasised by journalists, and at a time of change for the Italian media, the early elections caused limited interest in the campaign among both press and television journalists, and they gave it only limited coverage. Finally, the increasing amount of crime news, and the energetic representation of the economic crisis gave the electoral competition a general framework that was based on widespread feelings of uncertainty and collective concern over the security issue.

In this context, Berlusconi simply campaigned to strengthen his advantage by offering reassurance, while avoiding fuelling voters' expectations too strongly; whereas Veltroni tried to cultivate a climate of opinion based on more positive perceptions of the future, but was not entirely successful either at conquering the imagination of the media or – above all – at reaching those voters who might have made the difference. Lacking both Berlusconi's media resources and the Northern League's political machine through which to integrate mediated communication with daily, direct contact with people, aimed at communicating clear and genuinely shared messages, his campaign was destined to be an extremely difficult, and ultimately unsuccessful, enterprise.

Notes

1. The definition was also adopted by the founder of *la Repubblica*, Eugenio Scalfari. With regard to the analytic category see Marletti (1994).
2. On the 'pick and choose style' of consuming information see Blumler and Kavanagh (1999).
3. The lack of time arose both from the fact that the election, and thus the campaign, came about unexpectedly, and from the absence of the long period of increasing mobilisation that in the 2001 and 2006 elections had prepared the climate of opinion by allowing full exploitation of the unregulated period (Marini, 2002; Roncarolo, 2008a).
4. Prodi used the campaign bus for the first time in an Italian general election in the 1996 campaign and then, again, in 2006.
5. While Beppe Grillo's movement began through popular websites, in September 2007 it exploded onto Piazza Maggiore in Bologna as a street meeting of 80,000 people for V-Day (V standing for *Vaffanculo!*, Fuck off!) during which Grillo read the names of, and the charges against parliamentarians caught up in criminal proceedings. See McDonnell and Splendore (2008) and Donovan and Onofri (2008).
6. The article was by the editor of *la Repubblica*, E. Mauro, quoted by G. Dinmore in 'Prodi prepares for an autumn of discontent', *The Guardian*, 2 October 2007.

7. The general problem was exacerbated in 2008 by the large number of undecided voters who did not take (or at least did not express) a decision (sometimes concealing it even from themselves) until polling day itself. With regard to the political preferences of uncertain voters see De Sio (2008).

8. At present there are no data about the 'growing significance of leader effects in voting behaviour' which is the third indicator, but generally speaking in the Italian case there is no convincing empirical evidence for this trend. See Barisione (2006).

9. An analysis of Berlusconi's 2006 election campaign based on the presidentialisation theory is suggested by Pasquino (2006). For a critical reflection on the process of presidentialisation see, for example, Di Giovine and Mastromarino (2007) and Elia (2006).

10. See for example, on this point, what has been said by E. Macaluso in the editorial, 'L'illusione dei due pigliatutto' [The illusion of the two catch-all parties], *La Stampa*, 8 April 2008, p. 1.

11. The complete list of appearances, with data for all politicians, may be consulted at www.centrodiascolto.it. Under the *par condicio* law all main majority and opposition political forces (but, of course, not the leaders) must have equal media treatment, in terms of time and space.

12. This index was created from a daily compound score that assigned a value from 0 to 4 to each leader's visibility according to the following scale: 4 if the leader's name was in the title of the opening or editorial article; 3 if the leader's name was in the subhead of the opening or editorial article; 2 if the leader's name was in the title of another article on the front page; 1 if the leader's name was in the subhead of another article on the front page.

13. For a short account see A. Mattina, 'Il Pd lancia Veronesi. Rivolta dei cattolici' [PD launches Veronesi: Catholics in revolt], *La Stampa*, 23 February 2008, p. 4, and L. Accattoli, 'Famiglia Cristiana: Pd-Radicali, un pasticcio' [Famiglia Cristiana: Pd-Radicals, a mess], *Corriere della Sera*, 26 February 2008, p. 6.

14. The centre right had raised objections about the voting arrangements, complaining of a risk of large numbers of spoilt ballots since the ballot papers offered less space between the symbols of parties in coalition than they did between parties standing alone.

15. Sky TV – which had tried to circumvent the *par condicio* law's limits and organise a debate between Berlusconi and Veltroni – at the end of the campaign published a full-page advertisement in various newspapers with nine images of television election debates (from the confrontation between Blair and Howard in 2005 to the duel between Sarkozy and Royal in 2007 and that between Fisher and Ferrero Wainer in 2004). Beneath was the comment 'It is the Italians who come out the losers from this comparison' [Da questo confronto escono perdenti gli italiani].

16. At the beginning of March, Veltroni announced that he would not participate in Berlusconi's best-loved talk-show – 'Porta a porta' – during the last week before the vote, saying that he would only cancel some of his many electoral engagements for a face-to-face debate with the leader of PdL (thus obliging the producers to cancel Berlusconi's own appearance). After a lively protest, Berlusconi reacted by returning the snub, cancelling his scheduled participation in the programme presented by the left-wing journalist Lucia Annunziata (and thus also preventing Veltroni's participation). See the articles 'Veltroni non va a 'Porta a porta'. E così salta anche Berlusconi' [Veltroni not to appear on 'Porta a porta'. And so Berlusconi not to appear either] and 'Berlusconi diserta Raitre e la vieta

anche a Veltroni' [Berlusconi stays away from Rai3 and stops Veltroni from going either], both published in *Corriere della Sera*, on 8 and 29 March respectively.
17. The expression 'but also' was attributed to Veltroni by the comedian M. Crozza who did a 'glorious impersonation of Italy's centre-left leader [...] trying to reach the widest possible constituency' (Hooper, 2008).
18. We have considered electoral – or more generally 'political' – those issues on which one or more political actors take positions by expressing their views on it.

References

Barisione, M. (2006) *L' immagine del leader. Quanto conta per gli elettori?*, Bologna: Il Mulino.

Belluati, M. (2008a) 'Una leggera febbre', *Osservatorio sulla comunicazione politica*, www.dsp.unito.it.

Belluati, M. (2008b) 'La difficoltà della politica di parlare di sicurezza in campagna elettorale (ma non solo)', paper presented at the annual meeting of the Società Italiana di Scienza Politica, Pavia, 4–6 September.

Berselli, E. (2008) 'Partito democratico o partito ipotetico', *il Mulino* 57(3): 420–431.

Blumler, J. and Kavanagh, D. (1999) 'The third age of political communication: influences and features', *Political Communication* 16: 209–230.

Bobba, G. (2008) 'Chi ha vinto la sfida per definire l'agenda? La campagna elettorale vista attraverso i temi dei telegiornali', paper presented at the annual meeting of the Società Italiana di Scienza Politica, Pavia, 4–6 September.

Briquet, J.L. and Mastropaolo, A. (eds) (2007) *Italian Politics: The Center-Left's Poisoned Victory*, New York and Oxford: Berghahn.

Calise, M. (2005) 'Presidentialization, Italian style', pp. 88–107 in T. Pogutke and P. Webb (eds), *The Presidentialization of Politics: A Comparative Study of Modern Democracies*, Oxford and New York: Oxford University Press.

Cannone, F. (2008) 'Meno male che Alitalia c'è', *Osservatorio sulla comunicazione politica*, www.dsp.unito.it.

Di Giovine, A. and Mastromarino, A. (eds) (2007) *La presidenzializzazione degli esecutivi nelle democrazie contemporanee*, Torino: Giappichelli.

De Sio, L. (2008) 'Dove stanno davvero gli elettori fluttuanti?', *Rivista Italiana di Scienza Politica*, 36: 393–414.

Diamanti, I. (2007) 'Nel Paese debole esplode la voglia di un uomo forte', *la Repubblica*, 15 July, p. 1.

Diamanti, I. (2008) 'La geografia politica di Berlusconi', *la Repubblica*, 19 May, p. 1.

Dinmore, G. (2008) 'Taking the bus with Veltroni', *Financial Times*, 6 March.

Donovan, M. and Onofri, P. (2008) 'Instabilità, antipolitica e aspirazioni di cambiamento frustrate', pp. 51–65 in M. Donovan and P. Onofri (eds) *Politica in Italia: I fatti dell'anno e le interpretazioni,* 2008 edition, Bologna: il Mulino.

Elia, L. (2006) 'La presidenzializzazione della politica', *Teoria politica* XXII: 5–11.

Feltrin, P. and Natale, P. (2008) 'Elezioni politiche 2008. Primi risultati e scenari', *Polena*, 1: 143–167.

Hallin, D.C. and Mancini, P. (2004) *Comparing Media Systems: Three Models of Media and Politics*, Cambridge: Cambridge University Press.

Hooper, J. (2008) 'The "but also" man', *The Guardian*, 8 April.

Ignazi, P. (2008) 'La destra trionfante', *il Mulino* 57(3): 432–441.

Legnante, G. (2008) 'La campagna elettorale: leader e (pochi) temi in tv', pp. 121–134 in R. Mannheimer and P. Natale (eds), *Senza più sinistra*, Milan: il Sole 24 Ore.

Mannheimer, R. and Natale, P. (eds) (2008) *Senza più sinistra*, Milan: il Sole 24 Ore.

Marini, R. (2002) 'L'agenda della campagna elettorale "lunga" 2002–2001', *Comunicazione politica* III: 81–100.

Marletti, C. (1984) 'I settimanali come «quasi partito»: ascesa e declino del giornalismo di denuncia politica', pp. 83–94 in C. Marletti (ed.), *Media e politica*, Milan: Franco Angeli.

Marletti, C. (2006) 'Campagna permanente o campagna lunga? L'exploit di Berlusconi', *Comunicazione politica* VII: 249–258.

Mazzoni, M., Ciaglia, A. and Maimone, G. (2008) 'Agenda dei media e clima di opinione nella campagna 2008', paper presented to the annual meeting of the Società Italiana di Scienza Politica, Pavia, 4–6 September.

McDonnell, D. and Splendore, S. (2008) 'Web-populism? The political communication strategies of Beppe Grillo', paper presented to the annual meeting of the Società Italiana di Scienza Politica, Pavia, 4–6 September.

Norris, P., Curtice, J., Sanders, D., Scammel, M. and Semetko Holli, A. (1999) *On Message. Communicating the Campaign*, London: Sage.

Pasquino, G. (2006) 'Quasi una rimonta', *Comunicazione politica* VII: 219–227.

Petrocik, J.R. (1996) 'Issue ownership in presidential elections with a 1980 case study', *American Journal of Political Science* 40: 825–850.

Poguntke, T. and Webb, P. (eds) (2005) *The Presidentialization of Politics: a Comparative Study of Modern Democracies*, Oxford: Oxford University Press and European Consortium for Political Research.

Roncarolo, F. (2002) 'A crisis in the mirror. Old and new elements in the change of Italian political communication', pp. 69–91 in E. Neveu and R. Kuhn (eds), *Political Journalism*, London: Routledge.

Roncarolo, F. (2008a) ' "And the winner is…": competing for votes in the print and broadcast media', pp. 156–176 in J.L. Newell (ed.), *The Italian General Election of 2006: Romano Prodi's Victory*, Manchester and New York: Manchester University Press.

Roncarolo, F. (2008b) 'The news coverage of elections in the long transition of Italian democracy', pp. 308–323 in J. Stromback and L. Lee Kaid (eds), *Handbook of Election News Coverage Around the World*, London: Routledge.

Roncarolo, F. (2008c) *Leader e media. Campagna permanente e trasformazioni della politica in Italia*, Milan: Guerini.

Roncarolo, F. and Belluati, M. (2008) 'Surfing and trying to keep afloat. The political communication process in a highly fragmented coalition led by a "great mediator"', *Modern Italy* 13: 333–348.

Vaccari, C. (2008) 'La comunicazione nella campagna elettorale 2008', *Polena* 1: 177–184.

9
The New Technologies:
the First Internet 2.0 Election

Cristopher Cepernich

«PD sei grande? mah allora anche l'unione di prodi ti è piaciuta? Svegliati, è la stessa cosa! Cambia solo il nome...il presidente del pd? È prodi!!!!! Se vuoi controlla su wikipedia!» luomodellastrada

There is a widespread and deep-rooted belief among Italy's leading politicians that on-line election campaigning is a waste of time and resources 'because elections are not won on the Internet'. Certainly, all parties, even the smallest, have web sites brimming with information for voters and journalists, and making available a range of items of election propaganda (posters, flyers, gadgets and so on). The web site of the Partito Democratico (Democratic Party, PD) even featured the one and only party-based web TV channel in Italy, inherited from the site belonging to the Democratici di Sinistra (Left Democrats, DS). However, facilities for the most innovative features of web-based activity – networking, interactivity, the creation of spaces for discussion and spontaneous participation – are either not present, or are present to a degree that is insufficient or ineffective, or else – very significantly – when they are present, they are underexploited by surfers, who seem to prefer forums and blogs that are not the expression of politics in its institutionalised form.[1] Looking at this picture of politicians who 'do not like the Internet' (Ferraro, 2000) and of surfers who are uninterested in following the campaign on line, one has the impression that parties and leaders are on the web because the absence of an on-line presence would be more negative than presence on line is positive in its effects.

Thus, during the long and fruitless wait for the frequently predicted 'first on-line election campaign' to take place in Italy (Bentivegna, 1999, 2005, 2006; De Rosa, 2000; Jacobelli, 2001; Gazziano and Longo, 2005) – following which it would be possible to say that the Internet had counted for something in terms of votes – the first generation of web technologies has been overtaken by the second: the web 2.0 era has begun. In this phase of its development, the Internet is becoming more than ever a medium *produced by participation and which produces participation*. As some far-sighted social theorists had been able to predict (Lévy, 1994; Castells, 1996; De Kerckhove, 1996; Rheingold, 2000), the age of social networks (MySpace, Facebook), of user-generated contents (YouTube, Flickr) and of shared experience and knowledge (Wikipedia) has arrived. We live in an age of viral communication, of narrow- and ego-casting (Pira and Gaudiano, 2007).

In this chapter I intend to show how, on the occasion of the 2008 race, Italian politics, which has hitherto not been very receptive to the incorporation of technological innovations in its election campaigns, made its debut in the web 2.0 arena. With this in mind, we monitored YouTube,[2] the world's largest video-sharing community, throughout the 30 days of the official campaign period, seeking to establish how the Italian parties reacted to this opportunity and with what consequences.

That time when YouTube seduced the politicians...

2007 is the fateful year in which politics joined the web 2.0 era. In March, in fact, YouTube's senior executives opened the section entitled '*You Choose "08"*', a space where US presidential candidates participating in the primary elections could upload campaign advertisements, video-taped speeches and film clips. The same day, the space was joined by all the Republican and Democratic candidates. In addition, a new section of the site was soon inaugurated – 'News and Politics' – where every White-House candidate was invited to upload a video for a week, to await comments and to respond.

On 23 July a concrete step was taken towards consolidation of the so-called uploading democracy: with the first debate, held in Charleston, South Carolina, between the eight Democratic candidates participating in the primaries, old and new media brought about the long-awaited convergence. The debate was broadcast live by CNN, but the candidates responded to questions put directly by citizens through videos uploaded onto YouTube. The experiment turned out to be a success: more than 3,000 video-taped questions were sent to YouTube, a figure that would rise to 5,000 with the second CNN/YouTube debate, which the Republican party held on 28 November in St. Petersburg, Florida.[3] Obviously, from among all the videos submitted, CNN chose a smaller number, putting about 40 of them to the candidates.

Ex-British Prime Minister, Tony Blair, was the first major European politician to have had a significant web 2.0 presence. In April 2007, he announced the debut of the Labour Party's YouTube Channel (user name: theuklabourparty). In a brief video lasting 59 seconds, Blair lives up fully to YouTube's motto – Broadcast yourself – and declares:

> The purpose of this is so that people can get a proper idea of actually what we're trying to do in the Labour Party, of what we're about, of what we've done, what we hope to do in the future, to make sure that you can get a

proper look at all the question and answer sessions so that rather than simply everything going through the media you actually get to hear what it is we're saying, an explanation of the questions that people are asking.[4]

Upstaged, his Conservative rival, David Cameron, who was overhauling his party's web site, promptly established a YouTube link of his own (Benigni, 2008).

In common with politicians in other European countries, candidates for the Spanish premiership on 9 March 2008 posted videoed advertisements on YouTube. José Luis Zapatero, leader of the Spanish Socialist Worker's Party (Partido Socialista Obrero Español, PSOE) and outgoing prime minister, launched a series of appeals – designed to translate into images the slogan, 'Vote with all your might' – featuring a number of typical voters: for example, one episode recounts the story of a girl, just 18, who is voting for the first time. In face of all the cynicism about politics expressed by her father, the girl goes onto the Internet to access the candidates' web sites and concludes: 'I may still be young, but I'm not stupid. I watch and listen to politicians'. The candidate for the Partido Popular, Mariano Rajoy, also present on YouTube, chose more traditional advertisements, ones that simulated interviews about the harsh reality of Spain's economic situation.

In Italy, web 2.0 politics was inaugurated by the leader of Italia dei Valori (Italy of Values, IdV), Antonio di Pietro. The ex-public prosecutor and symbol of the 'Clean hands' investigations of the early 1990s, has been a real pioneer in the field of web-based politics in Italy. The first in the sclerotic world of political and electoral communication in Italy to do so, he transformed his web site into a blog, taking his lead from the technological exploits of Beppe Grillo. The first to do so, on 19 December 2006 he started a YouTube channel (IDVstaff), which currently numbers 2,368 subscribers and has reached a level of almost 70,000 views, not to mention the clicks on each of the 352 videos that are available. Having, in May 2006, taken on the role of Minister for Infrastructural Development in the centre-left government of Romano Prodi, Di Pietro commented once a month on the decisions taken by the Cabinet, beginning with the meeting that took place on 19 January 2007. In all the videos, the minister appears comfortably seated in an armchair in a living-room environment, almost always controlling his typically convulsive mode of speech and his direct and forthright language. Di Pietro was the first to appear on Second Life: the cyber-minister acquired the island of Neverland in the virtual world of the Linden Labs with the aim of establishing there a branch of his party. The following day, a group of aggrieved Second-Lifers protested by organising a sit-in on the promontory where the flag of IdV was already flying. Later on, the protesters would invade Di Pietro's personal residence on Neverland.[5] On 12 July 2007 the avatar of the leader of IdV opened his party's virtual headquarters with a conference lasting over eight minutes on the theme, 'The web protects democracy'.

To this day it remains the video with the most views on the YouTube channel. It should moreover be noted that for the French presidential contest in 2007, both Nicolas Sarkozy and Ségolène Royal established election committees on Second Life. Now, however, Di Pietro has already gone further: before the start of the election campaign he made a landing on Facebook;[6] his profile currently numbers 1,270 supporters. Driven more by a need to emulate him than by real conviction, the other party leaders – Walter Veltroni (with 2,512 'friends'), Bertinotti (263), Daniela Santanchè (51), Pierferdinando Casini (37) – followed him. Meanwhile, Silvio Berlusconi – of which there are a number of profiles, none of them active – stands out for his absence. In the 'groups' section of the network, all the parties were present, even if with very few signs of campaigning activity.

The consumer-generated media are potentially a very 'weighty' resource from the point of view of election campaigning. This is because (1) they allow candidates to manage the content of their communications directly, without any mediation; (2) they make it possible to have available a channel of transmission that is free or else costs very little; (3) they allow messages to be targeted with great precision; (4) infotainment may turn out to be a more effective vehicle of political communication than others (Street, 1997; Jones, 2005; Moy et al., 2005).[7] There is, however, another side to the coin: they make it practically impossible to control one's own image, and that can be a cause of serious problems for politicians (Thompson, 1996, 2000; Lull and Hinerman, 1997; Garrard and Newell, 2006; Cepernich, 2008) – due to gaffes, for example. Among those in this category we may recall videos that have become genuine YouTube classics: for example, the seven seconds of footage which, at the G8 summit in St. Petersberg in 2007, catches President Bush appearing to massage the shoulders of Angela Merkel. The Chancellor, clearly annoyed, shakes him off brusquely. Or again: on 8 June 2007, the newly elected Sarkozy is visibly high as he holds his first official press conference at the G8 in Heiligendamm, Germany. Sarkozy appears clumsy, tired and slightly unsteady; he perspires profusely and fails to hold back gratuitous giggles. Completely obscured by French television, the video was broadcast by 'La Deux', Belgium's second TV channel, and almost immediately became one of the most-watched videos on YouTube.

What distinguishes YouTube, however, are the caricatures, which also threaten to undermine the images of public figures. Take, among the many, the example of the clip that has immortalised the Democratic Senator John Edwards who, for two interminable minutes brushes his hair with manic precision before smothering it in lacquer prior to a TV interview. The excerpt, 'I feel pretty', based upon these images, has an irresistible comic effect. Once mounted on YouTube the video attracted 600,000 views in a single day (the number now standing at 1,267,716!).

An additional threat to the control of one's own image comes, finally, from amateur videos: well known is the case of the Republican senator, George

Allen, filmed while, in front of tens of people, he directs his attention, with a sneering smile, to the one non-white person in the group, calling him a 'macaca' a couple of times before extending him a bruising, 'Welcome to America'. The video, seen by hundreds of thousands of YouTube visitors, ruined his already slim chances of running as a presidential candidate. Especially in the United States, where denigrating messages are an integral part of campaign communication strategies, the recourse to videos of this kind has gone beyond the spontaneous postings of the initial phase to become a 'professionally organised' means of political conflict. It is said, for example, that one of the reasons why Joe Lieberman was defeated by Ned Lamont in the Democratic primaries in Connecticut in 2006 was because of the video of Bush embracing Lieberman: it was tangible proof of the closeness of the Democratic senator to Bush's positions concerning the war in Iraq. The clip, uploaded and parodied by large numbers of YouTubers, still has a high profile on the site and is often given the lapidary title, 'The Kiss'.

Then again, it can happen that when clips of this kind reach a high level of visibility and notoriety within the self-referential circuit of this community, they get taken up by the mass media (television, radio and the press). Then the likelihood of them damaging the reputation of the unlucky individual concerned grows in proportion with their popular success.

The 2008 election on YouTube

In Italy, the first elections in which the fascinations of web 2.0 played a role were those of 2008. This also meant a new era for election advertisements, which the *par condicio* regulations had de facto relegated to a secondary role by preventing them from being broadcast by the national television networks during the election campaign.[8] There thus emerged alternative advertising circuits in the 'non-spaces' (Augé, 1992) areas of cities, such as the entrance halls of railway and underground stations, or else on the Internet. This, we think, has made YouTube a significant area for investigation.

It should be said at once that every party and coalition had a YouTube presence that was proportional to the effort that was expended, in this area, by its staff and its supporters (cfr. Table 9.1). The lack of attention paid by some parties to YouTube is suggested by the following figure from our research: 75 per cent of the advertisements and official videos were uploaded by users whose nicknames are suggestive not of parties or of political associations, but of single individuals. The parties that were able to count on the most energetic 'web 2.0 activists' were above all the Lega Nord (Northern League, NL) (which had 31 uploads of which 3 were at the hands of party staff) and the Union of Christian Democrats and Centre Democrats (Unione dei Democratici Cristiani e dei Democratici di Centro, UDC) (of 10 clips not one was uploaded by its headquarters staff). By contrast, the Popolo della Libertà (People of Freedom, PdL) (only one of whose four clips appeared to owe its

Table 9.1   Election advertisements on YouTube

Party	No. of election advertisements appearing on YouTube	No. of clips uploaded
Popolo della Libertà	4	4
Partito Democratico	3	7
Unione Di Centro	3	10
Alleanza Nazionale	4	4
Italia dei Valori	5	5
La Sinistra – L'Arcobaleno	6	7
Lega Nord	11	31
La Destra	3	6
Partito Socialista	2	2
Total	41	72

presence to the initiative of a single individual at the time of the survey) and IdV (for which the corresponding proportion was one of five) kept firm control of their advertisements.

However, let us come to the central question. Which of the YouTube advertisements attracted the most viewings? Which attracted the greatest attention? Which ones, through the comments they elicited, gave rise to the greatest degree of interaction in the community of Internet users? In our opinion these are important indicators because if a video elicits large numbers of comments, then that means it has acted as a catalyst of viral communication. That is, it has activated, among and beyond users of the medium, that grapevine which now features centrally in the communicative strategies characterising post-modern campaigning (Norris, 2000; Marletti, 2007). In order to answer these questions, let us consider how the 15 most-watched videos are ranked.

As one can see, the video based around the PdL's campaign theme tune is the most-watched with 335,136 views. Even when grappling with non-textual forms of communication (Hartz Søraker, 2008) Berlusconi succeeds in adopting the most effective communicative strategy, turning his – frankly somewhat trashy – party anthem into a national-popular 'hit'. 'Menomale che Silvio c'è' ('Thank goodness for Silvio'), as it is entitled, is a ballad based on a classically Italian type of melody which the author, Andrea Vantina, an aspiring singer-songwriter from Verona wrote in 2002 the day after he had witnessed what he believed had been the umpteenth television debate to denigrate Berlusconi. The piece was heard by Berlusconi some years later, but in time for the elections of 2008. The text is a calm invocation which Silvio's fan addresses to his idol (the refrain being: 'Presidente siamo con te, menomale che Silvio c'è'[9]) to achieve the hoped-for victory ('Viva l'Italia, l'Italia che ha scelto di credere ancora in questo sogno'[10]). The anthem, sung by Vantina himself, was played cheerfully before the beginning, and at the end, of every rally held by Berlusconi. It showed, however, that the individual creativity of passionate supporters had already given way to the activity of electoral communication experts. The video clip that appears on YouTube is a highly professional product: improbable film extras representing, in turn, some sellers of ice-cream, a teacher, some bakers, a building worker, a troop of call-centre telephonists and a taxi driver, all sing the Berlusconi anthem urged on by a chorus of self-confident youths who look with unshakeable conviction to a future dominated by Berlusconi's party. Superimposed on the images, the words flow past as if they were urging some sort of mass karaoke.

What also helped to make the PdL the most viewed and commented-upon party were the advertisement 'Rialzati Italia' ('Italy, arise again!') with 138,644 views and 4,841 comments and the video, 'Le prime cose da fare' ('The most urgent things to be done') with 69,620 views and 3,878 comments. The first lists the emergencies the left in government is held to have provoked for the country: excessive taxation, high prices, crime, poor health care, the garbage crisis. The finale calls viewers to action with the cry, 'Rialzati Italia!' The second is an extract from a rally, addressed by Berlusconi, during which he lists the most important things to be done once he has won the elections. The numerous views and comments attracted by advertisements such as these, which – in contrast with 'Menomale che Silvio c'è' – are so traditional as to be banal, are also to be explained by the fact that they were both promoted on the home page of YouTube's Italian site through paid-for advertising.

There is, however, an important observation to make about Berlusconi's YouTube strategy. As Table 9.2 reveals, 'Menomale che Silvio c'è' has no comments. This is certainly not because of any lack of interest shown in the video by YouTubers – on the contrary, it became a real 'hit' as we have said – but rather because the video was uploaded with the comments feature disabled. Against every moral norm constitutive of the founding spirit of the on-line community, the video could not be commented upon.

The data presented here are in line with those published by the blog, 'Elezioni Politiche 2008',[11] which, throughout the campaign, surveyed the buzz of the main political leaders engaged in the electoral competition.[12] These data show that on two specific dates (19/20 March and 9/10 April) Berlusconi suddenly almost doubled his visibility on the Internet, reaching 500,000 citations at the time of the first hike and exceeding 900,000 at the time of the second. On that occasion, Berlusconi overtook, in terms of visibility, the undisputed leader of web 2.0 politics in Italy, Di Pietro, who, in the period under observation (21 February–13 April) reached, without any retreats, around 700,000 citations. Veltroni, by contrast, came, at the campaign's most crucial moment (10 April) slightly to exceed 200,000 citations. Perhaps the campaign staff of the Veltronis of this world have no faith in the medium, or are unable to use it effectively. It is, perhaps, no accident that the PD's only YouTube success was due to the efforts of a group

Table 9.2   The 15 election advertisements most viewed on YouTube during the 2008 campaign

Advertisement	Duration	Views	Comments
Meno male che Silvio c'è (Thank goodness for Silvio) – official campaign anthem of the PdL	3'14''	335,136	0
I am PD – A tutti quelli che pensano…si può fare! (I am PD – To all those who think…yes we can!)	3'31''	210,762	1465
Rialzati Italia (Italy, arise again!) – PdL	22''	138,644	4841
Le prime cose da fare (The most urgent things to be done) – PdL	4'19''	69,620	3878
Si può fare 2008 (Yes, we can 2008) – PD	2'40''	43,962	275
Il primo incontro su Second Life (The first meeting on Second Life) – IdV	8'40''	37,233	92
Possono toglierci la vita, ma non ci toglieranno mai la libertà! (They can deprive us of our lives, but they will never take away our freedom!) – Northern League	1'03''	14,675	302
Fai una scelta di parte (Make a choice of sides) – La Sinistra – L'Arcobaleno	2'30''	12,831	147
La Destra c'è (The Right is present) – La Destra	1'15''	9204	43
Borderline – Linea di confine tra disperazione e paura (Borderline – the frontier between desparation and fear) – Northern League	6'17''	8474	83
Vi chiedo un voto per un'Italia libera e pulita (I ask for your vote to build a free and honest Italy) – IdV	1'15''	8228	49
Per ridare l'Italia agli italiani (To restore Italy to the Italians) – La Destra	33''	7733	18
Più lontani da Roma, più vicini a te – Immigrazione (Further from Rome, closer to you – immigration) – Northern League	3'02''	7330	119
Con te! (With you!) – IdV	26''	6781	35
Oggi con il Partito Democratico si può fare – Spot ufficiale PD	3'02''	6237	54

of young people who were members of a branch of the party in Milan and who, it is said, produced the video, 'I am PD', by themselves, with a budget of €65. The video became the second most viewed (210,762) and the third most commented upon (1,465) during the election campaign. We will see in the next section what the main features of this success were. The characters in this video too are representative of specific social categories: a bar keeper, a newsagent, a doctor, a musician, a large number of students and the indispensable call-centre operators, a metaphor for job insecurity among young workers. Here too there is a play on the karaoke effect, the text being superimposed on the images in time to the music to allow the viewer to sing along with the festive melody of 'YMCA' the disco classic of the designer-clad Village People.

None of the other advertisements examined exceeded the threshold of 50,000 views and they attracted a rather small number of comments: in other words, there were no other significant web 'hits'. However, there are videos upon which it is worth dwelling briefly. Another one mounted in support of Veltroni was 'Si può fare 2008' ('Yes we can, 2008'), with 43,962 views and 275 comments, which was also the result of the commitment and political enthusiasm of certain young PD voters – in this case eight communications professionals (semiologists, directors, musicians, journalists etc.). They produced an elegant clip consisting of a series of face-on shots of ordinary people and show-business stars in poses that recall the world of everyday life, while the most well-known actors vocalise particularly suggestive extracts drawn from Veltroni's speeches. This example of activism is in many respects comparable to that of the Plataforma de Apoyo a Zapatero, a group of Spanish artists and intellectuals (Pedro Almodóvar, Miguel Bosé, etc.) who, at the time of the last Spanish elections supported the PSOE leader with a very entertaining video. This associated the very simple slogan, 'Yo estoy con Zapatero', with the hand gesture that is used in sign language to indicate the socialist leader's name and which, by means of the index finger being drawn to the eyes, reproduces the unusual triangular shape of the premier's eyebrows.

As has already been said, the most-watched video among the more than 350 which Di Pietro has so far uploaded to his YouTube channel is the one that shows the press conference to inaugurate IdV's Second Life headquarters (with 37,233 views and 92 comments) – thus demonstrating that integration and convergence between new media can have significant effects. By contrast, the video successes of the Lega Nord (Northern League, NL) are explained in a completely different way, being due, in one respect, to features strongly evocative of issues of social identity, above all membership of 'the Padanian people'. An example of this is the clip 'Possono toglierci la vita, ma non ci toglieranno mai la libertà!' ('They can deprive us of our lives but they will never take away our freedom!') with 14,675 views and 302 comments, a video adopting an epic tone and a fictional theme set in a fantasy world of chivalry which re-evokes the courage and determination with which the peoples of northern Italy defended their autonomy from the invaders during the age of the communes. In another respect, the NL's success is due to its ability to echo some of the most deeply rooted attitudes of a section of Italian voters: Thus, the video 'Borderline – Linea di confine tra disperazione e paura' ('Borderline – the frontier between desperation and fear') with 8,474 views and 82 comments and a good example of 'docufiction' lasting 6 minutes and 14 seconds, opens with a young woman, who is writing a letter: 'The letter will probably sit on this or some other desk without ever being read. But the anger and fear I experience every day deserve to be shouted about just as they deserve to be listened to. Because I am afraid'. At this point, fiction gives way to documentary material with interviews with ordinary people about hot topics such as crime, the cost of living, increasingly widespread poverty, the difficulty of finding a job and having a family, illegal immigration, prostitution, drugs. The girl is destined never to send her letter, but an anonymous figure wearing a tie in the green of 'Padania' symbolically transforms it into a vote for the NL.

YouTube: 'forum for debate' or 'terrace at a football stadium'?

Having mapped out the contours of the election propaganda present on YouTube, let us now examine how, from the point of view of the style and content of their communications, YouTubers interacted with this material. That is, let us consider whether, to what extent and how this material provided the basis for discussion of political and election issues. In order to do this we have concentrated our attention on 'I am PD', the video clip produced by the young Milanese activists belonging to Veltroni's party, and 'Borderline', the docufiction produced by the NL.

These videos are especially indicative and that is for at least two separate reasons. The first is that neither are official campaign advertisements, but clips produced by young activists or sympathisers familiar with the language of this genre: the MTV generation, in short, has come of age. It is no accident, we believe, that neither of the other election videos that became on-line 'hits' ('Si può fare 2008', and also, in part, 'Menomale che Silvio c'è') were the product of advertising agency talents. These videos, moreover, display not the usual point of view of politicians regarding ideas and programmes for the future, but rather, they are a portrayal of politics given, by groups of citizen-electors, to other citizen-electors. Is this a loss of the parties' monopoly on propaganda? Perhaps, but it is the highest expression of election-campaign narrowcasting. In the second place, by exploiting the logic of viral communication they, and especially the PD's video, had great success on the web, succeeding, as they did, in breaking down the barriers surrounding the self-referential communication of the on-line community, obtaining visibility and eliciting reactions through the traditional media (the press and television) too, thus reinforcing interpersonal election communication through informal grapevines.

The first step in this part of the enquiry involved analysing how the YouTubers posting comments on the two videos were aligned – if indeed they were – politically.[13] 33 per cent of the postings elicited by 'I am PD' could be attributed to people who in all probability were PD supporters. 26 per cent seemed to come from people who supported other parties, while 41 per cent – the majority – left no indication of their voting intentions or political affiliations. This obviously does not mean that they had no affiliations, but simply that we cannot know if they have any, and if so, what they are. The figure regarding the NL clip is also interesting: here, in fact, the comments of League supporters constitute the majority (39 per cent), with those posted by individuals expressing an intention to vote for an alternative party making up 27 per cent, those whose authors' affiliations are un-discernible, 34 per cent. This allows us to suggest that the traditional fidelity of League supporters to the ideals embodied by Bossi's party and the deep-rooted sense of belonging to the 'Padanian' community, can have effects as much in the virtual world with its absence of place, as in the off-line world.

Now let us consider how visitors engaged with the political content of the video. Let us preface this by pointing out that to view a YouTube advertisement is very different from seeing it on television: in the first case, in fact, individuals 'search out' the video instead of themselves 'being searched out'. Viewing a YouTube clip is the consequence of a pro-active stance towards the medium, driving the individual's intention to watch. That is to say that, in our opinion, there is a fundamentally political dimension to the action of one who sets out to watch these clips. In this respect, given that the type of political communication involved is highly theatrical and is sometimes a form of infotainment, it is not important to establish whether, in deciding to watch the video, the individual is driven primarily by a playful intent, by simple curiosity or by a logic of political mobilisation.

Let us now see how YouTubers engaged with the clips, beginning with the PD's advertisement (cfr. Table 9.3). Two figures strike one immediately: most of the comments posted by YouTubers supporting the PD (26 per cent) contain appeals to vote for Veltroni and the PD because their victory is possible as well as desirable. That is, they are a form of election campaigning. By contrast, the most recurring themes in the comments posted by those without apparent affiliations (40 per cent) or who support other parties, whether of the right, the centre or the extreme left (24 per cent), concern the aesthetic qualities of the video rather than its political content (including criticisms of its superficiality, lack of seriousness, ridiculous qualities, and so on).

However, even among the comments posted by PD supporters, the 'aesthetic question' has a larger place than the political if one takes account both of the 20 per cent expressing appreciation and of the 7 per cent expressing disapproval. In short, from the point of view of the audience, the infotainment formula seems to be the one best adapted to the medium and the target viewers, namely, the young and the very young users of YouTube.

The practice of attacking and insulting the leaders and supporters of the opposing line up is widespread: 12 per cent of the comments posted by PD

Table 9.3   Characteristics of comments on the video 'I am PD'

PD supporters	%	Party support unknown	%	Supporters of other parties	%
Appeals to vote for the PD	26	Criticisms of the video/satirical comments	40	Criticisms of the video/satirical comments	24
Expressions of appreciation of the video	20	Anti-political invective and arguments	10	Appeals to vote for another party	15
Criticisms and attacks on Berlusconi and his policies	12	Expressions of appreciation of the video	7	Insults and attacks directed at PD voters	13
Insults and attacks against centre and centre-right voters	9	Accusations of 'Veltrusconismo' (i.e., of being in cahoots with the PdL)	5	Attacks and insults directed at Veltroni (self-righteousness, opportunism etc.)	12
Criticisms of the video/satirical comments	7	Italy as a ridiculous country, in decline, without hope	4	Negative comments on the alliance decisions of the PD	7
Criticisms of the video, 'Menomale che Silvio c'è'	4	Requests for or provision of information about technical aspects of the video (names of the authors, those appearing in it, title of the theme tune etc.)	4	Attacks against the policies of the Ulivo and of Prodi (taxation, the garbage crisis, etc.)	4
Requests for or provision of information about technical aspects of the video (names of the authors, those appearing in it, title of the theme tune etc.)	2	Insults directed at the authors of the video	4	Insults directed at the authors of the video	3
Praise for voluntary political activity and expressions of commitment	2	Criticisms of the excessive and/or growing 'show-biz' qualities of politics	3	Homophobic remarks	3
Appeals to electors not to abstain	2	Appeals for a more serious style of politics	3	Accusations of 'Veltrusconismo' (i.e., of being in cahoots with the PdL)	2
Other	16		30		17

Note: N = 1465

supporters attacked Silvio Berlusconi personally as well as his policies, while 9 per cent contained generic attacks against those voting for the entrepreneur or his allies. From the other side of the left-right divide, 12 and 13 per cent of the comments respectively focus on Veltroni's supporters and on him as a prime-ministerial candidate – variously accusing him of being self-righteous, an opportunist, a liar, of having performed badly as mayor of Rome, and so on. Not a few of the comments of non-PD supporters criticise the electoral decisions of the new party of the left (7 per cent) – that is, the decision to exclude from the alliance the parties of the radical left and instead to include IdV and the Radicals of Emma Bonino and Marco Pannella – as well as the policies pursued by the Prodi government, above all the excessive tax burden (4 per cent). The 3 per cent containing attacks on homosexuals is explained by the fact that the YMCA music is a well-known icon within gay culture.

Finally, among the comments posted by those not openly affiliated with a party, the 10 per cent containing assertions classifiable as anti-political stand out. Such comments lay at the feet of the 'cast' of politicians generally responsibility for the grave problems afflicting the country, and protest against the waste and excessive costs of politics and the inadequacies of the Italian political class. To these can be added the 5 per cent expressing the view that there is no difference between Veltroni and Berlusconi because politicians 'are all the same'. This is a position that was well captured by the neologism 'Veltrusconismo' coined during the election campaign by the 'unwanted third party', Pierferdinando Casini. 3 per cent of the comments are not obviously anti-political but do call for a 'new', 'more serious' kind of politics.

Systematic scrutiny of the comments would show, in this author's opinion, that among the YouTubers without an obvious party-political placement, there are, besides a small number indifferent to political debate, a certain small percentage of centrist voters, supporters of Casini's UDC, but, more especially, a significant number of 'grillini', that is, supporters and faithful followers of the comedian Beppe Grillo and his anti-political proselytising activity – activity for the most part carried on through his widely followed blog. Finally, it is interesting to note that some of the comments – 3 per cent – complain about the excessive and growing 'show-biz' qualities of politics.[14]

Let us now examine the comments posted in relation to the video 'Borderline' (Table 9.4). League activists and sympathisers, not unlike their PD counterparts, have as their foremost thought encouraging members of the on-line community to vote for 'their' party (24 per cent). In our view this is a significant finding because it confirms that the new media are often approached with cognitive frameworks that are still the product of the old media. It may be the case that 'modernity is inseparable from its "own" media' (Giddens, 1991: 24) but it cannot fail to surprise to see the web used

Table 9.4　Characteristics of comments on the video 'Borderline' (Northern League)

League supporters	%	Party support unknown	%	Supporters of other parties	%
Appeals to vote for the League	24	Positive comments on the video	21	Defence of foreigners	23
Accusations of criminality against foreigners	15	Denunciations of urban decay and insecurity	21	Xenophic comments	14
Xenophic comments	9	Arguments defending foreigners	10	Criticisms of the video	12
Invocazioni e richiami alla Padania	7	Claims that the video is factually accurate	8	Insults aimed at League supporters	9
Appeals to help disseminate the video	7	Expressions of pessimism about the future	8	Anti-political arguments and invective	9
Claims that the video is factually accurate	6	Accusations of criminality against foreigners	6	Arguments and invective against Padania	6
Expressions of appreciation of the video	6	Anti-political arguments and invective	6	Claims that the video is factually accurate even though the author is not a League supporter	6
Denunciations of urban decay and insecurity	4	Calls for more effective crime-prevention measures	3	Expressions of opposition to policies of prohibition concerning drugs	6
Appeals for change	4	Complaints about excessive numbers of foreigners (but without labelling them as criminals)	3	Accusations that the traditional media give excessive emphasis to crimes committed by foreigners	3
Others	18		18		12

Note: N = 82

as if it were a megaphone. Consistently with the theme of the clip, 15 per cent of the posted comments take aim at foreigners, making them a scapegoat for rising crime and urban decay; 9 per cent of the comments contain xenophobic abuse. Finally 6 per cent express the view that the content of the video is highly accurate; 7 per cent express the hope that it will be circulated more widely; 6 per cent simply express appreciation for its good quality.

Among the non-aligned too, large numbers express appreciation of 'Borderline': 21 per cent of the comments in fact manifest approval of the form or the content. Indeed the profile of the non-aligned that emerges is one of individuals who are rather sensitive to the issue of security and criminality, since 21 per cent of the comments contain a denunciation of urban decay and manifest the widespread feeling of fear and insecurity; 8 per cent assert that the situation described in the film is confirmed by actual facts. Moreover, 6 per cent of those aligned with other parties believe that the video accurately mirrors reality. It is unclear whether they are of the left or the right. Among those aligned with other parties however, those presenting arguments in defence of foreigners (23 per cent) predominate. The arguments range from the need to distinguish between crime and immigration, to the usefulness of foreigners for the Italian economy and the importance of solidarity as a fundamental value. Xenophobic comments (14 per cent) are almost always accompanied by expressions of attachment to the party, La Destra, or other neo-fascist organisations.

Finally, the data shown in Figure 9.1 help to throw light on the rhetorical and debating styles that are prevalent in the interaction of YouTubers with the up-loaders of the videos and with other members of the on-line community. The data show that, in the election campaign-context, the prevailing model of interaction among participants is one based on symbolic warfare between antagonists rather than on discussion and dialogue. Not unlike what happens in a stadium during a football match, different factions engage each other in close, emblematic combat fuelled by: rigid assertions over whose content there is hardly ever any room for negotiation; yelling designed to lay claim to 'the last word'; 'head-on' insults; satire and glowering. Both videos attract comments the largest proportion of which are written like slogans and contain rigid assertions, unqualified statements and screams: 48 per cent in the case of the PD video, 44 per cent in the case

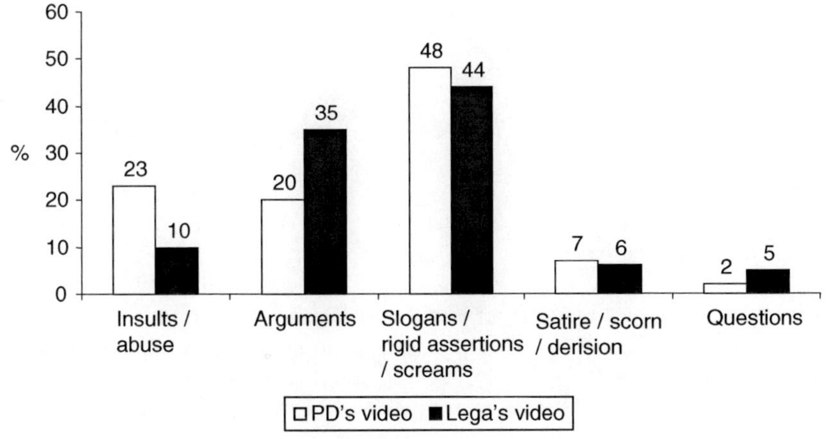

Figure 9.1   The rhetorical and debating styles shown by YouTube comments

of the video uploaded by the NL. This finding is to some extent explicable in terms of the 'fast' and 'liquid' nature of the medium. The same can be said for the satirical comments and the expressions of scorn and derision (practically the same in the two cases: 7 and 6 per cent).

The comments that contain slightly more thoughtful arguments amount to 35 per cent for 'Borderline' and only 20 per cent for 'I am PD'. This is an interesting difference, one that could be due to the different *genres* of the two clips: infotainment in the case of 'I am PD' versus the 'docufiction' of 'Borderline'. In order not to overstate the case, we will simply suggest that while the former may have led YouTubers to express themselves more – and perhaps more superficially – about the aesthetic qualities of the video, drawing attention away from the campaign issues that it did nevertheless raise, the second may have more successfully placed in the foreground the topic of the video rather than the video itself. This would then explain the lesser 'football-terrace' effect produced by the League's video – only 10 per cent of the comments contained insults – compared to that of the PD, which attracted comments 23 per cent of which contained insults towards PD voters and the authors of the video.

Conclusion

The data generated by this research show that only to a very small extent did YouTube prove to be a forum for the discussion of political issues. Those who had for this campaign seen in YouTube a new channel of democratic narrowcasting were brought up short by various items of empirical evidence. First, Silvio Berlusconi, great communicator and favourite to win the election, bought up advertising banners on YouTube and disabled the 'comments' option in connection with his most effective clip. True, a handful of the most determined YouTubers fully exploited the specific features of the medium and, through the tens of satirical videos and photographs they posted, made their comments regardless; other keen users resorted to repeated unauthorised uploads that were promptly blacked out; but thereby the crowded grandstand of those who *write* their comments was lost. The second piece of evidence concerns the members of the on-line community, who so far seem to have adapted to the logic of the new medium in some respects, but not in others: for the most part they show a preference for a rapid, sloganistic style of communication, which is sometimes creative but which in only a very few cases has a deliberative intention or can be considered genuinely informed and informative. Far more often campaign participation via YouTube takes place through slogans, insults and diatribe rather than through the creation of opportunities for dialogue and discussion. Notwithstanding the prospect of an end to the centrality of television (Menduni, 2007) it seems that the categories and cognitive frameworks that guide the communicative activities of those that plan election campaigns and – what is worse – of the citizens that follow them are still those peculiar to the old media. In the context of an election campaign, users of YouTube divide along lines corresponding to externally produced cleavages, especially those of political affiliation, and do battle with each other through the blows of slogans and insults, aligning themselves according to a logic of 'for or against' in ways not unlike those in which football supporters cheer on their favourite team. This leads us to conclude that a genuine network culture does not yet seem to be very widespread (Castells, 2001; Castells and Cardoso, 2006; Terranova, 2008).

Translated by James L. Newell

Notes

1. See, for example, the research carried out by Spindoc.it.
2. YouTube hosts 48.5 per cent of the videos present on the web with a monthly share of visitors amounting to 60 per cent (Nielsen data / NetRatings, February 2008). This means that every month more than 70 million people access the site from all over the world. Visitors consist predominantly of the young and the very young. For a detailed account of the YouTube phenomenon see Benigni (2008), and for an anthropological reading see Wesch (2008).
3. Research conducted by the Pew Center for The People and the Press (2007) reveals that in the US about 15 per cent of adult users of the Internet have seen or downloaded videos with a political content, with 2 per cent of respondents claiming to do so 'on a typical day'. Particularly successful is political satire – such as the caricature of the Clintons in the last episode of the series, 'The Sopranos'; 'I got a crush on Obama'; 'John McCain joking about bombing Iran', and the recording of John Edwards as he combs his hair lovingly before an interview. Over 44 per cent of the American public has heard of at least one of these videos, while 27 per cent has seen at least one. But the most interesting figure is the following: 68 per cent of respondents say they prefer questions to the candidates to be put by ordinary citizens rather than by journalists.
4. The video can be seen by clicking on the following link: http://it.youtube.com/watch?v=gul2U43solE. It had, at the time of writing, attracted 32,887 views.
5. Cfr. G. Nicoletti in *La Stampa*, 2 March 2007, p. 9; *La Stampa*, 3 March 2007, p. 7.
6. This is a social networking tool, created in 2004 by Mark Zuckerberg, originally with the intention of facilitating the efforts of old school and university friends to keep in touch with each other. Today Facebook is, in terms of number of members, the seventh largest social networking facility in the world, allowing users to stay in contact with friends, to make new friends, to upload an unlimited number of photographs and to share links and videos.
7. Another investigation carried out by the Pew Research Center (as cited by Vaccari, 2007) reveals that in the United States 61 per cent of citizens between 18 and 29 years of age and 39 per cent of those aged between 30 and 49 claim to obtain political information from light entertainment and comedy shows.
8. Law no. 28 of 22 February 2000, known as the *par condicio* law, was passed with the aim of assuring equality of treatment and impartiality for all political actors during election campaigns following Silvio Berlusconi's decision to 'take to the field' in 1994 (Cepernich, 2009).
9. 'Mr President we're behind you; Thank goodness for Silvio'.

10. 'Long live Italy, the Italy that has chosen still to believe in this dream'.
11. 'Elezioni Politiche 2008' is a blog devoted to the measurement and analysis of the on-line buzz of the 'social media' in relation to political parties and issues. See http://www.elezioni-politiche-2008.com
12. In the world of marketing, the term 'buzz' is used to indicate the 'noise' or 'stir', created by the way in which a message is spread by word of mouth within a social network. This viral marketing strategy makes it possible to reach, in the least time possible, what is called the 'swarm', that is, a group of users who, with respect to a theme, or a category of products or services, are homogeneous in terms of their interests.
13. The data are obtained by means of content analysis of the comments: sometimes their authors state their political affiliations explicitly; at other times they do so implicitly through what they say or through their nicknames. In any case, they do so in accordance with rather precise conventions that would be worth investigating further (Lange, 2008).
14. The percentages given in the last row in Table 9.3 and in Table 9.4 are made up of the sum of response types that, individually, have a maximum frequency of 3 per cent.

References

Augé, M. (1992) *Non-lieux*, Paris: Seuil.
Benigni, G. (2008) *La storia di YouTube*, Milan: Magazzini Salani.
Bentivegna, S. (1999) *La politica in rete*, Rome: Meltemi.
Bentivegna, S. (2005) *Politica e nuove tecnologie della comunicazione*, Rome: Laterza.
Bentivegna, S. (2006) *Campagne elettorali in rete*, Rome: Laterza.
Castells, M. (1996) *The Rise of the Network Society*, Oxford: Blackwell.
Castells, M. (2001) *The Internet Galaxy*, Oxford: Oxford University Press.
Castells, M. and Cardoso G. (2006) *The Network Society. From Knowledge to Policy*, Washington: Center for Transatlantic Relations and Johns Hopkins University.
Cepernich, C. (2008) *Le pietre d'inciampo. Lo scandalo come meccanismo sociale*, Rome: Aracne Editrice.
Cepernich, C. (2009) 'The changing face of media', in D. Albertazzi, C. Brook, C. Ross, and N. Rothenberg (eds), *Resisting the Tide. Cultures of Opposition in the Berlusconi Years*, London and New York: Continuum.
De Kerckhove, D. (1996) *Connected Intelligence. The Arrival of the Web Society*, Toronto: Somerville.
De Rosa, R. (2000) *Fare politica in Internet*, Milan: Apogeo.
Ferraro, G. (2000) 'La politica non ama internet? L'impiego della rete nella campagna elettorale', pp. 187–202 in M. Livolsi and U. Volli (eds), *Personalizzazione e distacco*, Milan: FrancoAngeli.
Garrard, J. and Newell, J.L. (eds) (2006) *Scandals in Past and Contemporary Politics*, Manchester and New York: Manchester University Press.
Gazziano, S. and Longo, L. (2005) *Internet e politica 2005. La rete e le elezioni: e se davvero la rivoluzione non fosse più in tv?*, Rome: BCM Editrice.
Giddens, A. (1991) *Modernity and Self Identity: Self and Society in the Late Modera Age*, Stanford: Stanford University Press.
Hartz Søraker, J. (2008) 'Global freedom of expression within nontextual frameworks', *The Information Society* 24: 40–46.
Jacobelli, J. (ed.) (2001) *Politica e internet*, Soveria Mannelli: Rubbettino.

Jones, J. (2005) *Entertaining Politics. New Political Television and Civic Culture*, Lanham, MD: Rowman & Littlefield.

Lange, P.G. (2008) 'Publicly private and privately public: social networking on Youtube', *Journal of Computer-mediated Communication* 13: 361–380.

Lévy, P. (1994) *L'intelligence collective. Pour une antropologie du cyberspace*, Paris: La Découverte.

Lull, J. and Hinerman, S. (eds) (1997) *Media Scandals. Morality and Desire in the Popular Culture Marketplace*, Cambridge: Polity Press.

Marletti, C. (ed) (2007) *Il leader postmoderno*, Milan: FrancoAngeli.

Menduni, E. (2007) *Fine delle trasmissioni. Da Pippo Baudo a YouTube*, Bologna: il Mulino.

Moy, P., Xenos, M. and Hess, V. (2005) 'Communication and citizenship. Mapping the political effects of infotainment', *Mass Communication & Society* 8(2): 11–131.

Norris, P. (2000) *A Virtuous Circle. Political Communication in Postindustrial Societies*, Cambridge: Cambridge University Press.

Pew Research Center for The People and the Press (2007) *Uploading Democracy: Candidates Field Youtube Questions*, http://people-press.org

Pira, F. and Gaudiano, L. (eds) (2007) *La nuova comunicazione politica. Dal volantino al blog, dalla radio a Second Life: strumenti, strategie e scenari*, Milan: FrancoAngeli.

Rheingold, H. (2000) *The Virtual Community*, Cambridge, MA: MIT Press.

Rheingold, H. (2003) *Smart Mobs. The Next Social Revolution*, Cambridge, MA: Perseus Books.

Street, J. (1997) *Politics & Popular Culture*, Cambridge: Polity Press.

Terranova, T. (2006) *Cultura Network*, Rome: Manifestolibri.

Thompson, J.B. (1996) *The Media and Modernity. A Social Theory of the Media*, Cambridge: Polity Press.

Thompson, J.B. (2000) *Political Scandal. Power and Visibility in the Media Age*, Cambridge: Polity Press.

Vaccari, C. (2007) *La comunicazione politica negli USA*, Rome: Carocci.

Wesch, M. (2008) 'An anthropological introduction to YouTube', lecture delivered at the Library of Congress, 23 June, video on http://www.youtube.com

Part IV
The Outcome

10
Italian Voters: Berlusconi's Victory and the 'New' Italian Party System

Alessandro Chiaramonte

From Prodi to Berlusconi

The traumatic breakdown of the centre-left coalition supporting the Prodi government, and the consequent early dissolution of Parliament, left no doubts about who would be the winner of the new elections. Silvio Berlusconi, and with him the alliance of the centre right, would present themselves once again as the stable alternative to the hotchpotch of parties of the left and centre left, which had demonstrated, if ever there had been any need, that they were incapable of governing together. The echo of the conflicts between the parties forming the Prodi government was, besides, already highly audible and was reflected in popularity ratings that were at minimum levels both for the coalition as a whole and for its leader and out-going Prime Minister. In this situation, Berlusconi would have an easy time getting the better of a battered opponent and, therefore, overturning the election result of just two years previously – which had, however, essentially been a tie.

Yet, at a certain point during the election campaign, it seemed that the outcome favourable to the centre right was not such a foregone conclusion after all. The impression, subsequently revealed to be fallacious, was one to which a series of factors contributed. They included, first, the novelties concerning the composition of the competing coalitions. There had been a veritable earthquake on the side of the political supply, giving rise to a number of uncertainties about how the electorate would respond. In particular, the decision of the Partito Democratico (Democratic Party, PD) to run in coalition only with Italia dei Valori (Italy of Values, IdV), excluding the parties of the radical left, had led to the creation of a 'rival show' in the shape of the list fielded by the Popolo della Libertà (People of Freedom, PdL) – consisting of Forza Italia (FI), Alleanza Nazionale (the National Alliance, AN) and a number of minor parties – and the decision of this new political entity to ally only with the territorial parties of the North – the Lega Nord (Northern League, NL) – and the South – the Movimento per le Autonomie (the Movement for Autonomy, MPA) – leaving the Unione dei Democratici Cristiani e dei Democratici di Centro (Union of Christian Democrats and Centre Democrats, UDC) to its fate. In the second place, the capacity of the PD leader, Walter Veltroni, to plan an election campaign of a prospective type – thus attempting to distinguish the destiny of the 'new' centre left coalition led by him from the already known and ill-fated one of the 'old' coalition headed by Prodi – resulted in a campaign that, at least initially, seemed to work. In the third place, uncertainty was increased by an electoral system, the one for the Senate, which seemed to have been conceived on purpose to prevent anyone from obtaining a solid majority of seats, above all in the case of close competition between two coalitions and/or between a number of coalitions or lists capable of overcoming the exclusion thresholds in the various regions.[1]

It was no accident that, on the afternoon the votes were counted, everyone's attention was focused on the outcome of the Senate election. This was less because a come-back by the centre left – the likelihood of which was believed in by only a few incurably optimistic supporters of that coalition – could realistically have undermined the expected result. Rather, it was because precisely in the Senate (but only here) the 'lottery' (D'Alimonte, 2007: 72–79) of the majority premiums, distributed region by region, might have prevented Berlusconi's coalition from obtaining a majority any larger than the one obtained by Prodi's coalition in 2006 – or even from obtaining an absolute majority at all. As the count proceeded, the outcome revealed itself to be what it was: a victory by a wide margin for Berlusconi's centre right which, in terms of votes, led the centre left by more than nine percentage points and, above all, obtained a solid majority in the Senate as well.

In order to understand how the centre right's victory came about, it is necessary to give a more detailed account of the significant changes that took place in the nature of the political supply, that is, how the various parties and coalitions are made up, as compared to only two years previously (section 2) and of the results of the Chamber and Senate elections with reference to the votes and seats obtained by the coalitions and the party lists (section 3). After that, we will seek to pin-point the principal factors that explain how the centre right was able decisively to overturn the defeat at the preceding elections and re-establish its control over the government of the country, focusing in particular on the effects of the restructuring of the supply of lists and coalitions and on the changes in voting preferences between 2006 and 2008 (section 4). Finally, we shall conclude by analysing the profound transformation which the Italian party system overall underwent at these elections, asking ourselves whether this is the contingent result of a largely unique set of circumstances, not to be repeated, or the latest phase in a process of structural change now under way for 15 years (section 5).

The 'earthquake' in the supply

The most sensational aspect of the general election of 2008 was surely the 'earthquake' that shook the supply of coalitions and lists. As far as the first are concerned, in the space of two years extra-large coalitions gave way to coalitions that were much less broad – both from the point of view of the number of parties they encompassed and from the point of view of the ideological distance between the parties. As for the lists, in the overwhelming majority of cases their denominations and their symbols are completely new.

Among the many novelties that were apparent on the side of supply in the elections of 2008, the first and perhaps the most important – because of the chain reaction it would provoke – was the electoral debut of the PD, born in 2007 from the merger of the Democratici di Sinistra (Left Democrats, DS) and the Margherita, with a leadership – that of Veltroni – legitimated by a direct vote (the so-called primaries) which saw the participation of no fewer than 3.5 million people.

The birth and the presentation of the unified list of the PdL, consisting of FI, AN and a number of minor formations, was almost a reflex action. In the intentions of Berlusconi and its other promoters, it represented, *in nuce*, the 'single' party of the centre right that would present itself as the direct alternative to the PD.

The other novelties of the electoral supply of 2008 derive from the decision of Veltroni to contest the elections separately from the parties of the 'radical' left and others, including in a coalition with the PD only the list fielded by Antonio Di Pietro (IdV).

Berlusconi took advantage of this, choosing not to ally with Pierferdinando Casini's UDC (which had previously refused to join the PdL) or with Clemente Mastella's UDEUR (which had in the meantime left the alliance of the centre left), but only with territorial parties like the NL and the MPA.

Three electoral cartels were then formed by the main parties that had been excluded by the two principal line-ups. The aim being to maximise the possibilities of overcoming the four per cent national threshold for the Chamber and the eight per cent threshold in each of the regions for the Senate, the cartels were: (1) La Sinistra-L'Arcobaleno (Rainbow Left, SA) which brought together the parties of the 'radical' left (RC, the PdCI, the Greens); (2) l'Unione di Centro (the Union of the Centre), that is, the alliance between the UDC and the Rosa bianca (White rose), which in practice was nothing other than a reunification a short time after a split within the UDC itself (it is no accident that the name of the alliance was Unione di Centro, whose acronym is precisely UDC); (3) la Destra-FT (the Right-Tricoloured Flame), which incorporated a number of pre-existing formations located in the area of the extreme right, together with a group of individual political figures then on their way out of AN.

The only two coalitions to be formed – Veltroni's on the centre left and Berlusconi's on the centre right – consisted of two and three lists respectively (in reality, from the point of view of the voters, the centre-right coalition too was composed of only two lists since where the PdL was allied with the NL, the MPA was absent and where it was allied with the MPA, the NL was absent). For the rest, as we have seen, there were only individual lists (even if they were formed of a number of parties), each of which was seeking to overcome the exclusion thresholds. This was a situation that was very different to the one in 2006 when the two coalitions consisted of 12 lists each.

Overall, then, the supply of lists and coalitions represented an absolute novelty, comparable almost to that of the elections of 1994 save only for the already tried and tested leadership of Berlusconi in the centre-right camp. But the degree of novelty was, as we have said, very significant. It is enough to bear in mind that all or almost all the labels for the various lists were appearing for the first time: PD, PdL, SA, la Destra, even UDC (as the Unione di Centro). Among the principal formations only the NL and Di Pietro's IdV ran using symbols already known to voters.

The results of the Chamber and Senate contests

Analysis of the results of the elections overall needs to distinguish not only what happened in the Chamber and the Senate, but also between what happened in the various arenas within which seats are assigned in the two branches of Parliament. The results of the election for the Chamber given in Table 10.1 are thus shown separately for the three arenas of which it is composed: the one in which the vote distribution determines the possible assignment of the majority premium; the single-member college of Valle d'Aosta, and the 'overseas' constituency.

The first of these arenas is the decisive one: here 617 of the total of 630 seats are at stake – as are the minimum of 340 seats that automatically go to the list or coalition with the largest number of votes. In other words, the line-up that wins here, even if it is by a margin of just one vote, obtains an absolute majority of seats. The margin of votes by which the coalition led by Berlusconi outstripped the one led by Veltroni was however much greater: the centre right obtained more than 17 million votes (46.8 per cent), while the centre left did not go much beyond 13.5 million votes (37.5 per cent), with a difference of about 3.5 million votes, equal to 9.3 per cent. This bore no comparison with the mere 24,755 vote difference (less than 0.1 per cent of the total of over 38 million valid votes) by which the Unione beat the Casa delle Libertà (CdL) in 2006. Overall, in the case of the Chamber, the final outcome of the distribution of seats was 344 for the centre right, 247 for the centre left, 36 for the UDC, 2 for the Südtirolervolkspartei (South Tyrolese People's Party, SVP and one seat for the movement for Italians resident abroad.

Table 10.1 Election results, Chamber of Deputies 2008

Lists/coalitions	ITALY (Majority Premium)				VALLE D'AOSTA		FOREIGN CONSTITUENCY		TOTAL	
	Votes		Seats		Votes	Seats	Votes	Seats	Votes	Seats
	No.	%	No.	%	No.	No.	No.	No.	No.	No.
PdL	13,629,089	37.4	272	44.1	13,877	0	314,357	4	13,957,323	276
Lega Nord	3,024,758	8.3	60	9.7	2,322	0	–	–	3,027,080	60
MPA	410,487	1.1	8	1.3	–	–	–	–	410,487	8
BERLUSCONI's coalition (tot.)	17,064,334	46.8	340	55.1	16,199	0	314,357	4	17,394,890	344
PD	12,092,969	33.2	211	34.2	–	–	331,567	6	12,424,536	217
IdV-Di Pietro	1,593,532	4.4	28	4.5	–	–	41,589	–	1,635,121	29
Aut. Lib. Dem.	–	–	–	–	29,311	1			29,311	1
VELTRONI's coalition (tot.)	13,686,501	37.5	239	38.7	29,311	1	373,156	7	14,088,968	247
UDC	2,050,309	5.6	36	5.8	–	–	81,450	0	2,131,759	36
La Sinistra L'Arcobaleno	1,124,428	3.1	0	0.0	–	–	28,353	0	1,152,781	0
La Destra-FT	885,226	2.4	0	0.0	–	–	14,609	0	899,835	0
PS	355,575	1.0	0	0.0	–	–	31,774	0	387,349	0
PCdL	208,173	0.6	0	0.0	–	–	–	–	208,173	0
SC	167,664	0.5	0	0.0	–	–	5,973	0	173,637	0
SVP	147,666	0.4	2	0.3	–	–	–	–	147,666	2
Italians resident abroad	–	–	–	–	–	–	83,585	1	83,585	1
OTHERS (tot.)	762,410	2.1	0	0.0	29,415	0	79,829	0	871,654	0
TOTAL	36,452,286	100.0	617	100.0	74,925	1	1,013,086	12	37,540,297	630

As far as the Senate elections are concerned, Table 10.2 shows the results for the 'domestic' and the 'overseas' segments separately. Within the national territory, the centre right won in all the regions in which the majority premium was at stake, with the exception of the traditional strongholds of the left (the four regions of the 'red belt' – Emilia Romagna, Tuscany, Umbria, Marche – plus Basilicata); and in winning 171 seats, it thereby obtained the absolute majority of senators. In addition, the centre right obtained three of the six senators representing the constituency reserved for Italians resident abroad – precisely the arena which had been responsible for the centre left's slender victory at the 2006 election (Chiaramonte, 2008). In total, then, the coalition led by Berlusconi could count on 174 seats, against 134 accruing to the alliance of the PD and IdV, 3 to the UDC, 2 to the SVP and one seat each to the movement for Italians resident abroad and the Vallee d'Aoste.

In contrast to 2006, this time the electoral system for the Senate did not prevent the winning coalition from obtaining a solid majority of seats and it did not therefore lead to government fragility. This was not, however, due to any particular virtues of the law, but rather to the change in the balance of power between the line-ups. Above all, it was due to the fact that many individual lists failed to reach the eight per cent regional thresholds. Such lists included the SA and the Destra-FT in every region, and also the UDC, which obtained seats only in Sicily, the result being to bring about the over-representation in Parliament of both the coalition of the centre right and the coalition of the centre left.

The elections of 2008 produced a clear and unambiguous result, one comparable – among the elections of the Italian transition – perhaps only to that of 2001. The line-up headed by Berlusconi obtained a large majority both in the Chamber and in the Senate, which should give the new Government – which also has the advantage of being composed only of the PdL and the NL – protection from the blackmail that in contrast undermined the preceding Prodi government. The fourth Berlusconi government was thus born in the most favourable circumstances, from the point of view of its own power, that had ever existed in the history of the Italian republic.

The votes cast for lists and coalitions between 2006 and 2008

The clear victory of Berlusconi and his coalition was essentially the product of the combination of two factors: the profound change in the nature of the political supply and the change in voters' preferences.

To begin with, the effects of the change in supply – which we have already described above – were very significant. Here, one has to bear in mind the loss of support to which the new coalitions of centre left and centre right were potentially subject thanks to their having broken the alliance with the radical left and the UDEUR on the one hand, and with the UDC and

Table 10.2 Election results, Senate 2008

| | ITALY | | | | FOREIGN CONSTITUENCY | | TOTAL | |
| | Votes | | Seats | | Votes | Seats | Votes | Seats |
Lists/coalitions	No.	%	No.	%	No.	No.	No.	No.
PdL	12,678,790	38.0	144	46.6	315,720	3	12,994,510	147
Lega Nord	2,644,247	7.9	25	8.1	–	–	2,644,247	25
MPA	355,076	1.1	2	0.6	–	–	355,076	2
BERLUSCONI's coalition (tot.)	15,678,113	46.9	171	55.3	315,720	3	15,993,833	174
PD	11,061,578	33.1	116	37.5	308,157	2	11,369,735	118
IdV-Di Pietro	1,414,118	4.2	14	4.5	37,985	0	1,452,103	14
SVP-Insieme autonomie	153,965	0.5	2	0.6			153,965	2
Aut. Lib. Dem.	26,375	0.1	–	–			26,375	0
VELTRONI's coalition (tot.)	12,656,036	37.9	132	42.7	346,142	2	13,002,178	134
UDC	1,898,886	5.7	3	1.0	55,450	0	1,954,336	3
La Sinistra L'Arcobaleno	1,093,135	3.3	0	0.0	26,664	0	1,119,799	0
La Destra-FT	703,685	2.1	0	0.0	12,929	0	716,614	0
PS	284,802	0.9	0	0.0	27,385	0	312,187	0
PCdL	180,454	0.5	0	0.0	–	–	180,454	0
SC	136,396	0.4	0	0.0	5,837	0	142,233	0
SVP	98,947	0.3	2	0.6	–	–	98,947	2
Vallee d'Aoste	29,186	0.1	1	0.3	–	–	29,186	1
Italians resident abroad	–	–	–	–	69,279	1	69,279	1
OTHERS (tot.)	636,556	1.9	0	0.0	70,057	0	706,613	0
TOTAL	33,396,196	100.0	309	100.0	929,463	6	34,325,659	315

the extreme right, on the other. This meant that the centre left 'gave up' approximately 15 per cent of the total of valid votes obtained in 2006;[2] for the centre right it meant 'giving up' about 8.5 per cent of that same total.[3] Considering that in 2006 the two coalitions – the Unione and the CdL – had for all practical purposes obtained the same number of votes, the tightening of the coalitional boundaries carried out by both in view of the elections of 2008 brought an advantage to the centre right of about 6.5 percentage points (precisely the difference between 15 per cent and 8.5 per cent, the theoretical 'sacrifices' of Veltroni and Berlusconi). In other words, the 'earthquake' on the side of the political supply, due to the competitive strategies adopted by the PD and the PdL, in itself altered the balance of power between the two main competitors, transforming what in 2006 had been substantially a tie into a large advantage for the centre right.

In order to win, Veltroni would thus have had to close this vote gap. He would have had to do it either by considerably broadening his base of support or else by hoping for a significant reduction in the base of support underpinning the coalition led by Berlusconi. It was not to be.

True, the PD/IdV coalition succeeded in enlarging its reservoir of support, above all thanks to IdV which almost doubled the number of votes it had obtained two years earlier. But it did it to an insufficient degree. Above all, the votes were not ones lost by Berlusconi's coalition, in which the PdL almost completely 'summed' the votes of its component parties, and the NL achieved the considerable feat of obtaining over three million votes, going from the 4.6 per cent of 2006 (with the MPA) to the 8.3 per cent of 2008 (without it). As a result of these gains, the gap between Berlusconi's centre right and Veltroni's centre left grew rather than diminished, passing from a theoretical value in 2006 of 6.5 per cent to an actual value in 2008 of 9.3 per cent.

Under these circumstances, the PD/IdV coalition, though losing the election, did not perform badly, even though Veltroni's hopes were for a completely different outcome. Comparison of the votes of 2006 with those of 2008 (Table 10.3) shows, however, that the electorate was without mercy in its treatment of the centre left as a whole – which lost almost 3.5 million electors as compared to just two years previously. Probably disappointed by the behaviour of their respective parties during the life of the Prodi government, most of these electors certainly abstained – as can be deduced both from the fall in turnout (down to 80.5 from 83.6 per cent) and from the first estimates of the flow of the vote made on the basis of both ecological (De Sio, 2008) and individual-level data (Feltrin and Natale, 2008). But another portion changed its voting behaviour, choosing the UDC (which, however, lost votes overall to the PdL) or a list belonging to Berlusconi's coalition. Such behaviour appears, however, to have been confined to certain areas of the South, confirming the fact that this is the only geographical area of the country where vote flows of any significance take place directly between the centre left and centre right.

Table 10.3 Vote and list differences 2006–2008, Chamber of Deputies

Lists 2008	Votes 2008		Lists 2006	Votes 2006		Difference 2008–2006	
	No.	%		No.	%	No.	%
La Sinistra L'Arcobaleno	1,124,428	3.1	Rifondazione Comunista	2,229,464	5.8	−2,398,129	−6.1
PCdL	208,173	0.6	PdCI	884,127	2.3		
SC	167,664	0.5	Greens	784,803	2.1		
IdV–Di Pietro	1,593,532	4.4	IdV–Di Pietro	877,052	2.3	+716,480	+2.1
PD	12,092,969	33.2	L'Ulivo	11,930,983	31.3	−588,199	−0.0
PS	355,575	1.0	Rosa nel Pugno	990,694	2.6		
			Socialisti Craxi	115,066	0.3		
SVP	147,666	0.4	SVP	182,704	0.5	−35,038	−0.1
			UDEUR	534,088	1.4	−534,088	−1.4
Centre-left Area	15,690,007	43.1		18,528,981	48.6	−3,483,806	−5.5
UDC	2,050,309	5.6	UDC	2,580,190	6.8	−529,881	−1.1
PdL	13,629,089	37.4	Forza Italia	9,048,976	23.7	−745,765	−0.3
			Alleanza Nazionale	4,707,126	12.3		
			Partito Pensionati	333,278	0.9		
			Dc–N.Psi	285,474	0.7		
Lega Nord	3,024,758	8.3	Lega Nord–MPA	1,747,730	4.6	+1,687,515	+4.8
MPA	410,487	1.1					
La Destra–FT	885,226	2.4	Alternativa Sociale	255,354	0.7	+399,366	+1.2
			Fiamma Tricolore	230,506	0.6		
Centre-right Area	19,999,869	54.8		19,188,634	50.3	+811,235	+4.5
Other lists	762,410	2.1	Other lists	435,728	1.1	+326,682	+1.0
Total valid votes	36,452,286	100.0	Total valid votes	38,153,343	100.0	−1,701,057	

The formation that paid the heaviest price for the general retreat of the centre left was the SA cartel, the victim of an outcome that was all the more spectacular for being so totally unexpected in terms of its dimensions. In 2006, RC, the Greens and the PdCI had together obtained 10.2 per cent of the vote in the election for the Chamber and 72 seats. In 2008 they obtained 3.1 per cent and no seats,[4] remaining, as they did, below the four per cent threshold. Even adding to the SA's votes those obtained by two formations that had broken away from RC – namely, the Partito Comunista dei Lavoratori (the Workers' Communist Party, PCdL) (0.6%) and Sinistra Critica (Critical Left) (0.5%) – it remains that case that the cartel lost almost two thirds of the support that the founding parties had obtained just two years before, equivalent to 2.4 million voters. The evenness in the geographical distribution of the losses sustained suggests that the SA's target electorate almost completely rejected the political project which the list itself represented, or at least that it rejected the mode and the timing of its construction. Analysis of the flows of the vote (De Sio, 2008; Feltrin and Natale, 2008) indicate, moreover, that of the 2.4 million voters moving away from the SA, about half abstained and half shifted towards the PD or IdV. A part of these latter probably cast a tactical vote, choosing not the party they most preferred but the one they least disliked among those having a realistic possibility of winning the majority premium and thus of governing.

The Italian electorate's turn to the right is shown by the centre right's growth in size of over 800,000 votes as compared to the elections of 2006, a very significant figure considering the large fall in turn-out. Thus, the 'weight' of the centre right with respect to the overall total of valid votes rose from about 50 to about 55 per cent.

Berlusconi's victory derives from this: from having known how to build a coalition sufficiently broad to enable him to maintain the position he had conquered in 2006 and then to capture additional votes both within his own field of reference – above all at the expense of the UDC, a part of whose supporters defected in the name of a 'useful' vote – and in the camp of his opponent by exploiting the change in the climate of opinion that many of the pre-election polls had already registered. Berlusconi knew how to 'read' exactly how things were going. And in these circumstances the extent to which Veltroni's was a 'mission impossible' emerges even more clearly.

A 'new' party system?

Looking at the party system that emerged from the elections of 2008, leads to the doubt that it has anything in common with the one that took shape during the course of the long Italian transition or even the one that characterised the last short legislature. Indeed, in making the comparison one has the sensation that one is looking at two different countries. The elections of 2008 present the picture of an Italian political system with two large formations – the PD and the PdL – which together account for more than 70 per cent of the votes and 78 per cent of the seats; with a parliament in which essentially five or six parties are represented and which is thus moderately fragmented; with a government composed of just two political entities – the PdL and the NL – and which enjoys a large majority in both chambers. There is no comparison with the Italian political system of just a few months before, with the two largest parties – the DS and FI – counting 43 per cent of the votes and seats between them;[5] with 19 parties represented in the Chamber of Deputies, in which there were no fewer than 11 parliamentary groups; with a government whose ministers belonged to eight different parties (and no fewer than 12 if we include the under-secretaries) and which, in addition, had a wafer-thin majority in the Senate, something that de facto conferred a disproportionate power of blackmail (to determine the life or the death of the government) not only on each party component of the coalition, but on each individual senator.

Until before the last elections, the Italian party system displayed levels of electoral and party fragmentation comparable, among the long-consolidated democracies, only with those of Belgium and Israel, countries which, however, have a structure of social and political cleavages much finer and more complex than the one in Italy. After the last elections, the level of fragmentation went down dramatically, reaching the average values for the consolidated democracies. As Figure 10.1 shows, in 2008, the effective number of electoral and parliamentary parties (Laakso and Taagepera, 1979)

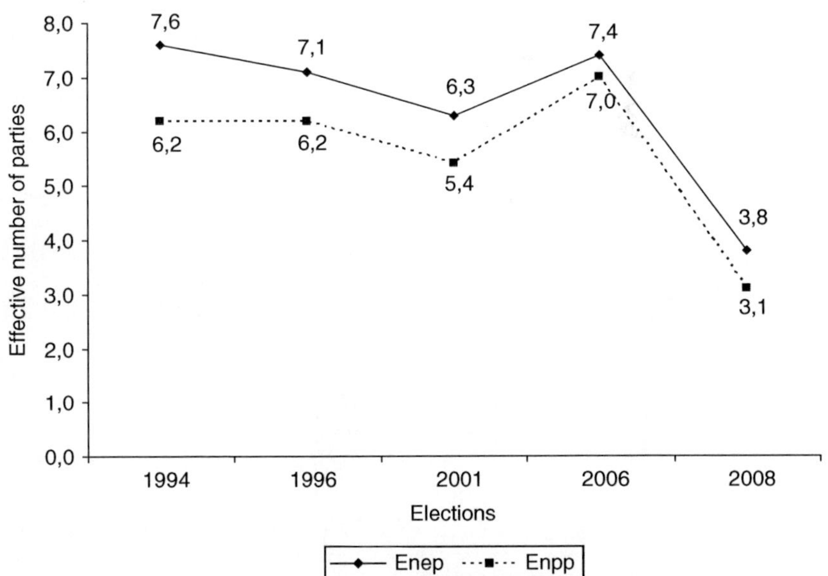

Figure 10.1   Effective number of electoral (Enep) and parliamentary (Enpp) parties, Chamber of Deputies 1994–2008

declined to the lowest level registered at any of the elections of the Italian transition (that is, from 1994), and indeed it has halved when compared to just two years ago.

Assuming that the PdL becomes before long a genuinely single entity – as the leaders of FI and AN, Berlusconi and Gianfranco Fini, have publicly hoped for – rather than remaining a mere electoral cartel, the Italian party system is, then, characterised (or would then be characterised) by the presence of two 'large' parties – precisely the PD and the PdL – whose absence has for too long been lamented. As already recalled, there has been a shift from a bi-party concentration equal to 43 per cent after the election of 2006 (and after every Italian election starting in 1994) to one of 70 per cent in terms of votes and 78 per cent in terms of seats in 2008 (Figure 10.2). To make a comparison with the other large European democracies: the two largest parties in France (following the 2007 election) account for 64.3 per cent of the votes and 86.5 per cent of the seats; in the United Kingdom (following the 2005 election) for 67.6 per cent of the votes and 85.9 per cent of the seats; in Germany (following the 2005 election) for 69.4 per cent of the votes and 73 per cent of the seats; in Spain (following the election of 2008) for 83.7 per cent of the votes and 92.3 per cent of the seats. In other words,

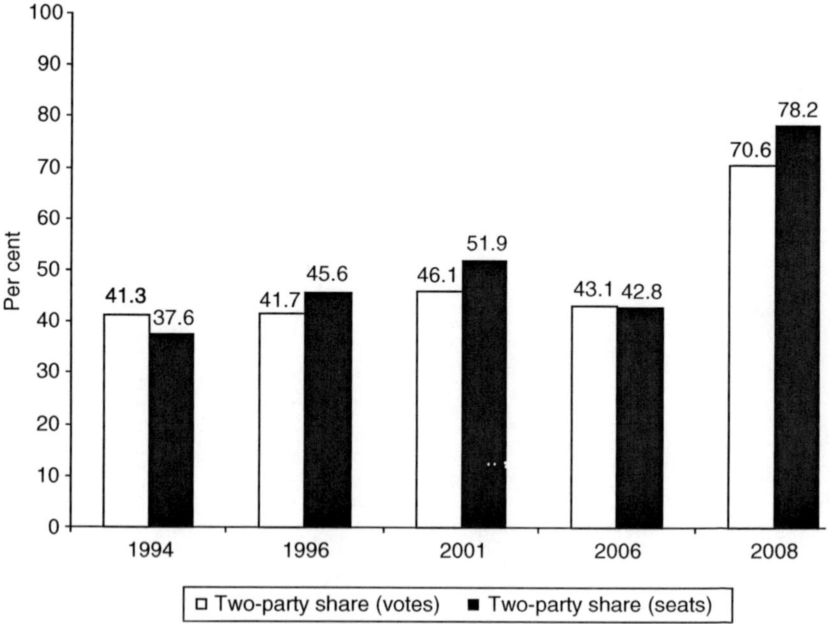

Figure 10.2 Concentration of votes and seats on the two largest parties, Chamber of Deputies 1994–2008

the overall size (in votes) of the two largest Italian parties is now in line with – if not, indeed, above – that of countries like France, the United Kingdom and Germany and significantly lower only than that of Spain; the overall size in seats is however above that of Germany, even though it does not reach the levels of France, the United Kingdom and Spain, which, however, have electoral systems that tend to over-represent the two largest parties to a much greater degree than does the Italian system.[6]

From another point of view, the elections of 2008 mark a retreat in the degree of bipolarism of the party system. After almost continuous growth from 1994, culminating in a level of concentration of votes and seats on the two largest coalitions equal to almost 100 per cent in 2006, in 2008 the combined votes of the two principal coalitions, those led by Berlusconi and Veltroni, dropped to 83.3 per cent – the lowest level, if one leaves aside the 'first' elections, those of 1994, of the period of the Italian transition. Meanwhile the combined seats fell to 93.8 per cent – below 2001 and 2006 (Figure 10.3).

In short, in 2008 less fragmentation, but also less bipolarism was apparent. On the other hand, the preceding elections had witnessed an increase of bipolarism and fragmentation. It is confirmation that, in the Italian

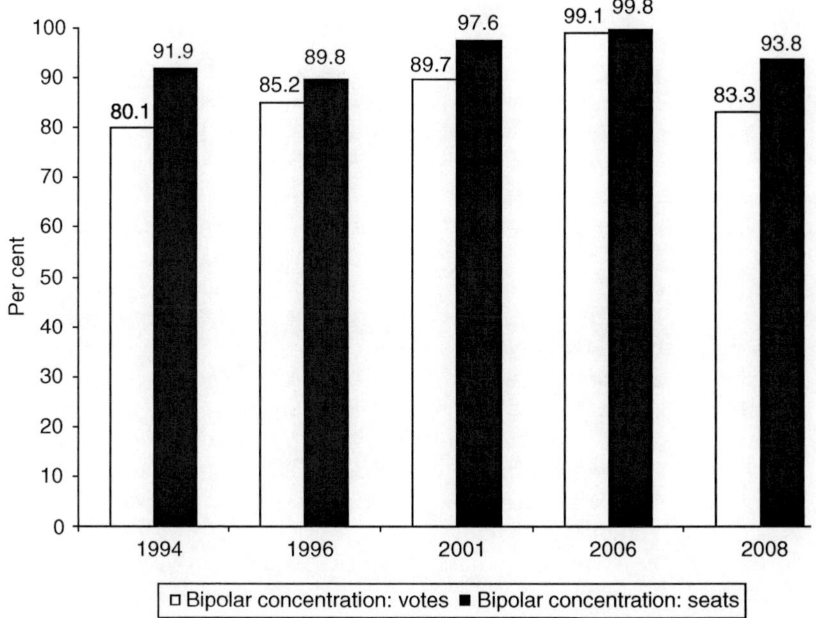

Figure 10.3   Bipolar concentration of votes and seats, Chamber of Deputies 1994–2008

transition, the two phenomena have always been inextricably linked. The consolidation of a fully bi-polar format has, in other words, been possible by virtue of a strategic coordination among the elites that has given priority to the inclusiveness of their coalitions over their homogeneity, thereby perpetuating and even encouraging party fragmentation (Chiaramonte, 2007).

Given this situation, after the 2006 elections, we wrote that

'in order to reduce the party fragmentation, the electoral system should be changed in such a way as to allow the larger parties of both line-ups to leave the minor parties to their fate – to under-representation or, even, no representation. One should, that is, avoid, giving an incentive to the broadest possible pre-electoral alliances, as in fact happens now through the assignment of a majority premium to the coalition that obtains the most votes' (Chiaramonte, 2007: 404).

Since then, and within the space of a few months, the larger parties have been reinforced – thanks to the birth of the PD and the PdL – and these have decided to form selective, no-longer catch-all, coalitions, excluding political forces like the parties of the radical left (subsequently excluded from Parliament) and the UDC (which was also significantly reduced in size, above all in the Senate). All this happened, however, in the absence of any electoral reform: how can it be explained?

The problem is to understand, in other words, if the party system that emerged from the 2008 elections is amenable to consolidation without institutional modifications to support it, or if it constitutes an exceptional and probably non-repeatable deviation with respect to that 'fragmented bipolar' format that had been becoming increasingly consolidated starting from the elections of 1994 until those of 2006 (Bartolini, Chiaramonte and D'Alimonte, 2004; Di Virgilio, 2006; Chiaramonte, 2007).

The incentive to create broad coalitions produced by the majority premium has often been emphasised, since – at least in the Chamber contest – it results in a national competition for the conquest of the largest number of votes and thus the absolute majority of seats. In the event that all have coalition potential, are driven by short-term rationality – that is, they are interested in the result of the current elections – and are office-seekers, the parties will thus tend to construct minimum winning coalitions. The 'breadth' of a coalition will thus be a function of the balance of power between the potential line-ups competing for victory.

In light of these considerations, it is understandable why, in 2006, the competing line-ups were so broad and omni-inclusive: since the competition was so close, even the few votes that a small party was able to contribute to a coalition would turn out to be decisive (and so it was, in effect); in other words, competition for the government of the country ensured that the parties – all the parties, even the smallest – had a mutual interest in coming together, to the point that no party capable of mobilising even as little as one per cent of the vote remained outside one of the two coalitions.

The action taken by Berlusconi in view of the elections of 2008 is also understandable – both the creation of the PdL – to counteract the PD's aspirations to the status of largest party – and, above all, the shrinking of the coalition's boundaries and thus the exclusion of the UDC. This had become a partner that was no longer necessary for victory after the 'old' centre left had disintegrated bearing in mind that the new PD-IdV alliance would not have represented a serious threat to the electoral victory. That is, in the new political situation that had come to be created with the breakdown of the alliance to the left, the UDC ended up paying for the loss of 'decisiveness' that its position and its votes had in the past had for the centre right line-up. And Berlusconi immediately called in his loan, freeing himself of an unruly partner that had in the meantime become superfluous.

Less understandable, but only apparently so, is the strategy pursued by Veltroni. It is entirely evident that the 'slimming down' of the centre left resulting from the exit of a wide range of parties, in particular those of the so-called radical left and Mastella's UDEUR, placed the line-up in a situation of clear disadvantage in relation to its opponents and thus reduced the possibility of victory even more. But Veltroni's intention was to reshuffle the cards, presenting himself as the leader of a great party with a 'majoritarian vocation' capable of governing alone or at the most with the support only of IdV, no longer a victim of the blackmail of the smaller parties located on its left and its right. He wanted to present himself at the head of a party and of an alliance that was restricted – but that was capable, however, both of attracting votes further to the left – through the appeal for a 'useful' vote, in contrast to a vote 'wasted' on formations without a hope of obtaining seats or seeing off Berlusconi's coalition – and of breaking through to the centre of the political spectrum, finally capturing the votes of that moderate sector of the electorate, without which aiming at success is unthinkable.

Veltroni's strategy was courageous, but ultimately the only one feasible in the specific political circumstances. Given the negative experience of the Prodi government, a re-edition of any coalition like that of 2006 would have been a losing proposition from the outset. *Perso per perso*, Veltroni aimed high, seeking to change the coalitional game and to attract new electors on different bases. He did not succeed in obtaining much: true, he drained off a significant proportion of the votes to his left – contributing to the debacle of the SA – but he was not able the channel the votes potentially available through demobilisation of the most disappointed of the voters of the left – who took refuge in abstention – nor even to capture a significant proportion of centrist voters. However much weight should be attributed to the unpopularity of the outgoing government in explaining the combined result of the PD and IdV, there is too little that is positive in the outcome for them that would justify the future maintenance of this format for the alliance of the centre left. On the contrary, if things remain as they are, it is difficult to imagine how the centre left could win again.

In short, the simplification of the political format which the elections of 2008 brought with them derives from a chain reaction set off by the decision of the PD to run practically alone, upon which followed the creation of the PdL, the exclusion of the UDC from the centre right, and the failure of the parties of the radical left, of the extreme right, of the UDEUR (which did not even field any candidates) and of a plethora of micro parties to achieve parliamentary representation. Given the nevertheless unfavourable results (holding little promise even for the future) which the PD's choice produced, it is legitimate to doubt the suggestion that the party system that has emerged from the last elections constitutes a situation of equilibrium. It is, in other words, legitimate to doubt that the PD will in the future be able to do without the votes of the radical left, and/or of the centrist formations and/or of the territorial or personal parties, which would thereby be allowed to re-join the political game, reproducing to a certain degree the vices of the lack of cohesion between allies and the fragmentation of the system that are familiar and that might seem only temporarily to have been put aside.[7] The only hope of avoiding a return to the worst of what we have witnessed in the recent past thus remains the path of institutional (and not only electoral) reform. In this legislature more than in those of the past, the conditions exist to enable the reforms to be enacted. It is now up to the Italian political class not to miss this opportunity.

Translated by James L. Newell

Notes

1. It is worth remembering that the electoral systems in place for the 2008 elections were the same as those used for the elections of 2006 and that they were the product of a 2005 reform introduced by Berlusconi and his centre-right coalition. Though based on the same principles of representation – that is, proportionality modified by the award of a majority premium – the systems for the Chamber and Senate differ from each other in a number of important ways. The most important concerns precisely the majority premium: in the Chamber it is designed in such a way as to attribute, automatically, a share equivalent to 55 per cent of the total number of seats to the coalition or the list with the largest number of votes. In the Senate, on the other hand, instead of being awarded on the national level, it is assigned in each region separately (with the exception of the regions of Trentino-Alto Adige, Molise and the Valle d'Aosta). This means that in the Chamber there is always a winner with 55 per cent of the seats, while in the Senate, this can by no means be regarded as certain. Given Italy's system of symmetrical bicameralism, with governments requiring the confidence of both chambers, it is not difficult to imagine the consequences: indeed

the outcome of the 2006 elections – with the centre left victorious in the Senate by a margin of only two seats – is one that reminds us of this. For a more detailed analysis of the electoral systems currently in force in Italy and of their potential effects, see: D'Alimonte and Chiaramonte (2006); D'Alimonte (2007); Chiaramonte (2008).

2. The figure reported here (15 per cent) takes account not only of the parties of the radical left (RC, the PdCI, the Greens) and of UDEUR, but also of other minor formations excluded from the coalition. These include the socialist component (subsequently the Socialist Party) of the Rosa nel Pugno (Rose in the Fist) and the Pensioners' Party, which transferred its allegiance to the PdL.

3. In this case too, the reported figure (8.5 per cent) takes account of the various minor formations left out of the coalition in addition to the principal exclusions – in this case, the UDC and the extreme right parties (Fiamma Tricolore and Alternativa Sociale notwithstanding the decision of the leader of the latter – Alessandra Mussolini – finally to join the PdL).

4. Having failed to obtain any seats, even in the Senate, the SA parties were excluded from Parliament entirely. As a result, Parliament is without any component still calling itself 'communist': it is the first time in the history of the Italian republic that this has happened.

5. Even if one took account of the emergence of the PD – and therefore of the fact that the Ulivo was present at the 2006 elections as a unified party entity – the combined percentages of the PD-Ulivo and FI would have been 55 in terms of votes and 57.9 in terms of seats, still very far from those of 2008.

6. It should be recalled, however that the level of bi-party concentration in terms of seats at the elections (78.2 per cent) is the highest of all the elections of the Italian republic, higher even than the 77.8 per cent achieved by the Christian Democrats and the Italian Communist Party at the election of 1976.

7. These considerations are equally applicable to the PdL on the other side of the left-right divide. It is, however, worth emphasising that consolidation of the PdL and the PD would constitute a dyke in the way of a return to levels of fragmentation like those present at past elections.

References

Bartolini, S., Chiaramonte, A. and D'Alimonte, R. (2004) 'The Italian party system between parties and coalitions', *West European Politics* 27(1): 1–19.

Chiaramonte, A. (2007) 'Il nuovo sistema partitico italiano tra bipolarismo e frammentazione', pp. 369–407 in R. D'Alimonte and A. Chiaramonte (eds), *Proporzionale ma non solo. Le elezioni politiche del 2006*, Bologna: Il Mulino.

Chiaramonte, A. (2008) 'How Prodi's Unione won by a handful of votes', pp. 203–222 in J.L. Newell (ed.), *The Italian General Election of 2006: Romano Prodi's Victory*, Manchester and New York: Manchester University Press.

D'Alimonte, R. (2007) 'Il nuovo sistema elettorale. Dal collegio uninominale al premio di maggioranza', pp. 51–88 in R. D'Alimonte and A. Chiaramonte (eds), *Proporzionale ma non solo. Le elezioni politiche del 2006*, Bologna: Il Mulino.

D'Alimonte, R. and Chiaramonte, A. (2006) 'Proporzionale ma non solo. La riforma elettorale della Casa delle libertà', *Il Mulino* 56(1): 34–45.

De Sio, L. (2008) 'Elettori in movimento', paper presented to the workshop, 'Elezioni del 14–15 aprile 2008: prime analisi' organised by Sise (Società Italiana di Studi Elettorali), Florence, 14 May, www.studielettorali.it.

Di Virgilio, A. (2006) 'Dal cambiamento dei partiti all'evoluzione del sistema partit-ico', pp. 173–206 in L. Morlino and M. Tarchi (eds), *Partiti e caso italiano*, Bologna: Il Mulino.

Feltrin, P. and Natale, P. (2008) 'Elezioni politiche 2008. Primi risultati e scenari', *Polena* 5(1): 143–167.

Laakso, M. and Taagepera, R. (1979) 'Effective number of parties: a measure with application to West Europe', *Comparative Political Studies* 12(1): 3–27.

11
A Different Legislature?
The Parliamentary Scene Following
the 2008 Elections

Federico Russo and Luca Verzichelli

Introduction: premises and promises of the XVI legislature

A number of the chapters in this volume, from different perspectives and using a variety of data, have already shed light on the peculiar outcomes of an election whose results were both decisive and largely expected. However, the longer-term implications of the election are, for the most part, difficult to decipher: The changes in the nature of the electoral supply and in the configuration of the party system would suggest the likelihood of a number of possible interesting developments in terms of the composition of Parliament, in the emergence of a new pattern of executive-legislative relationships and, in the longer term, in the overall mode of functioning of the political system. But to what extent are such possibilities likely to come to pass?

While the chapter by Gianfranco Pasquino deals with the most immediately relevant political consequence of the election – the formation of the new centre-right executive – in this chapter we will focus on the prospects for change in the parliamentary arena. Of course, our task is a difficult one since – writing a few weeks after the start of the legislature – we can more or less only guess, rather than evaluate on the basis of solid data, what is going on within the parliamentary institutions. However, there are a number of indicators that will help us to understand the respects in which the parliamentary environment has changed. Our starting question will therefore be as simple as it is ambitious: how different is the profile of the XVI legislature in comparison to those of legislatures of the recent past?

If our initial (and to a large extent still impressionistic) answer to the above question is confirmed, then we will be authorised to think that the XVI legislature is destined to be a crucial one, and that in the years ahead political actors will be able, after almost 15 years of regime transition, to put an end to some of the uncertainties that continue to overshadow the political system (Grilli di Cortona, 2007).

But such exploratory work as we will carry out here can also help us redefine research questions and agendas in a broader category of studies of the Italian political system – including elite studies and legislative studies. During the last ten years, our knowledge of the elements of change (as well as a number of elements of resilience and continuity) in parliamentary practices and processes has been augmented by a number of empirical contributions (Giuliani, 2008). However, a satisfactory general interpretation of the present role and performance of the Italian parliament – a traditionally grounded, institutionalised and very influential one – is still far from being achieved. Our goal is therefore to capture the essence of what is new about the legislative term that has just begun in order to evaluate it and the changes that can be expected to take place because of it.

Given these questions and goals, we shall proceed as follows: in the next section we will describe the principal contours of the XVI legislature, using simple indicators of party fragmentation and the concentration of power in the hands of the most relevant Parliamentary Groups (PGs). Subsequently, we will examine more closely the social backgrounds and political profiles of the parliamentary elite elected in 2008, in order to understand how much it has changed in comparison to the recent past. A third focus will be on some preliminary data concerning parliamentary activities, namely legislative initiatives and parliamentary questions, in order to establish the extent to which the period since the election has seen the emergence of an 'adversarial' pattern of interaction between two cohesive bodies, the majority and the opposition.

Quasi Westminster? The parliamentary setting following the 2008 elections

Our initial analysis concerns the magnitude of change in the patterns of political representation characterising the new legislature. Some of the data concerning the winners and losers of the 2008 elections have already been discussed by other contributors to this volume; but here we focus on the actors now represented in the parliamentary arena: Table 11.1 provides some basic descriptive information concerning the degree of political fragmentation, comparing the two legislatures elected on the basis of the electoral system, combining proportional representation with a majority premium, that was introduced in 2005.

The data reflect, unambiguously, the striking reduction in political fragmentation that has taken place thanks to the 2008 election. In absolute terms, the number of PGs in both chambers is the lowest since the war and decline in fragmentation also emerges when the more revealing indicator, the effective number of parties, is considered. The magnitude of the electoral change that took place in 2008 is even more evident when we deploy a measure of 'two-party concentration', the percentage of seats in

Table 11.1 Fragmentation in the parliamentary arena: Parties and parliamentary groups, 2006–2008

		2006			2008		
		N	ENP	% seats accounted for by two largest PGs	N	ENP	% seats accounted for by two largest PGs
Parties	Lower Chamber	20	7.5		9	3.1	
	Senate	18	6.7		10	2.7	
PGs	Lower Chamber	12 (13)	5.0 (5.5)	55.9 (51.9)	5	2.9	77.9
	Senate	9 (10)	4.9 (5.5)	53.4 (48.8)	5	2.7	82.3

Note: The Effective Number of parties (ENP) is found using the well-known Laakso and Tagepeera (1979) index of fragmentation. The unit of analysis, 'parties' includes all the parties which joined cartel lists or whose candidates were 'hosted' by and elected through lists fielded by other parties. The numbers given for PGs do not include the residual *gruppo misto* ('mixed group'). The figures in parentheses refer to the end of the XV legislature.

Source: Authors' elaboration of official data drawn from www.parlamento.it

each chamber accounted for by the two largest groups. Indeed, after the two historic elections of 1948 (which saw the impressive victory of the Christian Democrats (DC) over the 'Popular Front') and 1976 (when the concentration of votes on the DC and the Italian Communist Party reached its greatest extent) the overall size of the two largest PGs was less than 75 per cent in the Chamber and lower than 80 per cent in the Senate. Therefore, we can argue that in formal terms, the parliamentary profile that emerged in 2008 represents the most authentically 'Westminster-like' in Italian democratic history.

Another important suggestion emerges when we consider the growing parliamentary fragmentation that characterised the XV legislature. As is well known, this was due to the defection from their groups of origin of a large number of parliamentarians as a result of the birth of the Partito Democratico (Democratic Party, PD) in October 2007, and also to a number of individual switches to and from other parties. After the new elections, the reduction in the number of small parties in the centre of the spectrum and the disappearance of groups and components on the extreme wings should have reduced the opportunities for mobility of the parliamentary elite, and this allows us to argue that an important step in the direction of a more robust two-party format within Parliament has been taken, notwithstanding the positive results achieved by the Lega Nord (Northern League, NL) and Italia dei Valori (Italy of Values, IdV). However, some time will be required before the validity of this argument can be ascertained, as it will depend on how stable the two large Popolo della Libertà (PdL) and PD groupings, created at the beginning of the XVI legislature, turn out to be.

Data concerning institutional arrangements relevant to the work of Parliament at the beginning of the legislature also confirm the impression of a solid trend towards simplification in the Italian chambers. If we focus on the 'super-elite' consisting of those parliamentarians holding office in one of the legislature's institutions (Table 11.2), we have evidence of another important implication of the electoral change of 2008 for the daily life of Parliament: the concentration of agenda-setting powers in the hands of a leadership which, insofar as it is drawn mainly from the largest governmental actor (the PdL) and the largest opposition party (PD) is more homogeneous than before. Moreover, if we measure the distribution of these offices in terms of a weighted index of fragmentation of the PGs represented among the office holders, we are able to quantify the radical change the XVI legislature has brought with it – with its significant concentration of 'institutional power'

Table 11.2   Party distribution of office holders within Parliament, 2006 and 2008

	2006		2008	
	Lower Chamber	**Senate**	**Lower Chamber**	**Senate**
Speaker	1 RC	1 U	1 PdL	1 PdL
Deputy Speaker	2 U, 1 FI, 1 AN	1 U, 1 LN, 1 RC, 1 UDC	2 PdL, 1 PD, 1 UDC	2 PdL, 2 PD
Questors	1 U, 1 FI, 1 M	1 FI, 1 U, 1 M	2 PdL, 1 PD	1 PdL, 1 LN, 1 PD
Secretaries	3 U, 2 FI, 2 AN, 2 IdV, 1 RC, 1 LN, 5 M	3 U, 2 FI, 1 AN, 1 IU, 1 UDC, 2 M	4 PdL, 4 PD, 1 IdV, 1 LN, 1 M	4 PD, 3 PdL, 1 LN
Committee chairs	8 U, 4 M, 1 RC, 1 IdV	9 U, 1 RC, 1 FI, 1 IU, 2 M	10 PdL, 4 LN	13 PdL, 1 LN
Committee deputy-chairs	7 U, 7 FI, 4 AN, 2 RC, 2 UDC, 1 IdV, 1 LN, 4 M	7 U, 5 FI, 4 AN, 3 RC, 3 IU, 2 UDC, 1 LN, 2 M	12 PD, 11 PdL, 3 LN, 1 IdV, 1 UDC	13 PD, 11 PdL 3 LN, 1 IdV
Fragmentation index	4.8	4.4	2.7	2.2

Note:
U = Ulivo, FI = Forza Italia, AN = Alleanza Nazionale, RC = Rifondazione Comunista, IdV= Italia dei Valori, UDC = Unione di Centro, LN= Lega Nord, PdL = Popolo della Libertà; PD = Partito Democratico, M = gruppo Misto, IU = Insieme per l'Unione (Partito dei Comunisti Italiani and Verdi).
The Fragmentation index is a weighted application of the effective number of PGs to this small population of office holders. The weights are: Speaker 8, Deputy-speaker 7, Quaestor 2, Secretary 1, Committee chair 5, Committee deputy-chair 4.

Source: Authors' elaborations of official data drawn from www.parlamento.it

in the hands of the two largest parties – since the measure decreases by more than two points in both chambers from the first legislature to the second.

On the other hand, it must be borne in mind that time will also be required to verify the solidity of the seeming trend towards the concentration of institutional power in the two largest PGs, since the risks of internal division as well as the veto power of the 'minor' actors remain as real as ever. For instance, the process of allocating the parliamentary payoffs has been – even after the 2008 election – far from easy and straightforward: although the time required for the election of the chairs and deputy chairs of the permanent committees has been much shorter than before,[1] the NL claimed and received a number of offices, including the chairs of four committees in the Chamber and three in the Senate – an outcome that required a delicate process of negotiation within the majority. Moreover, allocation of the chair of the committee with responsibility for overseeing the system of public broadcasting has been especially problematic and time-consuming as the position has traditionally been reserved to the opposition and yet the majority has refused to vote in favour of the opposition's candidate, who is a representative, not of the PD, but of IdV.

Changes in candidate selection and in the profile of the parliamentary elite

As we have implied, the emergence during the election campaign of two large catch-all formations (or new-born parties) had generated expectations of significant change: these included expectations of change in the manner of candidate selection and more in general in the patterns of relationships between party 'selectorates' and voters. Moreover, changes were explicitly demanded in the composition and qualities of a political elite that appeared – just a few years after the onset of a dramatic period of political transition – already too old (Verzichelli, 2002) and inadequately qualified for its delicate role.[2] The sudden crisis of the Prodi II cabinet and the unusually short period of time that separated this event from the onset of the election campaign itself made impossible any kind of mobilisation that could make the process of political recruitment more open (Hazan, 2007): the process of candidate selection in Italy therefore remained – during the 2008 campaign as before – a rather centralised affair and not very open to the mobilisation of party activists and sympathisers.

However, it should be noted that, notwithstanding the short time available for the preparation of the campaign and the provisional status of its executive body, the PD was able to agree upon a set of formal rules for the selection of candidates,[3] which represents the first innovative step with regard to this issue in Italy for a number of years. A more open process of candidate selection, involving activists and voters, was only partially provided for by this document, whose first article exhorts 'the involvement of activists to the greatest extent possible' and recommends the use of a wide and inclusive process of consultation. But the most important innovation introduced by the regulations is the term limit imposed on incumbent parliamentarians (three terms or 15 years service in total). The limits do not apply to a number of leaders holding key offices within the party, but nonetheless the new rules had a more-than-marginal impact on the composition of the party's lists. Discussion of turnover of the lists led, indeed, to some controversial exclusions – such as that of former Prime Minister and Christian Democratic Party leader, Ciriaco De Mita, whose exclusion led to his immediate resignation from the PD in favour of the Union of Christian Democrats and Centre Democrats (Unione dei Democratici e dei Democratici di Centro, UDC) which fielded him instead.

On the side of the PdL, no formal decisions were taken and the process of candidate selection remained firmly under the control of the inner circles of the pre-existing parties, in particular Alleanza Nazionale (National Alliance, AN) and Forza Italia (FI): a restricted strategic committee was tasked with compiling the lists in all the constituencies without involving the parties' representatives in the localities, or the activists (who could, however, express their preferences about the policy platforms of the new party).

Such a situation led to a certain degree of continuity in parliamentary recruitment in 2008. About 80 per cent of former deputies and senators stood for re-election, and the percentage of incumbents that failed to be re-elected was, respectively, 14.4 per cent in the case of the Chamber and 29.7 per cent in the case of the Senate. Hence, if we leave aside the large number of incumbents that sought re-election through the lists that failed to reach the threshold necessary in order to be eligible to participate in the distribution of seats,[4] we can argue that a great deal of continuity in the parliamentary elite characterised the 2008 election outcome.

In order to understand the magnitude of such continuity, we now focus on recruitment through the two major lists, the PdL and the PD (Table 11.3). The data point clearly in the direction of a rather high degree of persistence of the political elite. This is particularly true in the case of the centre right's lists, where the rate of incumbent re-elections is close to 60 per cent and the two indicators of elite continuity (average seniority and the mean age of parliamentarians) are always higher than the corresponding figures for the group of PD representatives. However, the PD itself seems to have supported a large number of incumbents and the mean age of its representatives, although significantly lower than those of the PdL, remains quite high.

Another interesting indicator is given by the mean age of the newcomer parliamentarians – a measure which indicates the generation of access to Parliament. Again, the age of access to both chambers is rather far from the minimum required by the Constitution, showing the persistence of a 'generational divide' which keeps people younger than 50 away from the most high-profile political offices (Verzichelli, 2002).

Table 11.3 Turnover and circulation of parliamentarians elected in 2008

	New-comers	Directly re-elected	Interval re-elected	Average seniority	Mean age (newcomers)
Chamber of Deputies					
PdL	34.4	62.7	2.9	1.60	51.5 (48.2)
PD	38.2	56.3	5.5	1.06	50.3 (46.1)
All	37.4	58.3	4.3	1.34	50.8 (46.9)
Senate					
PdL	29.0	69.0	2.1	2.03	57.7 (55.7)
PD	27.7	64.7	7.6	1.37	55.2 (53.4)
All	31.3	64.2	4.5	1.62	56.0 (54.6)

Source: CIRCaP databases on the Italian parliamentary elite, University of Siena.

Table 11.4 Percentage of parliamentarians who are female, by parliamentary party, 2006–2008

	Chamber of Deputies		Senate	
	2006	2008	2006	2008
RC	31.7	–	38.5	
Ulivo/PD	20.9	28.6	17.8	30.3
UDC	7.7	5.7	4.8	0.0
FI	17.0		9.2	
PdL		20.1		8.9
AN	16.7		2.4	
LN	8.7	20.0	0.0	15.4
Total	17.3	21.2	13.9	18.1

Source: CIRCaP databases on the Italian parliamentary elite, University of Siena.

Other signs of continuity, or very partial and incremental changes, come from the gender distribution and the occupational profile of parliamentarians. With regard to the proportion of female parliamentarians (Table 11.4), the new record reached in 2008 (with more than 18 per cent female representatives in the Senate and 21 per cent in the Chamber of Deputies) has not done much to change the very low position of the Italian parliament in international rankings concerning the proportions of female members. With the victory of the centre right, the increase in the proportion of parliamentarians who are female has been at its most modest since the election of 1994. The disappearance from Parliament of parties like the communists and the greens may also have contributed to this outcome. However, it is evident from data not presented here that the failure of female representation significantly to increase is bound up with broader processes of recruitment of the parliamentary elite. For example, notwithstanding a number of optimistic predictions and the growth in the proportion of women presented as candidates, the two largest parties, particularly the PdL, found it difficult to place women in the most advantageous positions on their lists since to do so would have frustrated the expectations of re-election of several older male backbenchers. The result has been a very modest expansion in the number of female representatives in Parliament. Among the new PGs, only the NL – a party traditionally dominated by males – shows a significant increase in the proportion of its representatives who are females. In this, the NL is followed by the PD, the proportion of whose female parliamentarians has improved above all in the Senate.

Looking, finally, at the occupational backgrounds of the new parliamentarians (Table 11.5), here too, the situation does not seem to differ substantially from what has been observed in the recent past (for a detailed presentation of the data, not reported here for reasons of space, see Tronconi and Verzichelli, 2007 and Papavero and Verzichelli, 2008): professional politicians, trade unionists and the cluster of 'public sector' occupations are still more heavily represented in the ranks of the PD than in other groups, while the parties of the centre right are more inclined to represent the liberal professions, entrepreneurs, managers, journalists and other media occupations. NL parliamentarians continue to reflect a preponderance of the professional groups that have traditionally been attracted to this party (small farmers, craftsmen, small-business people) while the UDC continues to have a significant proportion of professional politicians.

The overall impression that emerges is that adaptation rather than dramatic changes characterised the processes of recruitment of parliamentary personnel at the 2008 elections. No doubt the disappearance from Parliament of some parties, and the emergence of new party actors like the PdL and the PD have had an impact on parliamentary recruitment. From this point of view, the most pronounced and genuine indicators of change came from the PD, whose lists were significantly overhauled through the inclusion as candidates of 'beginners' from civil society, of those in occupations found in the network of the third-sector associations, and also of a handful of people coming from the world of business. These included people like Matteo Colaninno (son of a famous industrialist and chief executive officer of a number of large companies) and Massimo Calearo (a leading figure in the new industrial elite from the very productive north eastern area). About 25 deputies elected for the PD, roughly 10 per cent of this party's current representatives, had no previous political experience in any of the pre-existing parties that gave life to the PD in 2007. This is per se a significant datum since, on the other side, where the largest proportion of

Table 11.5 Occupational backgrounds of members of the Chamber of Deputies, 2008 (%)

	PD	IdV	UDC	PdL	LN	All MPs
Professional politicians	28.6	13.8	17.1	15.0	10.0	19.4
Trade unionists	6.5	0.0	2.9	0.4	0.0	2.5
Manual workers	0.9	0.0	0.0	0.0	1.7	0.5
Craftsman/ Small business people/ Salesman	1.8	3.4	0.0	7.0	20.0	6.4
Landowners/ Small farmers	0.5	0.0	0.0	0.4	3.3	0.7
Industrialists	1.4	3.4	2.9	7.3	1.7	4.3
Lawyers	6.9	20.7	8.6	15.0	6.7	11.6
Architects/ Engineers	1.8	0.0	0.0	2.2	6.7	2.2
Doctors/ Pharmacists	3.7	6.9	8.6	5.1	1.7	4.6
Commercial consultants	1.8	0.0	5.7	4.0	11.7	3.8
Other professionals	2.3	0.0	2.9	1.8	8.3	2.5
Secondary-school teachers	6.9	3.4	5.7	3.3	5.0	4.9
University professors	9.6	13.8	8.8	2.6	0.0	5.6
University-based liberal professionals	1.0	0.0	2.9	0.4	0.0	0.7
Judges	0.9	3.4	0.0	1.1	0.0	1.0
Army officers	0.0	0.0	0.0	1.5	0.0	0.6
Senior public officials	4.1	6.8	5.8	6.2	3.3	5.1
Junior public officials	6.5	6.8	8.6	3.7	6.7	5.3
Senior private-sector managers	2.3	13.8	5.7	10.2	6.7	6.8
Private sector clerical workers	5.1	0.0	2.9	1.1	3.3	2.7
Journalists	7.4	3.4	11.4	10.6	1.7	8.1
Other professions	0.0	0.0	0.0	1.5	1.7	0.8
N	217	29	35	274	60	629

Source: CIRCaP databases on the Italian parliamentary elite, University of Siena

the PdL's elected representatives had already been active in FI and AN, only a handful of parliamentarians were directly recruited from civil society.

However, the profile and experience of those elected in 2008 suggest that the political elite has changed very little over the past 15 years. The degree of homogeneity of the candidates presented by the two largest parties is less pronounced than that of the candidates fielded by the parties of the First Republic. In the PdL group, for instance, the representatives of AN are more likely than the remaining members of this group to have relevant prior political and administrative experience, as well as a background in the party, while specific occupational backgrounds – for instance lawyers – are especially heavily represented here. FI representatives, on the other hand, normally come to Parliament having had a shorter political career and they are more likely to have a business background. Similarly, the patterns of political recruitment and career of PD representatives clearly differ depending on whether they are drawn from the Margherita or the Left Democrats. Of course such differences are likely to disappear only through slow and complex processes of institutionalisation within the new political formations; and the models of recruitment that today predominate – the vertical hierarchical model typical in the PdL and the compromise among local leaders and factions typical of the PD – are failing to allow the development of strong links between the national party elites and the localities (Folli, 2008).

The start of a decisive legislature?
Majority and opposition after the 2008 elections

Let us focus now on some behavioural data concerning the initial activities of the XVI legislature. A great deal of scholarly attention has traditionally focused on the inadequacies of the Italian parliament when it comes to the production of significant laws. These inadequacies have often been attributed to Parliament's bicameral structure or to the heterogeneity of the coalitions on which governments have had to rely in getting their initiatives approved (for a recent analysis see Zucchini, 2008a). The results of the 2008 election provide an ideal opportunity for a further test of the validity of these assumptions. In fact, the coalition supporting the Berlusconi IV government – with its large majority – is the least fragmented of all the governing coalitions to have taken office since the war, consisting as it does of just two groups both in the Chamber and in the Senate.[5] In addition, if compared with the variegated majority supporting the Prodi II cabinet, the ideological distance separating the two poles of the governing coalition has been considerably reduced. In summary, if the ability to pass effective legislation is primarily a function of the composition of the parliamentary majority and the number of party veto players, then we would expect the style of the legislative process to be very different from the one characteristic of the initial months of the XV legislature. In particular, the reduction in the number of governing parties and of the ideological distance among them is expected to decrease the need for continuous negotiations, favouring the emergence of a more productive and disciplined parliament. In order to assess whether and to what extent these expectations have been met, we will compare the main features of the legislative process during the first two months of the XIV, XV and XVI legislatures.

Before proceeding with the comparison, it will be helpful briefly to recall the basic characteristics of the Italian legislative processes that have come to symbolise the difficulties of the Italian parliament in legislating in a rational manner: governments' frequent recourse to decree laws and to the practice of making legislative proposals questions of confidence. The decree law – an instrument originally intended by the Constitution as a means of dealing with problems that were especially important and urgent – takes effect as soon as it has been decided upon by the Government and remains in force for 60 days. If, within this period, Parliament fails to ratify it by converting it into ordinary law, the decree in question loses its legal validity. Governments have often abused the instrument by, for example, the introduction of 'omnibus decrees' incorporating large numbers of disparate measures that could easily be included, instead, in ordinary legislative proposals.

Another means by which governments have attempted to overcome their weaknesses vis-à-vis the legislature has been by making their legislative proposals matters of confidence; in such cases parliamentarians are required to vote on the bill in question without the possibility of proposing any amendments. This strategy has had a twofold purpose: while it serves to reinforce the cohesion of the majority (since a defeat threatens the life of the Government) it also speeds up the legislative process, offering a means of circumventing obstructionism or the practice of filibustering on the part of the opposition.

What happened during the first two months of the XVI legislature (Table 11.6)? In this short but crucial time span of 60 days, Parliament approved seven laws (all of them laws converting government decrees into ordinary law), while the Government issued ten new decrees and asked for one vote of confidence. In the comparable period of time for the XV legislature, Parliament converted four decrees into ordinary laws, while the Government issued ten new decree laws and asked for three votes of confidence. If this initial evidence is confirmed over a longer time span (for instance a period of 18 months such as the one covered by Zucchini, 2008b), then we can predict that the XVI is likely to be a 'strong' legislature in terms of decisiveness and government steering capabilities; but the main features of legislative practice remain more or less the same. The parliamentary environment looks not very dissimilar to the one in which the Berlusconi II cabinet operated between 2001 and 2005. Indeed, the data for the beginning of the XIV legislature are more similar than are the data for the beginning of the XV legislature to those of the latest one, with seven converted decrees, eight decrees issued and two confidence votes attached to legislative bills.

Table 11.6   Legislative activity in the first two months of the legislature, 2001, 2006 and 2008

	Laws approved	Decree laws issued	Confidence votes
XIV legislature (Berlusconi II)	7	8	2
XV legislature (Prodi II)	4	10	3
XVI legislature (Berlusconi IV)	7	10	1

Source: Authors' elaborations of official data drawn from www.parlamento.it

Hence, the evidence from the first two months of legislative activity in the new parliament is rather mixed. On the one hand, the prevailing style of law-making seems to have remained unchanged, since decrees and converted decrees continue to be the primary sources of legislation: despite the large and cohesive majority on which the Government can rely, the ordinary legislative process looks like remaining rather marginal even in the XVI legislature. On the other hand, a comparison of the first two months of the XV and of the XVI legislature suggests signs of discontinuity: most notably, the majority is now much more capable of passing legislation on the floor and it can do so without resorting to the tool of the confidence vote. While the style of the legislative process appears to be characterised by its usual features (a considerable use of decrees) the productivity of Parliament has increased (a higher number of laws approved) together with the cohesion of the majority (fewer votes of confidence). In fact, during the short period considered here, with only three exceptions, the Government never lost a vote on the floor of the assembly: in one case it was beaten on a minor amendment due to the absence of a number of its supporters, while some days later the NL voted twice against the Government to pass amendments proposed by the opposition. This had less to do with the specific content of the amendments, than it did with the League's decision to vote with the opposition in order to express its opposition to the highly symbolic transfer of €150 million to Naples to address the notorious 'garbage crisis'. In short, although the majority in the XVI legislature is much more cohesive than the centre-left coalition which supported the Prodi II cabinet, when it comes to the long-standing North-South divide there are still signs of conflict between the NL and PdL. This does not mean that the impact of party veto-players is comparable to the power they were able to wield during the previous legislature, but it does mean that intra-coalitional tensions are likely to reappear in Parliament when sensitive issues (such as federalism, welfare and infrastructure) are discussed.

As mentioned elsewhere in this book, the outcome of the 2008 election not only created a cohesive majority but also a less fragmented opposition. In fact the parliamentary group representing the main opposition party (the PD) numbers about 75 per cent of the whole opposition in the Chamber of Deputies and almost 80 per cent in the Senate. Given this, it should not be a matter of surprise that the PD formed an unofficial 'shadow cabinet' whose portfolios mirror those of the Government. Although it is not the first example of such action,[6] the emergence of a shadow cabinet suggests that the opposition is seeking to adopt a new style, more appropriate to an adversarial style of parliamentary interaction. The PD's shadow cabinet consists of 22 members (including Walter Veltroni, the leader of the PD) plus eight collaborators with specific functions but without a formal portfolio. Among the shadow ministers, 14 are members of the Chamber of Deputies, five are members of the Senate and three are not parliamentarians. In such a system we would expect the primary responsibility of shadow ministers to be that of scrutinising and controlling their counterparts: to facilitate these tasks most are members of the permanent committees that correspond to their portfolios.[7]

Here, however, we are more interested in the behavioural aspects: how are shadow ministers performing their roles? Are they challenging their opponents in public or do they prefer to avoid open conflict? To answer these questions we can look at their parliamentary activities during the first two months of the XVI legislature. In particular, it can be helpful to check whether, and to what extent, shadow ministers scrutinise their counterparts. In the Italian parliament there is a wide range of procedures through which parliamentarians can ask questions of ministers; these include questions for written reply, questions for oral reply, question time, interpellations and questions for reply in committee. Question time and interpellations are the procedures that attract by far the most public attention as they are often picked up by the media; by contrast, the other procedures are more suited to extracting information than to influencing the public agenda. If the PD wants to present the shadow cabinet as a credible alternative then we expect shadow ministers to make extensive use of questioning procedures to challenge their respective opponents. However, data from the first two months do not bear out such an expectation. 9 of the 19 shadow ministers who are also parliamentarians did not present a single question in this period: moreover, the least active are the political heavyweights of the PD's PG.[8] The other 10 shadow ministers asked 24 questions: 11 questions for written reply, 6 questions for oral reply, 6 questions for reply in committee and only 1 interpellation. From this evidence, it can be said that at the very beginning of the legislature the shadow cabinet did not engage in open confrontation with the Government, preferring to act in less adversarial ways. As to the reasons for this choice, it is still too early to draw any firm conclusions: however, it could be argued that the shadow cabinet needs some time to learn how to play its role, and interaction may become more adversarial as the legislature progresses. Alternatively, it is possible that the shadow cabinet will continue to adopt a relatively mild style as a matter of strategic choice. In fact, as discussed elsewhere in this book, the style of the PD's election campaign was designed to convey an image of moderation, one that refused to embrace the aggressive rhetoric that had previously characterised the centre-left coalition.

Though the shadow cabinet has not so far made extensive use of parliamentary questioning, the same cannot be said of Parliament as a whole: in the first two months of the legislature's life, no fewer than 1,712 questions were put. Taking a closer look at this questioning activity can tell us something about the relations between the Government and its majority, between the opposition and the Government, and among the parties of the opposition. Table 11.7 shows that in the Chamber of Deputies, the number of questions asked by the representatives of a group tends to be proportional to the size of that group: the PdL is the group that asked the most questions, followed by the PD and so on. Nevertheless, and quite surprisingly, while the PD asked slightly fewer than its natural share of questions, the party led by Antonio Di Pietro, the combative IdV,[9] has been the most active scrutiniser in Parliament.

The data in table 11.7 suggest that, however disciplined it may be when it comes to the legislative process, the majority is far from submissive. It might be true that a dog that barks a lot never bites, but such a large number of parliamentary questions asked by the major government party is quite uncommon. At this stage it is possible to list only some likely explanations – in respect of which closer analysis and a longer period of observation will be necessary in order to draw firmer conclusions. According to some scholars (Martin and Vanberg, 2004), oversight procedures are often employed to manage intra-coalitional conflicts. It may be that members of the PdL have used questions as a way of controlling the actions of ministers whose political backgrounds differ from their own. Indeed we must not forget that the PdL is not yet a genuinely single party but an electoral alliance consisting of two parties (FI and AN). However, a considerable proportion of questions are likely to address local issues and/or deal with specific interests, showing that majority backbenchers are more active than usually thought. Looking at the opposition, after noting the activism of the small IdV, one might ask whether and to what extent the parties in opposition are operating in alliance. Data on parliamentary questions suggest that at the beginning of the legislative term, cooperation has been minimal. The PD and IdV are the only opposition parties to show any degree of coordination, and even that has been sporadic, the two having asked 17 questions together. By contrast, the UDC has asked only one question with IdV and two with the PD. Competition rather than

Table 11.7 Parliamentary questions asked during the first two months of the Berlusconi IV government by parliamentary group in the Chamber of Deputies

	Questions	%	Seats	%
PdL	512	44.1	273	43.3
PD	358	30.9	218	34.6
IdV	93	8.0	28	4.4
LN	131	11.3	60	9.5
UDC	100	8.6	35	5.6
Mixed group	17	1.5	16	2.5
Total	1,160		630	

Source: Authors' elaborations of official data drawn from www.parlamento.it

cooperation seems to be the key to understanding relations among the three opposition parties in the initial months of the legislature.

Conclusion: what kind of parliament?

In this chapter we have presented a number of indicators of the profile of Parliament at the beginning of the XVI legislature. Our description has offered confirmation of the most important changes brought about by the vote of April 2008: political fragmentation has decreased considerably in both chambers and the ideological distance within the parliamentary coalition supporting the executive has been drastically reduced. The allocation of offices and responsibilities in Parliament now follows the pattern of a 'quasi two-party system', and the advantages enjoyed by the current government, in terms of the cohesiveness of its parliamentary majority and therefore its legislative autonomy are astonishing in comparison to the situations in which previous recent governments have found themselves. It should be noted that these changes chime closely with what was implied by many of the promises made by the two leaders that dominated the political stage during the election campaign: in emphasising the positive performance of his cabinets in terms of accountability and policy effectiveness, Berlusconi's main electoral pronouncements insisted on the legislative autonomy of the executive. But the campaign strategies chosen by Walter Veltroni and the PD too clearly took their distance from the consensus democracy paradigm, reflecting the choice in favour of a more compact base of political support and sending the clear message that Parliament needed to be rationalised through a greater delegation of power to the executive.

The significance of these indicators of change should not be overestimated. We know from previous research (Capano and Giuliani, 2003; Zucchini, 2008a) that legislative practices and Parliament's standing orders have rendered parliamentary behaviour highly resistant to change and that very often actual differences between a *then* and *now* are much less evident than what was expected on the basis of the 'political conditions' pertaining at the start of a given legislature. The XVI legislature is characterised, like those before it, by a number of features whose effects may be to counteract those of the changes and promises we have discussed above. For instance, the effective emergence of a solid 'two-party' pattern of interaction with a clear distinction of roles between two homogeneous entities called a 'majority' and an 'opposition' could be endangered – even in the course of the current legislative term – by repeated attempts at blackmail and sudden changes in the policy agenda, generated by elements within the majority coalition (i.e., the NL). Correspondingly, excessively intense competition among the different 'tendencies' within the parliamentary minority could destroy efforts to build a constructive opposition, giving minor parties (i.e., IdV) a much more visible and combative role than they would other-wise be entitled to.

It is unrealistic to think that in a context such as that of the Italian political system, Parliament can suddenly change the way it operates. The image of a parliament which is really able suddenly to switch to another model can hardly come true in a political system like the Italian one. This is likely to be, in the end, an important constraint that, notwithstanding the signs of transformation we have been able to observe, all the protagonists of the XVI legislature will have to take into account.

Notes

Although the chapter has been produced collectively by the two authors, Federico Russo is particularly responsible for the last three sections while Luca Verzichelli wrote the first two.

1. However, one should remember, in comparisons with the past, that after the 2006 election, election of the President of the Republic kept parliamentarians busy for a couple of weeks at the beginning of the legislative term.
2. It is appropriate here to recall the amazing success, during the two years of the XV legislature, of a book written by the *Corriere della Sera* journalists, Sergio Rizzo and Gian Antonio Stella (2007), who described in detail the enormous power and privileges of *la casta* – an extensive but close-knit and dominant political elite whose sphere of influence extends from the local to the national level.
3. The *Regolamento per le candidature* [Rules for the selection of candidates] was approved on 20 February by the PD's provisional executive and included 11 articles.
4. A not insignificant sector of the political elite was thus excluded from Parliament. It included, in the case of the Chamber, 32 incumbents who stood for election as representatives of the La Sinistra L'Arcobaleno, 7 as representatives of the Partito Socialista and 2 as representatives of La Destra. In the Senate, 11 incumbents stood for election as representatives of the La Sinistra L'Arcobaleno.
5. The government is also supported by the Movimento per l'Autonomia, whose 8 deputies and 2 senators are members of the residual Gruppo Misto.
6. The Communist Party formed a shadow cabinet in 1989, during the X legislature.
7. There are some exceptions, because there are more ministers than permanent committees.
8. In the period considered the following shadow ministers did not ask any questions as 'main questioner' (*primo firmatario*): Piero Fassino (Foreign Affairs), Marco Minniti (Interior), Pierluigi Bersani (Economy), Matteo Colaninno (Economic Development), Enrico Letta (Welfare and Labour policies), Alfonso Andria (Agriculture), Giovanna Melandri (Communications), Maria Paola Merloni (EU), Michele Ventura (Implementation of the electoral programme).
9. IdV took a very aggressive stance in the aftermath of the elections. From the outset of the legislature the party rejected the formation of a single PG incorporating the two main parties of opposition (as it had agreed to as part of the pre-electoral pact with the PD) and it accused the PD of being too soft on the Berlusconi government, repeatedly claiming that it was 'the only real opposition'.

References

Capano, G. and Giuliani, M. (2003) 'The Italian parliament: in search of a new Role?', *Journal of Legislative Studies* 9(2): 8–34.

Folli, S. (2008) 'Senza legami con il territorio', *Il Sole 24 ore*, 20 March.

Giuliani, M. (2008) 'Brand new, somewhat new or rather old? The Italian legislative process in the age of alternation', *South European Society and Politics* 13(1): 1–10.

Grilli di Cortona, P. (2007) *La transizione politica in Italia*, Rome: Carocci.

Hazan, R. (2007) 'Selezione delle candidature e conseguenze delle elezioni interne ai partiti', pp. 171–197 in L. Bardi (ed.), *Partiti e sistemi di partito*, Bologna: Il Mulino.

Laasko, M. and Taagepera, R. (1979) '"Effective" number of parties: a measure with application to West Europe', *Comparative Political Studies* 12(1): 3–27.

Martin, L. and Vanberg, G. (2004) 'Policing the bargain: coalition government and parliamentary scrutiny', *American Journal of Political Science* 48(1): 13–27.

Papavero, L. and Verzichelli, L. (2008) 'The elections and the XV legislature', pp. 223–244 in J.L. Newell (ed.), *The Italian General Election of 2006: Romano Prodi's Victory*, Manchester and New York: Manchester University Press.

Rizzo, S. and Stella, G.A. (2007) *La Casta. Così i politici italiani sono diventati intoccabili*, Milan: Rizzoli.

Tronconi, F. and Verzichelli, L. (2007) 'Il ceto parlamentare alla prova della nuova riforma elettorale', pp. 335–368 in R. D'Alimonte and A. Chiaramonte (eds), *Proporzionale ma non solo*, Bologna: Il Mulino.

Verzichelli, L. (2002) 'Da un ceto politico all'altro. Il mutamento nel personale legislativo Italiano (1992–2001)', pp. 319–362 in R. D'Alimonte and S. Bartolini (eds), *Maggioritario finalmente. La transizione elettorale 1994–2001*, Bologna: Il Mulino.

Zucchini, F. (2008a) 'Dividing parliament? Italian bicameralism in the legislative process (1987–2006)', *South European Society and Politics* 13(1): 11–34.

Zucchini, F. (2008b) 'An afterword – but not the last word', *South European Society and Politics* 13(1): 111–117.

12

The Formation of the Fourth Berlusconi Government

Gianfranco Pasquino

Introduction

In the period between 1946 and 1993, that is, before the reform of the electoral law along majoritarian lines and the transformation of the Italian party system, the processes of government formation in Italy were long and complicated, and never easy to understand or explain. Nevertheless, as Verzichelli and Cotta (2000) have accurately and intelligently shown, the rules applying to them can be identified, even though they are somewhat Byzantine. Therefore, the suggestion of Schofield and Sened – that 'understanding Italian politics in terms of coalition theory has proved very difficult' (2007: 101) – is only partially correct and would apply only to those coalition theorists who focus exclusively on the office-seeking perspective. Some not totally bizarre and unpredictable criteria were always at work (as imaginatively reconstructed by Mershon, 2002). The paramount rule was that decisions regarding which governing coalition would be formed, among which partners and with what allocation of portfolios to the different parties, could be taken only after the results of the election were fully known. Since alternation among totally different coalitions was impossible – both because it lacked sufficient votes and because of Italy's membership of the Western camp, the Communist Party could not enter any governmental coalition – Italian voters knew in advance at least which party was in any case going to be excluded from the governmental arena. That said, before the elections Italian voters could not know precisely the kind of coalition that would follow and even less were they informed beforehand of the name of the prospective Prime Minister. Though the variations were limited and the surprises quite rare, the entire process of government formation remained firmly in the hands of the parties and, in some cases, of faction leaders, especially of powerful Christian Democratic faction leaders.

The most dramatic change produced by the 1993 electoral law was that it became imperative to construct pre-electoral coalitions (see Campus and Pasquino, 2006). Therefore, since 1994 Italian voters have been able to deliver a virtual mandate to the winning coalition. Moreover, it has become important for the two (major) coalitions clearly to indicate the names of their respective candidates for the office of Prime Minister, so much so that, starting with the 2001 elections and, then again at the 2006 and 2008 elections, coalitions included the names of their prime-ministerial candidates as parts of the symbols of the parties willing to support them. Though of doubtful propriety from a constitutional point of view, as we will see below, this innovation has been considered positive from a political point of view. Nevertheless, as Italy is a parliamentary republic, the Prime Minister can still be defeated in Parliament and replaced by Parliament notwithstanding the unfounded and misleading opinion of those who claim that he has been 'elected' by the voters. To prove this point *ad abundantiam* there are several instances one can cite:

i. the December 1994 crisis of the first government led by Silvio Berlusconi gave birth to a government led by Lamberto Dini (January 1994–February 1996);

ii. the October 1998 defeat of the first government led by Romano Prodi opened the way to a government supported by a slightly different parliamentary majority and led by Massimo D'Alema (October 1998–December 1999) who then

iii. led a second government (December 1999–April 2000) only to be replaced within more or less the same centre-left coalition by

iv. another government led by Giuliano Amato (May 2000–April 2001).

v. Even Silvio Berlusconi suffered a similar fate, having, in July 2005, to renegotiate the terms of engagement of the four parties within his centre-right coalition.

However, when Romano Prodi's second government went through a minor crisis in mid-February 2007, the President of the Republic, Giorgio Napolitano, allowed Prodi to regain/retain office only after a renewed vote of confidence, solemnly warning him and his majority that a subsequent crisis would lead to a dissolution of Parliament if no other majority could be formed. True to his correct interpretation of the Constitution, following yet another parliamentary defeat for the Prodi government, in mid-January 2008, after a brief round of constitutionally necessary consultations with the various party leaders, President Napolitano came to the conclusion that no other majority was possible in that legislature. Hence, he dissolved what was the shortest-lived Italian parliament (April 2006–February 2008) and called new elections to be held on 13–14 April 2008.

In the following paragraphs, I will briefly analyse the election outcome as the product of, among other things, fateful decisions made by the leaders of the two major coalitions (or parties). I will then focus on the new coalition politics in Italy – a new politics largely caused by the birth of the

Democratic Party. The bulk of the chapter will be devoted to explaining the process of government formation and portfolio allocations, providing some hopefully meaningful comparisons with the previous governments of the transition that started in 1994. I will also try to explain why the parties within Berlusconi's government desired certain specific portfolios and why the personal-political power of Silvio Berlusconi has grown significantly.

The election outcome

Bitterly disappointed by the fall of his government, Prodi decided not to run for office again and, as expected, the newly elected leader of the recently created Democratic Party, former Left Democrat Walter Veltroni, resigned from the office of Mayor of Rome in order to assume the burden of leading the party's election campaign. As in 2001, the person who had to face the challenger on the centre right, once more Silvio Berlusconi, was not the centre left's incumbent. Paradoxically, Veltroni was unable, on the one hand, to exploit the advantages of incumbency (such as they were), or, on the other, to rid himself of the negative evaluations and the dismal levels of approval and popularity of Prodi's government. In short, Veltroni suffered the worst of both worlds. He also made a fateful decision, a decision that some considered an act of political courage and others a desperate gamble. Annoyed by the conflicts and the tensions repeatedly produced and fed by the various small parties of the centre left that had, if not doomed, certainly severely weakened Prodi's government, Veltroni decided that his Democratic Party would 'run alone'. He also challenged Berlusconi to do the same. The existence as part of the electoral law of a sizable majority bonus to be attributed to the party polling just one more vote than its competitors, nationally for the Chamber of Deputies and region by region for the Senate, suggests that launching a duel between the Democratic Party and the 'People of Freedom' (the name chosen by Berlusconi for the party created by the merger of Forza Italia and the National Alliance) was indeed a very hazardous political act; for it flew in the face of all the available polling evidence – which showed a significant and unchanging lead for Berlusconi.

The only surprising feature of the Democratic Party's defeat was its scale. The third victory of Silvio Berlusconi, who has fought all five elections held since 1994, was almost taken for granted. Two phenomena had not been predicted: the significant electoral growth of the Northern League, which obtained more than eight per cent of the national vote, and the disappearance from Parliament of the so-called radical left that had run in an improvised party cartel called La Sinistra L'Arcobaleno (or 'Rainbow Left') and proved unable to surmount either of the two thresholds – four per cent nationally for the Chamber of Deputies; eight per cent in each region for the Senate – it had to surmount in order to gain access to Parliament. In the election's immediate aftermath, the traditional, and much-to-be-deplored, fragmentation of the Italian party system seemed a problem of the past. Only five parties are represented in the 2008 Parliament. From right to left they are: the People of Freedom, the Northern League, the Union of the Centre (which, against all the odds, succeeded in almost holding its own), Italy of Values (Antonio Di Pietro's political organisation), the Democratic Party. Leaving aside any consideration concerning the quantity and quality of political representation, the simplification of the party system could not but have positive consequences for the process of formation of the new government.

Pre-electoral coalitions

As I said, the coalitions were formed well before the elections. In 1998 and again in 2008, the fragmented, litigious, and ideologically rigid extreme left bore much of the responsibility for the fall of Prodi's governments. Because of these negative experiences, and in order to get rid of Mastella and the Democratic Union for Europe (Unione Democratici per l'Europa, UDEUR) as well as Lamberto Dini (whose disloyal behaviour was, in the end, the decisive factor in the outcome of the last fateful Senate vote), Veltroni decided that the Democratic Party would run 'alone'. In the light of the survey evidence, this decision was not so much a courageous act, as fans of the Democratic Party tried to convince commentators and voters, but, as I have already said, almost a desperate gamble. Since the election, the issue of coalition formation has remained more alive than ever for the Democratic Party if it wants to continue governing at the local level.[1] For his part, Berlusconi appeared to have solved the problem well before the day of the elections. His solution, certainly made necessary in the wake of the decision to create the Democratic Party, was to ask the National Alliance to join a new party, that is, to merge with his Forza Italia in what he called the People of Freedom (Popolo dell Libertà). In fact, the offer was also extended to the Northern League and to the Union of Christian Democrats and Centre Democrats (Unione dei Democratici Cristiani e dei Democratici di Centro, UDC). Both parties, however, wanted to retain their own precious visibility. Berlusconi had no objection to the League retaining its name and symbol, but the same treatment was not given to the UDC. When the leader of the UDC expressed his opposition to absorption by the People of Freedom, declaring his willingness to follow the same path as the League, Berlusconi rejected this solution and practically obliged the UDC to run alone. In order to understand why preferential treatment was given to the League, benevolent treatment to the National Alliance, and hostile treatment to the UDC, one may draw on ideas deriving from coalition theory. Without in any way discounting the importance of the geographical concentration of the Northern League that significantly contributes to its bargaining power, I will use three of these ideas: programmatic compatibility; political and ideological contiguity; information saving.

The programmatic differences among Forza Italia, the National Alliance, and the Northern League on all the major campaign issues – immigration, security, taxes – were limited and, indeed, almost non-existent.[2] On some of these issues the UDC's positions were extremely close to those of the People of Freedom, but there were clear differences when looking at the proposed policies. While Forza Italia kept a very low profile on the issue of the utmost importance to the Northern League, that is, federalism, the National Alliance, true to its emphasis on the 'nation', was never adamantly favourable. However, federalism was presented as part of a larger package of institutional reforms, among them the strengthening of the powers of the Prime Minister, something that was potentially favourable to the fortunes of both Berlusconi and Gianfranco Fini. Not in principle opposed to federalism, the UDC was lukewarm towards the idea of giving stronger powers to the Prime Minister. Where the UDC was farthest apart from its previous governmental partners was in terms of its attitude to the electoral law. The leader of the party, Pierferdinando Casini, expressed a deep desire for a truly proportional electoral law and identified the German model as his preferred solution. Deprived of any significant socio-economic issue on which to keep high the profile of his party, Casini decided to stress the importance of so-called ethical-biological issues (especially assisted reproduction, living wills and stem-cell research). On all of them he took or faithfully interpreted the stances formulated by the Vatican. While no doubt doing so for opportunist reasons, the remaining centre-right parties constantly expressed their agreement with the Vatican and the Pope. In the end, however, Veltroni's refusal to debate ethical-biological issues during the electoral campaign won out: he succeeded in preventing them coming to the surface – knowing that they risked provoking the explosion, within his party, of the divisions between the Catholic and 'secular' politicians – and Casini saw his most important asset nullified.

Though it favoured a proportional law, the Northern League had no objection to retaining the existing electoral law as long as it could share the fruits of the majority bonus. As to political and ideological compatibility, the four parties of the centre-right had solved this problem a long time ago, and in any case, definitely before the 2001 elections. Indeed, it must be stressed that the centre right coalition has constantly been more homogeneous than the centre left and has behaved accordingly. It was their political and ideological compatibility that made the merger between Forza Italia and the National Alliance not only possible, but almost uncontroversial. Only a small fraction of the National Alliance decided to keep alive the tradition and the themes of the post-war Italian extreme right by running, together with the Fiamma Tricolore, as La Destra-FT (the Right – the Tricoloured Flame) – achieving a rather poor election result and no representation in Parliament. The sore point, almost an insult, was the fact that in the Summer of 2005, the then Secretary of the UDC, Marco Follini (Casini was the Speaker of the Chamber of Deputies at the time) had brought about the demise of

Berlusconi's government, preventing him from achieving a much-coveted record: leading one government capable of lasting the entire Parliamentary term. Follini had then moved gradually to join the ranks of the centre left in the Senate, eventually becoming an elected Senator for the Democratic Party. But Berlusconi made Casini pay the price of that betrayal.

Finally, as we know from the theory of coalition-making, time and the knowledge of political and portfolio preferences are important factors in facilitating the construction of a governmental coalition and in speeding up the process. In the case of Forza Italia, the National Alliance, and the Northern League, not only had the party organisations not changed at all, but since 1994 their leaders had remained the same. By contrast, the centre left had fought the five national elections between 1994 and 2008 each on the basis of a different coalition arrangement, carrying a different label, and under three different leaders, none of whom ever acquired or was in full control of his coalition.

Government formation and the allocation of portfolios

By the time of the 2008 elections, the leaders of the centre right knew each other intimately, from a political point of view. They had learned that, united behind Berlusconi, their chances of winning were huge. Briefly, they had no problem in communicating, in exchanging information, or even in bargaining. They were perfectly aware of the personal preferences of each of their allies and of the political preferences of their electorates, their party supporters, their senior collaborators. Once the leader of the National Alliance, Gianfranco Fini, had been elected Speaker of the Chamber of Deputies, attention shifted to the allocation of the Cabinet portfolios. Berlusconi's patience, bargaining abilities and persuasiveness did the rest. Of course, there were conflicts and tensions, but they remained subdued and had no significant consequences. It was no surprise, then, that the entire list of ministers was already in his pocket when he was received by the President of the Republic to be officially entrusted with the task of forming the new government, his fourth. Again, in line with his eagerness to perform unprecedented acts, Berlusconi succeeded in becoming the only Prime Minister ever in the history of the Italian Republic to have accepted a presidential appointment to form a government without reservation and to have immediately handed him the entire list of the ministers of which it was to be composed.

The Italian constitution states that it is the task of the President of the Republic to appoint the President of the Council of Ministers (the Prime Minister). While this is not the place to dwell on why it was that the makers of the Constitution decided on a provision of this kind, it is certainly necessary to emphasise that the Constitution does not in the least suggest or imply that the President of the Council of Ministers is or should be directly elected by the voters.[3] But it is also true that the 'temptation' to reform the

Constitution on this point has often arisen, usually as response to two pressures. First, it is crystal-clear that direct popular election would automatically strengthen the Prime Minister vis-à-vis Parliament, at the same time curtailing the powers of the President of the Republic. Second, direct election would automatically reduce the power of the parties to the same extent and prevent them from acting irresponsibly in Parliament. The opponents of direct election, who have so far narrowly carried the day, respond that such a provision would be incompatible with a parliamentary regime, that it would create unnecessary rigidities and risk transforming parliamentary and political crises into institutional crises. Despite the absence of a reform concerning the manner in which the President of the Council of Ministers is chosen and the powers of the office, the fact is that many voters, analysts, commentators and, most importantly, politicians have come to think and behave as if not only were the leader of the victorious coalition indeed automatically entitled to the office of Prime Minister, but also that no Prime Minister should be replaced by Parliament, especially not by a parliamentary majority different from the one he led. In practice, however, there have been three instances in which the Prime Minister has been replaced in Parliament, and two of those Prime Ministers had succeeded in carrying their respective coalitions to victory.

Curiously, in both cases, though widely, but in my opinion wrongly, criticised, the same President of the Republic, Oscar Luigi Scalfaro (1992–1999), supervised the processes. In the first case, which in 1994 led to Berlusconi's replacement by Dini, some critics maintained that the President went beyond his constitutional powers, by lending Dini so much personal and institutional support as almost to create a 'Government of the President'. The second case was the one which, in 1998, saw the President facilitate the transition from Prodi to D'Alema. Precedents such as these help one to understand the complexity and the delicacy of constitutional conventions, and why it is that the rules are often stretched, and political actions performed outside them.

Throughout his political career, President of the Republic Giorgio Napolitano has always shown deep respect for the rules of the game, especially those of the institutional game. While not denying the need for constitutional reform, his clearly formulated position was and is that as long as there is no reform, the old rules hold and must be applied in their entirety. His subsequent behaviour has been fully consistent with his declarations.

In spite of the fact that the two major coalitions have since 2001 included the names of their respective leaders and prime-ministerial candidates as part of the party/coalition symbols that have appeared on the ballot papers, President Napolitano solemnly announced in the wake of the 2008 elections, that he would keep to the constitutional rules and to previous practices. Hence he proceeded with the convention of consulting former Presidents of the Republic (a convention whose rationale derives from the presumed political wisdom of these people and their knowledge of the politicians involved) and the leaders of the parties represented in Parliament. In doing so he acted exactly as he had already done in appointing Romano Prodi to the office of Prime Minister in May 2006. However, two significant political changes had broken the surface of the stagnant waters of the Italian political system. On the one hand, all of the minor parties of the left had disappeared from Parliament because of their inability to cross the electoral thresholds, as we have seen. On the other hand, and again as I have already indicated, following Veltroni's success in creating a unified party of the centre left, the Democratic Party, Berlusconi and Fini had decided to follow suit and to merge Forza Italia and the National Alliance in a new party called the People of Freedom. The overall electoral outcome was a 'terrible', that is, drastic, simplification of the party alignments in the 2008 Parliament. Thanks to these two important occurrences, the presidential consultations could be extremely swift. Much was known and little remained to be discovered as to the coalitional preferences of the major political actors and their choice of Prime Minister. As a consequence, there was absolutely no need for the President of the Republic to protract the consultations with the 'political forces', as the Italian jargon would put it, or to postpone the expected and inevitable appointment of Berlusconi. Always in search of striking and extraordinary accomplishments, Berlusconi submitted to the President of the Republic the list of the ministers of his fourth government the day after he received his formal appointment on 7 May.

For several reasons, Berlusconi had an easy task, achieving something that no previous Prime Minister had ever been in a position to attempt. Even before winning his third national election (his two earlier victories had taken place in 1994 and 2001) he had made several references to the composition of his future government. Criticising the exaggerated size of poor Prodi's government – 25 Ministers and 76 Deputy Ministers and Undersecretaries – he promised to give birth to a lean cabinet consisting of 12 Ministers only, eight men and four women. He almost succeeded in keeping his word. Among his 12 ministers with portfolio there are two women (Stefania Prestigiacomo, for the Environment, and Mariastella Gelmini, for Education). The number four is reached by adding two women who were appointed as ministers without portfolio: Mara Carfagna, with responsibility for Equal Opportunities, and Giorgia Meloni, with responsibility for Policies for the Young. There are nine ministers without portfolio so that the total number of Ministers is 21. Adding to them the 39 undersecretaries (of which only five are women), the total becomes 60, considerably fewer than the members of Prodi's government. The list of ministers, the ministries for which they are responsible, and their party affiliations are provided in Table 12.1.

The two necessary votes of confidence took place without drama, in the new climate of 'dialogue' that the leader of the opposition, Walter Veltroni,

Table 12.1   Composition of Berlusconi's fourth government

Prime Minister
Silvio Berlusconi (Forza Italia)

Ministers with Portfolio
Foreign Affairs: Franco Frattini (Forza Italia)
Home Affairs: Roberto Maroni (Northern League)
Justice: Angelino Alfano (Forza Italia)
Defence: Ignazio La Russa (National Alliance)
Economy and Finance: Giulio Tremonti (Forza Italia)
Economic Development: Claudio Scajola (Forza Italia)
Agriculture, Food and Forests: Luca Zaia (Northern League)
Environment: Stefania Prestigiacomo (Forza Italia)
Infrastructure: Altero Matteoli (National Alliance)
Labour: Maurizio Sacconi (Forza Italia)
Heritage: Sandro Bondi (Forza Italia)
Education: Maria Stella Gelmini (Forza Italia)

Ministers without Portfolio
Relations with Parliament: Elio Vito (Forza Italia)
Federal Reform: Umberto Bossi (Northern League)
Legislative Simplification: Roberto Calderoli (Northern League)
Relations with the Regions: Giancarlo Fitto (Forza Italia)
Equal Opportunities: Mara Carfagna (Forza Italia)
European Union Policies: Andrea Ronchi (National Alliance)
Public Administration and Innovation: Renato Brunetta (Forza Italia)
Policies for the Young: Giorgia Meloni (National Alliance)
Implementation of the Government's Programme: Gianfranco Rotondi (Christian
    Democrats for Regional Autonomy)

sought to pursue from a position of clear, but perhaps underestimated, weakness. On 14 May, Berlusconi's government obtained the vote of confidence of the Chamber of Deputies with 335 votes for the motion, 275 against, 1 abstention and 14 absent; and on 15 May it was the turn of the Senate where there were 173 for the motion, 137 against, 2 abstentions and 9 absent. Because of the sizable parliamentary majority won by Berlusconi, thanks to the electoral law and its majority bonus, neither vote was ever in question. Both debates in Parliament were characterised by a total lack of drama, the opposition led by Walter Veltroni appearing and, perhaps, being, substantially tamed and resigned. On 15 May, Veltroni announced the composition of his Democratic Party's shadow cabinet, which was received without fanfare and whose shadow ministers have yet to master an uncertain and imprecisely defined role. It may be of some interest to recall that the first attempt to import the idea of a shadow cabinet from the United Kingdom into the totally non-British Italian context had been made in 1990 by Achille Occhetto, then the secretary of a Communist Party that was engaged in the process of transforming itself into the Democratic Party of the Left. For several, not all unpredictable, reasons, the experience proved to be brief and was certainly not attended by much enthusiasm or success.

More on portfolios

There are two approaches that can be of help in analysing the composition of the fourth government to be led by Berlusconi. The first involves following the path inaugurated by those who study coalitions (for an overview see Laver and Schofield, 1990). The second one, much more rarely pursued, consists in comparing the 2008 government with the 2001–2006 experience.[4] Following the first approach, one can assess whether the allocation of portfolios has been made according to some precise criterion and has followed any specific rules. For instance, one may ask the very traditional questions concerning the kind of relationship that exists between the votes obtained by the parties and the portfolios allocated to their representatives. This type of analysis is made slightly more complicated by the fact that the respective electoral strengths of Forza Italia and the National Alliance cannot be precisely measured with reference to the votes gained by each of them because they ran together under the label of the People of Freedom. All this taken into consideration, of the 12 Ministers with portfolio, eight belong to Forza Italia, two belong to the National Alliance and two belong to the Northern League. Looking at the nine Ministers without portfolio, four of them belong to Forza Italia, two each to the National Alliance and the Northern League, one to the so-called Christian Democrats for Regional Autonomy. Hence, of the 21 Ministers overall, the distribution is: twelve for Forza Italia; four each for the National Alliance and the Northern League; one for the Christian Democrats for Regional Autonomy.

Two elements clearly stand out. Having polled just over eight per cent of the Chamber vote, the Northern League is significantly overrepresented since it has the same number of Ministers as the National Alliance whose electoral support would, in all likelihood, amount to approximately 12 per cent. However, in counting and weighing the 'spoils', one must not underestimate the importance of the office of President of the Chamber of Deputies allotted to the leader of the National Alliance, Gianfranco Fini. The second important element to be taken into consideration for an overall evaluation of the allocation of political power (of the 'coalition payoffs' in the terminology of Laver and Schofield, 1990) is that Forza Italia clearly has the upper hand in the Government. In addition to the office of Prime Minister, Forza Italia has obtained three ministries usually considered extremely important: Foreign Affairs; Economy and Finance; Justice. To all this it is appropriate to add the office of Speaker of the Senate – which occupies second place in the hierarchy of Italian political institutions since, when necessary, the Speaker officially stands in for the President of the Republic. It was given to Forza Italia's former group leader in the Senate,

Renato Schifani. Figures 12.1, 12.2, and 12.3, which build on Campus' useful chapter (2002), offer both a synthesis of some available data and a comparison with post-1994 governments.

As is well known, the number of portfolios attributed to the various parties making up a governing coalition is important in satisfying their overall expectations. However, some parties also have clear preferences with regard to the precise types of portfolios (their ranking in terms of importance, their prestige, their domain of activities) they would like to obtain. From this point

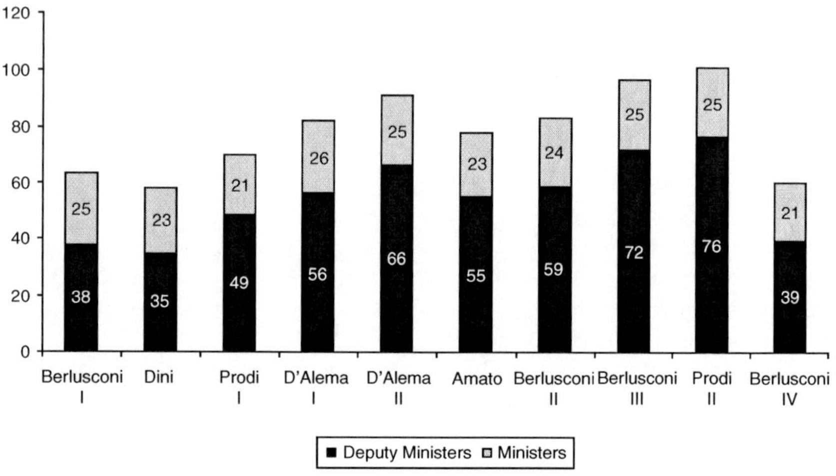

Figure 12.1   Numerical composition of post-1994 Italian governments

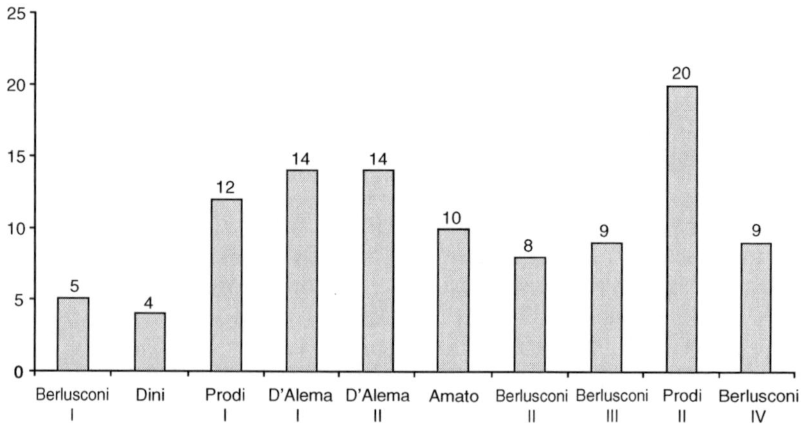

Figure 12.2   Number of female members of post-1994 Italian governments

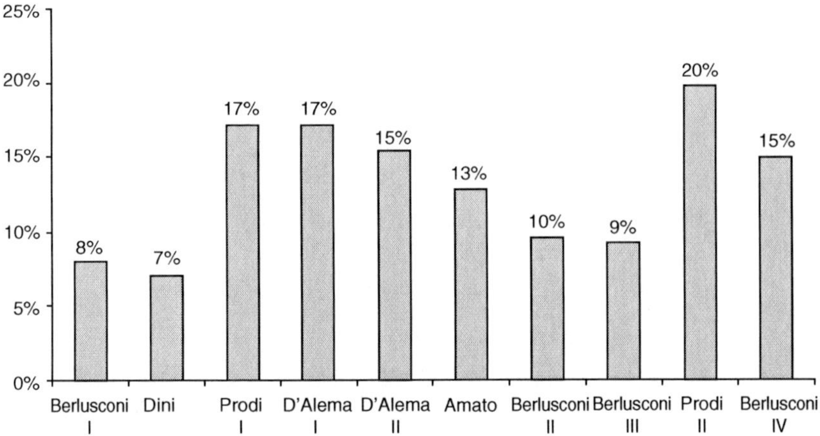

Figure 12.3   Per cent female of post-1994 Italian ministers

of view, the Northern League emerges as the clear winner. The three most important issues on which it ran its election campaign, and that go a long way towards defining its profile – federalism, security and immigration – were precisely translated into the portfolios they asked for and duly obtained. The Minister for Home Affairs, Roberto Maroni, will in fact deal with security and immigration, two issues that in the perception of many in the Italian electorate are closely intertwined. The very title of the portfolio given to the leader of the Northern League, Umberto Bossi – Federal Reform – suggests that the League has won at least the semantic battle for the devolution of political and administrative power to the regions. The rather obscure and unprecedented post of minister for Legislative Simplification is meant to indicate that Minister Roberto Calderoli will attempt to eliminate many unnecessary 'national' laws and proceed to legislative decentralisation. Finally, it is no surprise that the League has also been granted the Ministry of Agriculture, Food and Forests. Not only does Northern Italy boast a highly productive agricultural sector, but in the recent past, under the previous Berlusconi government, Italy engaged in a prolonged battle with the European Commission concerning quotas for the production of milk and the payment of fines imposed on the Italian government.

Judging by the number and the importance of the portfolios it obtained, one could say that the National Alliance emerged as a clear loser. Only two of its representatives, incidentally both former leaders of the party's parliamentary groups in the Chamber and Senate, obtained portfolios of any significance: Defence, and Infrastructure and Transport. On the other hand, by far the most important portfolios were those allocated to Forza Italia. On the issues that, in one way or another, the Prime Minister considers especially important, he allocated the relevant portfolios to loyal collaborators. Berlusconi's fourth government also represents a shrewd combination of experienced ministers and new entries. The experienced Ministers are instances of what I would like to call the 'certified and pre-owned'. On the whole, they have returned to the ministerial offices they had in the 2001–2006 period: Foreign Affairs (Franco Frattini), Home Affairs (Roberto Maroni), and the Economy and Finance (Giulio Tremonti) (the process of government formation in 2001 has been carefully analysed by Campus, 2002). To these one should add Economic Development because Claudio Scajola, for a time in charge of the organisation of Forza Italia, is a powerful figure. The new entries are a more diversified lot. On the one hand, there are figures powerful in their respective parties – individuals such as, for instance, Ignazio La Russa, coordinator of the National Alliance, at Defence; on the other hand, there are representatives of Forza Italia chosen because of their staunch loyalty – such as, for instance, Sandro Bondi (Cultural Affairs) – or their competence – such as Maurizio Sacconi (Labour, Health and Social Policies). Of course, there are also several cases of untested and unknown capabilities such as Forza Italia's Angelino Alfano at Justice and Mariastella Gelmini at the important Ministry of Education. That said, simply from the point of view of its composition, Berlusconi's fourth government appears better balanced and, on the whole, more competent than his previous ones. But, of course, if the proof of the pudding is in the eating, the proof of any government must be in its activities.

To the above analysis can be added the observation that Berlusconi has gained a greater degree of domination of his coalition allies than at any time in the past – so much so that he has even left in the background any discussion or proposals for constitutional reform. Only Bossi and the Northern League can act as effective counterweights to Berlusconi's power, but on too many issues their outlooks coincide. On the other hand, when it comes to sheer institutional power, Berlusconi has not gained much. As a tribute to the wisdom of the makers of the Italian Constitution, he will still find himself battling with the President of the Republic, the Higher Council of the Judiciary, the Constitutional Court, and, in spite of his sizable majority, even with Parliament. Fortunately and rightly so.

Coda

Immediately after his electoral and political defeat, the leader of the opposition, Walter Veltroni attempted to establish a less conflict-ridden relationship with the Prime Minister, what he called a 'dialogue'. To a large extent, at least for tactical reasons, Berlusconi seemed inclined to reciprocate. He could count on a high level of trust in his government on the part of Italian voters since, at the beginning of June, 55 per cent expressed some or much trust, as against 42 per cent saying little or none.[5] However, the thaw between the leaders of the two major parties lasted *l'espace d'un matin*. What Veltroni certainly underestimated and, even, at times, neglected, is that the monumental conflict of interests involved in the decisions Berlusconi will have to take as Prime Minister and the consequences they will have for his entrepreneurial assets and activities, remains unsolved. In fact, the first two decisions taken by the government went exactly in the direction of protecting Berlusconi the entrepreneur. He rejected the decision of the European Court of Justice that his Rete 4 Channel ought to be shifted to satellite broadcasting and that Europa 7 had the right to replace it. He had an amendment passed by Parliament that postpones his trial for giving money to a British lawyer, David Mills, in order to corrupt judges. Indeed, Berlusconi's conflict of interests will not only affect his governmental performance and, perhaps, his barely concealed ambition to become the next President of the Republic, but it remains a major obstacle in the way of Italy's path to becoming a liberal-democratic regime. Nevertheless, because of his sizable parliamentary majorities both in the Chamber of Deputies and in the Senate; because of the lessons learned in the past by himself and his governing partners and, above all, because of the confusion and the near disarray of the opposition, Berlusconi's fourth government has the unprecedented chance of lasting for the entire parliamentary term, that is until April 2013. However, there are those who hypothesise that the Prime Minister might want to ask for a dissolution of Parliament before then, perhaps in the wake of some electoral success and/or positive poll findings concerning his popularity and evaluations of his government's performance. He might want to do that in order to have a fresh parliamentary majority to elect him to the office of President of the Republic whose mandate will come to an end in May 2013. Knowing Berlusconi's larger-than-life ambitions, this scenario is by no means farfetched. As for Veltroni, his leadership does not appear uncontroversial and no doubt the 2009 local and European elections will put it to a very serious test.

Notes

1. Indeed, in quite a number of important local administrations for which elections are due in the Spring of 2009, the Democratic Party runs the risk of being ousted if it is unable to count on the support of several small left-wing groups.
2. See the, perhaps too complicated, attempt to identify these differences made by Ieraci (2008).
3. I have dealt with all these issues in Pasquino (2002).
4. Though I have no space to pursue the suggestion of Warwick and Druckman (2006), it is apparent that the allocation of portfolios has favoured the Northern League not because of its seat share, but, as the two authors would claim, because of its considerable bargaining power.
5. *la Repubblica*, 10 June 2008, p. 7. According to the same survey, the most popular ministers were, in the following order: Tremonti, Brunetta, Frattini, and Maroni, all enjoying an approval rate of over 60 per cent. Brunetta's popularity may be

explained by the fact that in his role as Minister dealing with the bureaucracy, he had promised to punish civil servants not performing their tasks adequately (the so-called *fannulloni*, or 'do-nothings') and he was in fact actively working towards that goal.

References

Campus, D. (2002) 'La formazione del governo Berlusconi', pp. 275–294 in G. Pasquino (ed.) *Dall'Ulivo al governo Berlusconi. Le elezioni del 13 maggio 2001 e il sistema politico italiano*, Bologna, Il: Mulino.

Campus, D. and Pasquino, G. (2006) 'Leadership in Italy: the changing role of leaders in elections and in government', *Journal of Contemporary European Studies* 14(1): 25–40.

Ieraci, G. (2008) *Governments and Parties in Italy. Parliamentary Debates, Investiture Votes and Policy Positions (1994–2006)*, Leicester: Troubador Publishing.

Laver, M. and Schofield, N. (1990) *Multiparty Government. The Politics of Coalition in Europe*, Oxford: Oxford University Press.

Mershon, C. (2002) *The Costs of Coalition*, Stanford: Stanford University Press.

Pasquino, G. (2002) *Il sistema politico italiano. Autorità, istituzioni, società*, Bologna: Bononia University Press.

Pasquino, G. (2008) 'The political context 2001–2006', pp. 15–32 in J. L. Newell (ed.) *The Italian General Election of 2006: Romano Prodi's Victory*, Manchester and New York: Manchester University Press.

Schofield, N. and Sened, I. (2007) *Multiparty Democracy. Elections and Legislative Politics*, Cambridge: Cambridge University Press.

Verzichelli, L. and Cotta, M. (2000) 'Italy: from "constrained" coalitions to alternating governments?', pp. 433–497 in W.C. Müller and K. Strøm (eds), *Coalition Governments in Western Europe*, Oxford: Oxford University Press.

Warwick, P. V. and Druckman, J. N. (2006) 'The portfolio allocation paradox: An investigation into the nature of a very strong but puzzling relationship', *European Journal of Political Research* 45(4): 635–665.

Conclusion: a Watershed Election?

James L. Newell

Introduction

The Italian general election of 2008 was, in one respect at least, very similar to the four that had preceded it; for, in its immediate aftermath, each left the observer with the feeling that what had just taken place would very likely turn out to be a watershed in Italian politics. The reasons for such an impression are not hard to discern: the Italian political system is widely viewed as having been undergoing a process of more or less fundamental transformation since the early 1990s with the outcome of that process continuing to appear uncertain. Partly because of this, campaigns have tended to have a dramatic quality, as if what were at stake was less the governance of a polity for the subsequent few years than a choice between competing civilisations. Moreover, as Mastropaolo points out, the profile of the political products on offer has always varied considerably from one election to the next (often with complete name changes, as Chiaramonte points out). This too has fed the impression of a process of change in which the election outcomes have represented likely turning points. That 2008 was no exception to any of this is confirmed by Edmondo Berselli (2008: 420) when he notes that, according to a widely held view 'the never-ending Italian transition' had, with the 2008 outcome, 'reached an initial milestone'. If such a reading was hardly surprising in view of the dramatic reduction in party-system fragmentation which took place, the analyses presented in this volume offer ample material for an assessment of the sense in which, and the extent to which, the view of 2008 as a watershed is an appropriate one. There are several perspectives from which such an assessment can be carried out. Here we draw on the preceding chapters briefly to consider the perspectives of: voting behaviour; the party-system and institutions; the Italian transition, and government performance.

Voters

As the analyses of Mastropaolo and Chaiaramonte suggest, from the point of view of voting behaviour, 2008 held relatively few surprises. That is, if the April outcome came as a shock, then this was to be attributed more to the profound changes in the nature of the political supply than to changes in voters' actual preferences. True, voters were clearly not static: the UDC lost votes to its right in the name of a *voto utile*, as did the SA, for the same reason. A significant proportion of former supporters of the SA parties abstained. The PD's gains from the parties to its left were to a degree offset by losses to the UDC. The League and IdV made dramatic gains. But as at previous elections, once again, shifts overwhelmingly took place within the centre left and centre right rather than across them so that the change in the distribution of voting preferences between the two was much less dramatic than the underlying shifts. If we add up the votes of the parties on each side of the basic left-right dividing line, and compare these totals with those obtained by centre left and centre right at the previous four elections, we find that the 11 per cent lead enjoyed by the centre right in 2008 differed little from the lead it had enjoyed at earlier consultations (Table C.1).

The figures confirm the basic structural deficit in support for the centre left discussed by Mastropaolo and thus throw a spotlight on Pasquino's point that notwithstanding Veltroni's attempt to revolutionise the party system, the issue of coalition formation – with the possibility of having to re-admit to the political game some of the smaller parties 'expelled' from Parliament by the election outcome – remains very much alive for him.

Table C.1   Chamber of Deputies election results, 1994–2001

	Centre left		Centre right		Others	
	No.	%	No.	%	No.	%
1994*	13,298,244	34.3	17,944,799	46.4	7,474,000	19.3
1996*	13,017,475	34.7	19,775,087	52.7	4,696,765	12.5
2001*	12,976,189	35.0	18,433,911	49.7	5,673,061	15.3
2006**	19,497,354	49.7	19,367,032	49.4	343,028	0.9
2008***	16,158,574	43.0	20,426,484	54.4	955,239	2.6

Notes:

* Figures are for the votes cast in the proportional arena.

** The three sets of figures are the totals for the Unione, the Casa delle Libertà and others across the three arenas (the domestic arena, the overseas constituency amd the single-member college of Valle d'Aosta) within with Chamber seats are distributed.

*** Centre left = the total across the three arenas for Veltroni's coalition plus SA, the Socialists, the PCdL, SC and SVP; centre right = the total across the three arenas for Berlusconi's coalition plus UDC, La Destra-FT.

Sources: Figures for 2001 and 1996 elections taken from 'Riepilogo elezioni politiche', http://brunik.altervista.org/20030922221253.html; Figures for 1994 elections taken from http://www.rassegna.it/elezioni/indice.htm and from http://elezionistorico.interno.it/liste.php?tp=C&dt=27/03/1994&cta=I&tpEnte=A&tpSeg=C&numEnte=&sut1=&sut2=&sut3=&descEnte=&descArea=ITALIA; Figures for 2006 election taken from Chiaramonte (2008, table 10.1); Figures for 2008 election taken from Chiaramonte (this volume, table 11.1).

Veltroni's problem is two-fold. On the one hand, the centre left is penalised by those same cultural factors to which Cavazza and Corbetta (2008: 445) have drawn attention in seeking to account for the Lega Nord's (Northern League's, NL's) striking advance (and it is because the factors are cultural that the centre left's deficit is structural):

> Insecurity…emerges…from a representation of the present and, above all, of the future, based as much as ever on the uncertainty that creates a feeling of precariousness even for those who have not yet had to deal with the consequences first hand…In this respect, then, it cannot be denied that the mass media have a key role…The space devoted by the most popular programmes and at the peak viewing times to ever more thorough analyses of cases of crime (especially if the protagonists are non-EU immigrants), to the daily show of the middle-class family suddenly or gradually impoverished, and to the landings of illegal immigrants, contributes without a shadow of a doubt to…the capacity of the centre right easily to exploit the structure of communication and to transmit a strategically advantageous representation of reality. To assert that the success of the League is evidence of the lack of influence of television on voting choices given that its spokespersons are not among those most frequently seen on screen is a superficial argument.

Second, therefore, unless Veltroni can find a way of broadening the base of his support to both his right and his left, the only chance he has of winning is by means of an appropriate alliance strategy. As Table C.2 shows, with one minor exception, the largest formation on the centre left has remained smaller than the largest centre-right formation, even when the centre left has won, at every election since 1994. Leaving aside the conundrums that would in any case be involved in attempting to expand support to both left and right simultaneously, the PD has the additional difficulty – to return to the point made by Cavazza and Corbetta – of finding a means of successfully framing issues in such a way as to avoid having to adopt the language of its centre-right adversaries and so reinforce their credibility. Veltroni is thus left with this awareness: if he runs alone, he is always likely to be beaten by Berlusconi. Given the difficulties of winning over new supporters in the short term, this argues in favour of the construction of alliances.[1] On the other hand, the construction of alliances is not without its own problems. That is, if Veltroni seeks to beat Berlusconi by building coalitions with other parties, then, as the run-up to 2008 shows (when his decision to run alone enabled Berlusconi to do without the UDC), what this does is to alter the strategic context within which Berlusconi has to make his own alliance decisions. In other words, the almost certain result of a centre-left decision to re-admit other parties to the political game is that the centre right would do the same.

Table C.2   Percentage of the vote won by the two largest lists fielded by the centre right and centre left respectively, Chamber of Deputies elections, 1994–2008

	Election				
Largest list for:	**1994**	**1996**	**2001**	**2006**	**2008**
Centre right	21.0	20.6	29.4	36.0	37.3
Centre left	20.4	21.1	16.6	31.3	33.2

Notes: In order to compare 'like with like', for each of the elections, the lists on the basis of whose scores the above percentages are arrived at, are as follows: in 1994: Forza Italia (FI) and the Partito Democratico della Sinistra (Democratic Party of the Left, PDS); in 1996: FI and the PDS; in 2001: FI and the Democratici di Sinistra (Left Demorats, DS); in 2006: the combined vote of FI and Alleanza Nazionale (National Alliance, AN), for the centre right, and the Ulivo (formed of the DS and the Margherita), for the centre left; in 2008: the Popolo della Libertà (People of Freedom, PdL) formed of FI and AN for the centre right, and the Partito Democratico (Democratic Party, PD) formed of the DS and the Margherita, for the centre left.

So, in terms of the question with which we began – namely the degree to which 2008 is likely to be a watershed in Italian politics – from one perspective at least, the election outcome represents something of a paradox: in revealing stability in the left-right distribution of the vote, it has confirmed the sheer enormity of the task facing the centre left if it is ever to win again, thus rendering even more dramatic the victory of Berlusconi.

The party system and institutions

As the chapters by Chiaramonte and by Russo and Verzicehlli show in some detail, the party-system consequences have been considerable given the reduction in fragmentation and the consolidation of bi-polar competition. This, in turn, has had actual and potential institutional consequences. The actual consequence has been that the government that has taken office has done so with prospects of lasting the entire legislature better than those of any other since the war: the small number of its parties and the narrowness of the ideological space they cover free it from the blackmail to which the previous government was exposed; the power of the incoming Prime Minister was symbolised by the fact that he is said to have gone in to the customary post-election meeting with the President with the list of ministers already prepared, as Pasquino notes. Not surprisingly then, the number of days separating the date of the election and the date the new government formally assumed office was the shortest in the history of the Republic: 24, for a post-war average of 46.

The potential consequence has to do with the capacity of Parliament to influence the content of public policy and, vice versa, the capacity of the executive to subordinate the legislature to its will. Governments' capacities to control legislative decision-making remained weak even after the 1990s party-system upheavals enabled pre-constituted coalitions successfully to seek absolute majorities of seats. This was because the party system remained fragmented and because the rules governing the passage of legislation – both those embodied in the Constitution and those embodied in the standing orders – contained significant provisions decentralising decision-making within the legislature and protecting minority interests (Newell, 2006).[2] Hence, prompted to take the lead in the field of legislation by such external pressures as those arising from European integration, executives from the early 1990s increasingly resorted to laws of delegation – in effect becoming more autonomous with regard to legislation by governing outside Parliament altogether (Capano and Giuliani, 2003).[3] As Russo and Verzichelli point out, if in some respects, initial evidence points in the direction of 'a "strong" legislature in terms of decisiveness and government steering capabilities' (as the decline in fragmentation would lead us to expect), the evidence for the emergence of an 'adversarial' pattern of interaction between two cohesive bodies, the majority and the opposition, is so-far mixed. Therefore, the extent to which the XVI legislature will see the emergence of a fundamentally new relationship between it and the executive remains uncertain, with much depending on changes in the policy agenda and what this does for intra-coalition tensions on both the governing and opposition sides.

The Italian transition

This then throws a spotlight on a third perspective from which the watershed quality of the election may be assessed – the implications of the outcome for the so-called Italian transition – for here too, much is likely to depend on the impact of unpredicatble political events on relations within each of the two main coalitions. The idea that the Italian political system has, since the early 1990s been in a state of regime transition, derives from two considerations, conceptual and empirical. Conceptually, 'transition' refers to a state of 'movement' from one regime to another, where the term 'regime' means that complex of rules, norms and procedures which govern: recruitment to positions of political authority (e.g., as a consequence of the electoral system); the functioning of political institutions (e.g., Parliament); the definition of the political community itself (Pasquino, 2000: 202). Empirically, the relevance of the concept to Italy stems from the way in which the 1990s *party-system* transformation seemed to have led the *political system* as a whole to acquire more of the features than it allegedly had of a 'normal majoritarian democracy': electoral coalitions enabled voters collectively to decide on the party composition of governments, directly; alternation in office between competing coalitions was possible; governments, through greater recourse to legislative decrees, had a stronger role in Parliament (Capano and Giuliani, 2001, 2003; Newell, 2006; Vassallo, 2007). On the other hand, the two coalitions which, by the first election of the new millennium had emerged as apparently permanent features of the political landscape were fluid and unstable. So, while the average life of governments during the First Republic was somewhat less than a year (322 days), in the period from the 1994 election to the election of 2001 it was just over a year (422 days). Thus it was, that, in addition to the electoral reform of 1993, more thoroughgoing institutional reform was thought to be necessary in order to consolidate the changes that had been achieved thus far and to overcome the continuing weaknesses in the political system's mode of functioning, in particular, the lack of cohesion of governing majorities and thus their capacity for efficient and effective policy making.

But the conditions that underpinned convictions of the necessity for further institutional change were precisely those that made it difficult, if not impossible, to achieve that change. Already with the failure of the Bicameral Commission for Constitutional Reform under Massimo D'Alema in 1997, it was clear that party-system fragmentation had turned large numbers of parties into partisan veto players (Tsebeliss, 2002) all wanting change, but changes going in contrasting directions so that a majority in favour of any given set of changes became impossible to construct.

If this served to sustain the view that the Italian political system was somehow caught *in mezzo al guado*, in a 'never-ending' transition, as some authors called it, then in the immediate aftermath of the 2008 campaign, it looked for a while as though a breakthrough might have been achieved. First, fragmentation on both governing and opposition sides had declined dramatically. Second, the Partito Democratico (Democratic Party, PD), had made conspicuous efforts to conduct a campaign that abandoned the demonising, anti-Berlusconi rhetoric of the past: wanting to convey an image of novelty for his party and to encourage 'prospective' voting, Veltroni sought to avoid references to Berlusconi's conflict of interests and past performance, as a focus on the past would inevitably have revived memories of the Prodi government – which was the last thing he wanted to do, as Favretto notes. Having, then, put aside, or at least considerably attenuated, reciprocal denials of the claims of the other to legitimacy, the two main coalitions had thereby forgone a style of competition that had hitherto contributed significantly to rendering institutional reform intractable, as well as being self-reinforcing. Third, the two-party concentration of seats, at 78 per cent, was such as to give the PdL and the PD the parliamentary support required to enable them to produce constitutional reform with a good chance of lasting. That is to say, Article 138 of the Italian Constitution provides that amendments must be passed with support of two thirds of the members of both chambers – otherwise, they may potentially be overturned by means of a popular referendum, as happened in 2006 when constitutional reform passed by the centre right with a simple majority, in opposition to the centre left, provoked the request for a vote which the centre right lost by a margin of almost two to one.

It was therefore not altogether surprising that in May, the Prime Minister and the leader of the opposition seemed intent on a regular set of meetings with a view to finding mutually acceptable institutional reforms – even less surprising given the clear incentives both men had: successful reform arguably offered the opportunity of a place in Italian political history as the fathers of a new constitutional settlement, something that seemed likely to be especially attractive to the aging Berlusconi, reputed to want to crown his career at the end of his term as Prime Minister with election to the Presidency.

On the other hand, as Pasquino points out, 'the thaw between the leaders of the two major parties lasted *l'espace d'un matin'*, Veltroni having underestimated the extent to which the decisions Berlusconi would have to take as Prime Minister would be affected by his unsolved conflict of interests – two of the Government's earliest decisions sending this conflict right to the top of the political agenda and in so doing tying Veltroni's hands in any potential dialogue with Berlusconi.

So the likely impact on the transition of the election outcome for the moment appears unclear, its prospects seeming to be dependent on at least the following factors on each side. On the centre left, though Veltroni succeeded in expelling the far left from Parliament, he has not succeeded in eliminating it as a force within the wider political system. Given the possibility that he may be obliged to re-admit it to the political game, the positions he is able to take in constitutional reform negotiations with the Government may be correspondingly restricted.

On the centre right, the positions that Berlusconi is able to take in negotiations are likely to be significantly influenced by the fact that the NL is numerically indispensable to the Government's survival and the PdL is not yet a fully-fledged single entity. On these fronts, economic developments are likely to be particularly significant. Italy is suffering at least as much as other European countries from the economic uncertainties instigated by the crisis of the US sub-prime mortgage sector and in the second quarter of 2008, recorded growth, at 0 per cent, was at its lowest level for five years (Troja, 2008: 12). If the Government starts becoming unpopular and looks like going down, the League will certainly not want to go down with it. In such circumstances, issues central to the League's appeal, such as taxation and fiscal federalism, may provide major tests; for the decisions taken in these areas will have a significant impact on the coalition's ability to deal with pressures to stimulate the economy and enhance household purchasing power at a time of deteriorating external conditions – while also preventing a reversal of the recent improvement in Italy's public finances (the *Economist*, 2008). So the difficulties of concluding any trade-off agreements that may be necessary to enable the executive *both* to agree constitutional reform with the opposition *and* to retain the internal unity necessary for survival may go up considerably. A very similar hypothesis might be advanced with respect to unity of the PdL.

On the other hand, Berlusconi's announcement at the beginning of August that the PdL was to become a political party within three months and hold its first national congress in January suggested moves to consolidate the unity of the body's components as quickly as possible. As for the League, its loyalty might be assured by the knowledge that it has been the clear winner in terms of the share out of government positions. This means that in any situation of tension with its allies, the calculation of whether, in terms of its support, it does better by breaking, or by staying on to exploit the potential of its offices is a much more difficult one to make than it would have been had its offices more closely reflected its share of the vote. Moreover, as long as any package of proposed constitutional and institutional reforms includes 'federalism', the NL may not care very much about many of the remaining matters. If, for example, the two largest parties were to agree on a reform of the electoral law based on the two-ballot system with single member constituencies as the PD's programme proposed, then it could have little to object to given the geographical concentration of its vote.

The Government's performance

In August 2008, the American news magazine, *Newsweek*, published an article under the title, 'Miracle in 100 days', praising Berlusconi for having, as it put it, 'brought order to chaotic Italy', especially in relation to the Naples garbage crisis and illegal immigration (Barigazzi, 2008). Thereby, it seemed to offer confirmation that in bringing to office a strong executive based on a seemingly compact, ideologically homogeneous coalition, the election had led to a significant improvement in the quality of Italian government. What seems likely is that, regardless of its actual performance, the Government will succeed in convincing citizens that it represents a new departure in this respect. The reason is two-fold. On the one hand, as compared to the governments that preceded it, and especially as compared to the Prodi government, it is well placed, precisely because of its compactness, to use communication as a tool in the battle to control the political agenda and therefore to engage in permanent campaigning. For this reason, it will be much less vulnerable than its predecessor was to the media's need for conflict, much less vulnerable to 'the lack of balance of an information system that continuously swings between an old form of parallelism and new adversarial attitudes towards politicians' (Roncarolo and Belluati, 2008: 340). On the other hand, therefore, the Government is likely to be able to benefit from a sharp contrast betweem *its* image and that of a predecessor which, because it was litigious and unpopular for most of its life, is widely perceived as having been ineffective.

If such a contrasting image does take root then – unless Berlusconi's government really is as effective as its predecessor in terms of such essential variables as the rate of growth, the level of unemployment, tax evasion and the public debt – it is likely to be misleading, because, as detailed in the chapters by Capriati and Fois, the Prodi government had some notable achievements to its credit, ones that were – one might add – 'especially notable precisely *because* of its structural weaknesses' (Paolucci and Newell, 2008: 284): as Roncarolo and Belluati (2008: 340) point out,

> When in January 2008 the centre left government lost by 161 votes to 156, few appeared to remember that it had succeeded in reaching agreement between supporters and opponents of radical reforms in various policy fields. Few appeared to remember either that – just a few days previously – it had won backing for a budget that offered some reason for agreement to all parties.

In concluding the volume dedicated to the general election of 2006 (Newell, 2008: 255) I noted that the government that then took office did so at 'a time of considerable economic difficulties, the pressures to reduce the budget deficit and the level of public debt bequeathed by its predecessors leaving it very little room for popular public spending measures'. Under these circumstances, some commentators had been

> prepared to argue that the most likely scenario [was] that of a government diligently delivering austerity measures and thereby paving the way for defeat at the next election by a right-wing coalition once again enjoying all the conditions necessary to allow it to raise levels of public spending and reduce taxes.

The prediction is one which, looking back in the light of Capriati's analysis, seems not to have been too wide of the mark.

Of the predictions for the Government's prospects that might be made in the aftermath of the latest election a not implausible one is that in producing an opposition keen to engage 'constructively' with a man like Berlusconi, 2008 could prove, in relation to a range of significant issues, paradoxically to have freed the Government from the pressures usually operating in bipolar party systems. Specifically, dialogue to achieve constitutional reform, if such takes place, might have perverse consequences for proper mechanisms of accountability, preventing the opposition from ensuring that the Government remains effectively as well as formally responsible. This appeared to be the message of the one other major effort of cooperation to have taken place since the start of the transition: the work of the Bicameral Commission for Constitutional Reform in 1997. Then, the centre left had been widely criticised for refraining, for the sake of retaining Berlusconi's cooperation, from legislation that would effectively deal with the entrepreneur's conflict of interests as owner of the country's three largest private TV networks and as a potential prime minister: in the end, Berlusconi withdrew cooperation anyway, leaving constitutional reform in tatters but his media empire intact. As, in May and June, the Government tabled a range of radical proposals on immigration and security, along with others widely criticised as representing a re-edition of the so-called *ad personam* laws salient in the legislative activity of the last Berlusconi government,[4] the notably restrained reaction of Veltroni's party led many to have visions of a re-edition of the previous experience – of cooperation in institutional reform (to which Berlusconi is reputedly rather indifferent) being traded for what, for him, are matters of substance. If such a scenario comes to pass, then it will suggest this verdict on the 2008 election: that it has above all brought us the latest striking application of Tancredi's famous advice, 'If we want things to stay as they are, things will have to change'.

Notes

1. Especially in view of the local elections due in 2009 when, as Pasquino suggests, the PD will be in danger of losing a number of important local authorities if it refuses to ally itself with the far left.
2. Examples include (1) the constitutional provision that bills, once presented, must be considered in committee – where they may be amended or combined with other bills so that the text referred for decision to the plenary session may differ considerably from the original; (2) the constitutional provision giving the power of legislative initiative to individual parliamentarians as well as to the Government – thus preventing executives from choosing, on their own authority, the procedure to which their bills will be subject or deciding the priority its bills will be given in the parliamentary timetable; (3) the provisions, in Parliament's standing orders, which place planning in the hand of the Committee of Parliamentary Group Leaders, whose decisions require two-thirds majorities.
3. Seeking to retain a significant role for itself, Parliament responded by giving greater emphasis in its activities, to the functions of oversight and scrutiny – leading observers to discern the development of an informal division of labour between executive and the legislature, the former formulating public policy, the latter providing *ex-ante* guidance and direction (motions and resolutions), and *ex-post* controls (questions and interpellations).
4. The proposals essentially revive 2003 legislation which sought (before being ruled unconstitutional) to provide immunity from prosecution for the holders of the offices of President of the Republic, President of the Senate, President of the Chamber of Deputies, President of the Council of Ministers (i.e., the Prime Minister). Critics view them as part of a move designed to save Berlusconi from conviction in a corruption trial involving David Mills, former husband of the British government minister, Tessa Jowell.

References

Berselli, E. (2008) 'Partito democratico o partito ipotetico', *il Mulino* 57(3): 420–431.
Capano, G. and Giuliani, M. (2003) 'The Italian parliament: in search of a new role?', *Journal of Legislative Studies* 9(2): 8–34.

Cavazza, N. and Corbetta, P. (2008) 'Quando la difesa del territorio diventa voto', *il Mulino* 57(3): 441–448.
Chiaramonte, A. (2008) 'How Prodi's Unione won by a handful of votes', pp. 203–222 in J.L. Newell (ed.), *The Italian General Election of 2006: Romano Prodi's Victory*, Manchester and New York: Manchester University Press.
Newell, J.L. (2006) 'Characterising the Italian parliament: legislative change in longitudinal perspective', *Journal of Legislative Studies* 12(3–4): 386–403.
Pasquino, G. (2000) *La transizione a parole*, Bologna: il Mulino.

Index

Page references for notes are followed by n and the note number, eg, 148n6